W9-AGB-941

PENGUIN CLASSICS

A Complete Annotated Listing of
Penguin Classics, Twentieth-Century Classics,
Nature Classics and the Pelican Shakespeare Series

Visit our Web site at www.penguinputnam.com

CONTENTS

* Indicates a new edition of a Penguin Classic that has undergone substantial revisions
and/or has additional and enhanced apparatus

PUBLISHER'S NOTE

For more than fifty years, Penguin has been the leading publisher of the classics in the English-speaking world. Since the publication of the first Penguin Classic in 1946—E. V. Rieu's translation of *The Odyssey*—we have dedicated ourselves to making sure that the great books of all time speak to the present day by reflecting the state of the art in scholarship, translation, and book design. We also continue to honor our founder Allen Lane's original mission: to make these great books available at a reasonable cost.

This new catalog provides complete, annotated descriptions of all books currently available in our Classics and Twentieth-Century Classics series as well as the Penguin Nature Classics and Pelican Shakespeare series.

From Renaissance philosophy to the poetry of revolutionary Russia, from the spiritual writings of India to the travel narratives of the early American colonists, from the Age of Homer to the Beat Generation, there are Classics here to educate, provoke, entertain, and enlighten readers of all interests and inclinations. We hope this catalog will inspire you to pick up that book you've always been meaning to read, or the one you may not have heard of before.

Write to us with your comments about the Penguin Classics, and ask us to include your name on our mailing list to receive updates and other information at Penguin Classics, Dept. CC, 375 Hudson Street, New York, NY 10014 or e-mail us at reading@penguin.com. Visit the Classics area on our Web site at www.penguinputnam.com.

Flatland
A Romance of Many Dimensions

Introduction by Alan Lightman

Abbott's delightful mathematical fantasy about life in a two-dimensional world brilliantly satirizes Victorian British society.

128 pp.   0-14-043531-X $8.95

The Letters of Abélard and Héloïse

Translated with an Introduction by Betty Radice

This collection of writings offers insight into the minds of two prominent Christian medieval figures—the French scholastic philosopher Peter Abélard and his beloved Héloïse, who became a learned abbess—and their celebrated but tragic love affair.

312 pp.   0-14-044297-9 $11.95

The Education of Henry Adams

Edited with an Introduction and Notes by Jean Gooder

In this memoir Adams examines his own life as it reflects the progress of the United States from the Civil War period to the nation's ascendancy as a world power. A remarkable synthesis of history, art, politics, and philosophy, *The Education of Henry Adams* remains a provocative and stimulating interpretation of the birth of the twentieth century.

624 pp.   0-14-044557-9 $12.95

Esther

Edited with an Introduction and Notes by Lisa MacFarlane

Originally published in 1884 under a female pseudonym and set in Old New York, *Esther* is a memorable love story and an insightful portrait of a confident age encountering the tensions between science, art, and religion.

256 pp.   0-14-044754-7 $9.95

Mont-Saint-Michel and Chartres

Introduction by Raymond Carney

A philosophical and historical meditation on the human condition, Adams's journey into the medieval consciousness synthesizes literature, art, politics, science, and psychology.

448 pp.   0-14-039054-5 $14.95

JANE ADDAMS
1860 – 1935, AMERICAN

Twenty Years at Hull-House

Introduction by Ruth Sidel

Addams's account of the famed settlement house she founded and of the principles of social justice that inspired her, tells in lucid, unsentimental prose the real stories of the people fictionalized in the novels of Theodore Dreiser and Upton Sinclair.

320 pp.   0-14-043691-X $12.95

JOSEPH ADDISON

See Sir Richard Steele.

ADOMNÁN OF IONA
C. 628 – 704, IRISH

Life of St. Columba

Translated with an Introduction by Richard Sharpe

This biography, written one hundred years after the death of St. Columba (597) and drawing on both oral and written materials, presents a richly detailed portrait of religious life in the sixth century.

432 pp.   0-14-044462-9 $13.95

AESCHYLUS
525 – 456 B.C., GREEK

The Oresteia
Agamemnon/The Libation Bearers/ The Eumenides

Translated by Robert Fagles with an Introduction, Notes, and Glossary by Robert Fagles and W. B. Stanford

The Oresteia—the only trilogy in Greek drama that survives from antiquity—takes on new depth and power in Fagles's acclaimed modern translation.

336 pp.   0-14-044333-9 $9.95

The Oresteian Trilogy

Translated with an Introduction by Philip Vellacott

Justice, vengeance, and the forces of fate provide the themes for *Agamemnon, The Choephori,* and *The Eumenides.* Vellacott's verse translation is presented with a short introduction to Greek mythology and the historical context of the trilogy.

208 pp.   0-14-044067-4 $9.95

Prometheus Bound and Other Plays

Translated with an Introduction by Philip Vellacott

Prometheus Bound, The Suppliants, Seven Against Thebes, and *The Persians,* presented here in verse translation, demonstrate that reason, not violence, is the proper principle of civilized life.

160 pp.   0-14-044112-3 $9.95

AESOP
c. 6TH CENT. B.C., GREEK

The Complete Fables

*Translated by Olivia and Robert Temple
with an Introduction by Robert Temple*

This definitive and fully annotated
modern edition is the first translation
ever to make available the complete
corpus of 358 fables attributed to Aesop.
Revealing a rawer, racier, very adult aesthetic, this version includes 100 fables
not previously published in English.

288 pp.   0-14-044649-4 $8.95

ANNA AKHMATOVA
1889 – 1966, RUSSIAN

Selected Poems

*Translated with an Introduction and
Notes by D. M. Thomas*

Akhmatova's poems bear witness to the
terrors of Stalinism, the loss of all
whom she loved, and the blessings of
memory. These outstanding translations by novelist D. M. Thomas do
honor to the works of one of the greatest poets in modern history.

20TH-CENTURY CLASSICS

160 pp.   0-14-018617-4 $12.95

HENRI ALAIN-FOURNIER
1886 – 1914, FRENCH

Le Grand Meaulnes

Translated by Frank Davison

The only novel by Alain-Fournier, follows
a young man killed in action in World
War I, and is a masterly exploration of the
transition from boyhood to manhood.

20TH-CENTURY CLASSICS

208 pp.   0-14-018282-9 $12.00

LEON BATTISTA ALBERTI
1404 – 1472, ITALIAN

On Painting

*Translated by Cecil Grayson with an
Introduction and Notes by Martin Kemp*

The first book devoted to the intellectual rationale for painting, Alberti's
discussion of the process of vision,
painting techniques, and the moral and
artistic prerequisites of the artist
remains a classic of art theory.

112 pp.   0-14-043331-7 $12.95

LOUISA MAY ALCOTT
1832 – 1888, AMERICAN

The Inheritance

*Edited with an Introduction by
Joel Myerson and Daniel Shealy*

Alcott's first novel, written in 1849,
when she was seventeen, is the captivating tale of a young orphan girl whose
inheritance is a secret locked in a long-
lost letter. Inspired by the sentimental
novels and Gothic romances of her day,
The Inheritance illuminates Alcott's
early influences and foreshadows her
mature style.

208 pp.   0-14-043666-9 $10.95

Penguin Readers Guide Available

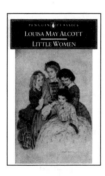

Little Women

Edited with an Introduction by Elaine Showalter and Notes by Siobhan Kilfeather and Vinca Showalter

Alcott's beloved story of the March girls —Meg, Jo, Beth, and Amy—is a classic American feminist novel, reflecting the tension between cultural obligation and artistic and personal freedom.

544 pp.   0-14-039069-3 $7.95

Work
A Story of Experience

Edited with an Introduction by Joy S. Kasson

A story about a nineteenth-century woman's search for a meaningful life through work outside the family sphere, *Work* is at once Alcott's exploration of her personal challenges and a social critique of America.

384 pp.   0-14-039091-X $11.95

ALFRED THE GREAT
849 – 899, ANGLO-SAXON

ASSER
D. C. 908, ANGLO-SAXON

Alfred the Great

Translated with an Introduction and Notes by Simon Keynes and Michael Lapidge

This comprehensive collection includes *Asser's Life of Alfred*, extracts from *The Anglo-Saxon Chronicle*, and Alfred's own writings, laws, and will.

368 pp.   0-14-044409-2 $13.95

HORATIO ALGER, JR.
1832 – 1899, AMERICAN

Ragged Dick and Struggling Upward

Edited with an Introduction by Carl Bode

Alger's characteristic theme of youths achieving the American dream through hard work, resistance to temptation, and goodwill is presented in these two tales that reflect nineteenth-century life.

304 pp.   0-14-039033-2 $9.95

KINGSLEY AMIS
1922 – 1995, BRITISH

Lucky Jim

Introduction by David Lodge

Originally published in 1954, this hilarious story of Jim Dixon's adjustment to teaching in the stultifying world of the university was the first modern British novel to plumb the comic possibilities of academic life.

20TH-CENTURY CLASSICS
256 pp.   0-14-018630-1 $11.95

AMMIANUS MARCELLINUS
c. 330 – 395, ROMAN

The Later Roman Empire
(A.D. 354–378)

Selected and Translated by Walter Hamilton with an Introduction and Notes by Andrew Wallace Hadrill

Considered to be the last great Roman historian, Ammianus Marcellinus continues the histories of Tacitus, describing the reigns of the emperors Constantius, Julian, Jovian, Valentinian, and Valens.

512 pp.   0-14-044406-8 $15.95

MULK RAJ ANAND
B. 1905, INDIAN

Untouchable
Preface by E. M. Forster

Anand, hailed as his country's Charles Dickens, presents a portrait of India's untouchables written with an urgency and fury that has made this his richest and most controversial novel.

20TH-CENTURY CLASSICS

160 pp.   0-14-018395-7 $11.95

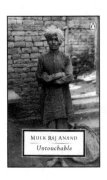

SHERWOOD ANDERSON
1876 – 1941, AMERICAN

"Sherwood Anderson was the father of all my works—and those of Hemingway, Fitzgerald, etc. We were influenced by him. He showed us the way."

—WILLIAM FAULKNER

The Egg and Other Stories
Edited with an Introduction by Charles E. Modlin

Anderson profoundly changed the American short story, and this collection of his mature work shows him at the peak of his storytelling art. Placed alongside masterworks like "The Egg," "Death in the Woods," "An Ohio Pagan," and twenty other classics are five stories rescued from unpublished manuscripts.

20TH-CENTURY CLASSICS

400 pp.   0-14-118079-X $11.95

Winesburg, Ohio
Introduction by Malcolm Cowley

Anderson's 1919 volume of interconnected stories about an ordinary small town whose citizens struggle with extraordinary dreams and grotesque disappointments has become an emblematic saga of American loneliness.

20TH-CENTURY CLASSICS

256 pp.   0-14-018655-7 $8.95

ANNA COMNENA
1083 – C. 1148, BYZANTINE

The Alexiad of Anna Comnena

Translated with an Introduction by
E. R. A. Sewter

A Byzantine emperor's daughter vividly records the turbulence that marked the rule of her father, Alexius I (1081–1118).

560 pp.   0-14-044215-4 $14.95

ANSELM OF AOSTA
C. 1033 – 1109, BRITISH (B. ITALY)

The Prayers and Meditations of St. Anselm

Translated with an Introduction by
Sr. Benedicta Ward and a Foreword by
R. W. Southern

Combining personal ardor and scrupulous theology, *Prayers and Meditations* offers an intimate view of this Archbishop of Canterbury, most noted for his acceptance of rational inquiry into the mysteries of faith.

288 pp.   0-14-044278-2 $12.95

MARY ANTIN
1881 – 1949, AMERICAN (B. RUSSIA)

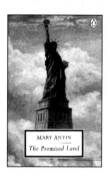

The Promised Land

Introduction and Notes by Werner Sollors

Interweaving introspection with political commentaries, biography with history, *The Promised Land* (1912) brings to life the transformation of a Russian Jewish immigrant into an American citizen. Antin not only describes her own personal journey but illuminates the lives of thousands.

20TH-CENTURY CLASSICS

400 pp.   0-14-018985-8 $10.95

APOLLONIUS OF RHODES
C. 3RD CENT. B.C., GREEK

The Voyage of the Argo
The Argonautica

Translated with an Introduction by
E. V. Rieu

Apollonius used the manner and matter of epics but wrote from a personal viewpoint, as a critical observer, in his *Argonautica*, the fullest surviving account of Jason's voyage in quest of the Golden Fleece.

224 pp.   0-14-044085-2 $12.95

APPIAN
C. 2ND CENT. A.D., GREEK

The Civil Wars

Translated with an Introduction by
John Carter

Covering the period from 133 to 35 B.C., this exploration of the decline of the Roman state details the struggles of Marius against Sulla, Caesar against Pompeius, and Antonius and Octavian against Caesar's assassins, Brutus and Cassius.

480 pp.   0-14-044509-9 $13.95

APULEIUS
C. A.D. 125 – 180, NORTH AFRICAN

The Golden Ass
Translated with an Introduction and Notes by E. J. Kenney

Lucius, a young man who believes witchcraft can transform him into a bird, instead becomes a donkey. Anticipating the modern novel, Apuleius combines satire and buffoonery with deep moral seriousness, and magic and fantasy with sincere religious feeling.

304 pp. 6 maps 0-14-043590-5 $10.95

THOMAS AQUINAS
1225 – 1274, ITALIAN

Aquinas: Selected Writings
Edited and Translated with an Introduction by Ralph McInerny

Though he was controversial in his day, Aquinas would significantly influence Catholic tradition and dogma. Arranged chronologically, this volume includes sermons, commentaries, responses to criticism, and important extracts from one of Christianity's supreme masterpieces, the *Summa Theologica*.

880 pp. 0-14-043632-4 $14.95

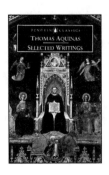

HANNAH ARENDT
1906 – 1975, AMERICAN (B. GERMANY)

Between Past and Future
Arendt's penetrating analysis of the complex crises of meaning in modern society and political philosophy is presented with her impassioned exercises for guiding readers toward the reinvigoration of the concepts of justice, reason, responsibility, virtue, and glory.

20TH-CENTURY CLASSICS

320 pp. 0-14-018650-6 $13.95

Eichmann in Jerusalem
A Report on the Banality of Evil
Arendt's internationally famous and controversial report on the trial of Nazi leader Adolph Eichmann deals with the problem of the human being within a modern totalitarian system. This posthumously revised edition contains a postscript by Arendt and further factual material revealed after the trial.

20TH-CENTURY CLASSICS

320 pp. 0-14-018765-0 $13.95

On Revolution

This pioneering analysis of the principles that underlie all revolutions discusses three classic revolutions— the American, the French, and the Russian—and shows how both the theory and practice of revolution have developed.

20TH-CENTURY CLASSICS

352 pp.   0-14-018421-X $13.95

LUDOVICO ARIOSTO
1474 – 1533, ITALIAN

Orlando Furioso

Translated with an Introduction by Barbara Reynolds

A dazzling kaleidoscope of adventures, ogres, monsters, barbaric splendor, and romance, this epic poem stands as one of the greatest works of the Italian Renaissance.

Part I: 832 pp. 0-14-044311-8 $16.95

ARISTOPHANES
C. 447 – C. 380 B.C., GREEK

The Frogs and Other Plays

Translated with an Introduction by David Barrett

The Wasps, The Poet and the Women (Thesmophoriazusae), and *The Frogs* use parody and low comedy to convey the spirit of Athens during the long, tragic war against Sparta.

224 pp.   0-14-044152-2 $9.95

HANNAH ARENDT

Born in Hanover, Germany, in 1906, Hannah Arendt moved with her family to Königsberg when she was three years old. Her mother interested her in contemporary politics, in particular the Spartacist faction of the Social Democratic Party and its leaders, Rosa Luxemburg and Karl Liebknecht. Arendt studied philosophy at the University of Hamburg with Martin Heidegger in 1924 and with Karl Jaspers from 1925 until 1929. She married Gunther Stern in 1929 in Paris, returning in 1933 to avoid the Nazis and living there until 1940. After escaping to New York, Arendt served as one of the premier members of the faculty of the New School for Social Research and also as a Visiting Fellow of the Committee on Social Thought at the University of Chicago. She originated the concept of the "banality of evil" in *Eichmann in Jerusalem*, her account of Adolf Eichmann's war-crimes trial, and wrote extensively on political and Jewish issues. She died in 1975.

The Knights/The Peace/The Birds/ The Assembly Women/Wealth

Translated with Introductions by David Barrett and Alan H. Sommerstein

Representing Aristophanes's sharply satirical comedy, this collection is prefaced by an introduction to the history and literary style of the author.

336 pp.   0-14-044332-0 $10.95

Lysistrata and Other Plays

Translated with an Introduction by Alan H. Sommerstein

Lysistrata, The Acharnians, and *The Clouds* comedically reflect Aristophanes's longing for the return of peace and honest living in Athens.

256 pp.   0-14-044287-1 $7.95

ARISTOTLE
384 - 322 B.C., GREEK

The Art of Rhetoric

Translated with an Introduction and Notes by Hugh Lawson-Tancred

With this book, Aristotle established the methods of informal reasoning, providing the first aesthetic evaluation of prose style and detailed observations of character and emotions.

304 pp.   0-14-044510-2 $13.95

The Athenian Constitution

Translated with an Introduction and Notes by P. J. Rhodes

This is the single most important extant source for the study of the institutions of classical Athens. "Clearly and accurately translated....Lucid introduction and notes, and excellent analytical summaries, introduce each chapter."
—S. M. Burstein, California State University, Los Angeles

208 pp.   0-14-044431-9 $9.95

De Anima (On the Soul)

Translated with an Introduction and Notes by Hugh Lawson-Tancred

Considering the nature of life, Aristotle surveys and rejects the ideas of Plato and the pre-Socratics, developing his philosophy of the soul and mind, and introducing the central concepts of form and matter to explain perception, thought, and motivation.

256 pp.   0-14-044471-8 $12.95

Ethics

Translated by J. A. K. Thomson with an Introduction and Bibliography by Jonathan Barnes and Revised with Appendices and Notes by Hugh Tredennick

In a work that had tremendous impact on Western moral philosophy, Aristotle treats ethics as a practical rather than a theoretical science, and introduces psychology into the study of human behavior.

384 pp.   0-14-044055-0 $10.95

The Metaphysics

Translated with an Introduction by Hugh Lawson-Tancred

One of the cornerstones of Western speculative thought, *The Metaphysics* is

Aristotle's first mature statement of his own understanding of reality. An extraordinary synthesis of the natural and rational aspects of the world that probes some of philosophy's deepest questions, it is now available in a highly readable translation.

528 pp.   0-14-044619-2 $11.95

Poetics

Translated with an Introduction and Notes by Malcolm Heath

In one of the most perceptive and influential works of criticism in Western literary history, Aristotle examines the literature of his time, describing the origins of poetry as an imitative art and drawing attention to the distinctions between comedy and tragedy.

144 pp.   0-14-044636-2 $10.95

The Politics

Translated with an Introduction by T. A. Sinclair and Revised and Re-Presented by Trevor J. Saunders

The search for the ideal state and the best possible constitution is the basis for the last great work of Greek political thought.

512 pp.   0-14-044421-1 $12.95

See *Classical Literary Criticism.*

ARRIAN
2ND CENT. A.D., GREEK

The Campaigns of Alexander

Translated by Aubrey de Sélincourt and Revised with a New Introduction and Notes by J. R. Hamilton

Written four hundred years after Alexander's death, this is the most reli-able account of the conqueror's life, character, and achievements.

432 pp.   0-14-044253-7 $13.95

ASSER

See Alfred the Great.

FARID UD-DIN ATTAR
c. 1142 – c. 1220, PERSIAN

The Conference of the Birds

Translated with an Introduction by Afkham Darbandi and Dick Davis

Consisting of a group of stories bound together by a pilgrimage, this great twelfth-century poem is an allegorical rendering of the *Way of the Sufi*, the secretive and paradoxical form of Islamic mysticism.

240 pp.   0-14-044434-3 $12.95

JOHN AUBREY
1626 – 1697, BRITISH

Brief Lives

Selected and Edited with an Introduction, Glossary, and Notes by John Buchanan-Brown and a Foreword by Michael Hunter

Vividly evoking Elizabethan and Stuart England, Aubrey's deft prose portrays a host of both well-known and forgotten but fascinating statesmen, poets, philosophers, and scientists. *Brief Lives'* mixture of entertainment and erudition revolutionized the art of English biography. This edition also includes "An Apparatus for the Lives of Our English Mathematical Writers" and "The Life of Thomas Hobbes of Malmesbury."

528 pp.   0-14-043589-1 $15.00

JOHN JAMES AUDUBON
1785 – 1851, AMERICAN
(B. SANTO DOMINGO, RAISED IN FRANCE)

Selected Journals and Other Writings

Edited with an Introduction by Ben Forkner

Known universally for his vivid paintings of American birds, John James Audubon was equally capable of bringing nature to life with a pen. Gathered in this volume are the fruits of his literary talent: journals, letters, bird biographies, a memoir of his early years, and stories of the American frontier—writings dedicated to the appreciation and preservation of nature's beauty.

NATURE CLASSICS

**576 pp.   8 pp. of color plates
0-14-024126-4 $15.95**

SAINT AUGUSTINE
354 – 430, NORTH AFRICAN

City of God

Edited by David Knowles and Translated by Henry Bettenson with an Introduction by John O'Meara

Augustine examines the inefficacy of the Roman gods and of human civilization in general. Blending Platonism with Christianity, he created the first

Christian theology of history—planning a city based not on the Roman pantheon but on Christian love.

1,152 pp.   0-14-044426-2 $15.95

Confessions

Translated with an Introduction by R. S. Pine-Coffin

This autobiography is both an explanation of Augustine's own conversion to Christianity and an attempt to convince the reader that it is the one true faith.

352 pp.   0-14-044114-X $8.95

JANE AUSTEN
1775 – 1817, BRITISH

Emma

Edited with an Introduction and Notes by Fiona Stafford

Considered by most critics to be Austen's most technically brilliant achievement, *Emma* sparkles with ironic insights into self-deception, self-discovery, and the interplay of love and power.

448 pp.   0-14-043415-1 $7.95

Lady Susan/The Watsons/Sanditon

Edited with an Introduction by Margaret Drabble

These three works—one novel unpublished in her lifetime and two unfinished fragments—limn an intriguing picture of Jane Austen's development as a great artist.

224 pp.   0-14-043102-0 $7.95

Mansfield Park

Edited with an Introduction and Notes by Kathryn Sutherland

Mansfield Park is Jane Austen's most sustained examination of family life, and while it echoes and extends the themes of *Pride and Prejudice*, it is more serious in both tone and intent.

480 pp.   0-14-043414-3 $6.95

Northanger Abbey

Edited with an Introduction by Marilyn Butler

During an eventful social season at Bath, Catherine Morland is invited to Northanger Abbey, where she believes she has discovered all the trappings of the Gothic novels she so loves reading. As she learns to distinguish literature from life, Catherine must also confront the trials of imperiled love, true-life danger, and, especially, the inevitable necessity of learning to think for herself.

288 pp.   0-14-043413-5 $6.95

*Persuasion

Edited with an Introduction by Gillian Beer

Anne Elliot, the heroine of Austen's last and most mature novel, overcomes social obstacles, her father's selfishness, and a seven-year misunderstanding in order to win the love of and marry the man she desires.

272 pp.   0-14-043467-4 $5.95

Pride and Prejudice

Edited with an Introduction and Notes by Vivien Jones

Published in 1813, *Pride and Prejudice* announced the arrival of the comedy of manners, a welcome change from the stiff, moralistic novels of the past.

384 pp.   0-14-043426-7 $7.95

Penguin Readers Guide Available

JANE AUSTEN

Regarded by many as the finest English-language novelist, Jane Austen lived in and wrote about Regency England. She died in 1817 at the age of forty-two after having written six novels, four of which were published during her lifetime. Austen's novels concern the marriage prospects of young upper-class women and are renowned for their flawless style, wit, and pointed social satire. She herself never married.

Sense and Sensibility

Edited with an Introduction by
Ros Ballaster

In her first novel, Austen is already mistress of gentle irony and keen observation, sparing no one in this lively study of the constraints placed on gentry-women in the eighteenth century.

368 pp.   0-14-043425-9 $6.95

Penguin Readers Guide Available

JANE AUSTEN
1775 - 1817, BRITISH

CHARLOTTE BRONTË
1816 - 1855, BRITISH

The Juvenilia of Jane Austen and Charlotte Brontë

Edited by Frances Beer

This collection provides the opportunity to discover the first examples of Austen's neoclassical elegance and Brontë's mastery of the romantic spirit.

400 pp.   0-14-043267-1 $9.95

See Charlotte Brontë.

MARY AUSTIN
1868 - 1934, AMERICAN

The Land of Little Rain

With an Introduction by
Terry Tempest Williams

Mary Austin calls it the Country of Lost Borders—the desert and foothill lands between Death Valley and the High Sierras. To most travelers it is a parched, empty territory, unwelcoming and unforgiving. But in this classic collection of essays, Austin breathes life into the landscape, describing in loving

and knowing detail its savage beauty, opening our eyes to a wider world.

NATURE CLASSICS

128 pp.   0-14-024919-2 $10.95

ISAAC BABEL
1894 - 1941, RUSSIAN

Collected Stories

Edited and Translated with an
Introduction and Notes by David McDuff

These stories, including Babel's masterpiece, "Red Cavalry," illuminate the author's lifelong struggle both to remain faithful to his Russian Jewish roots and to be free of them, a duality of vision that infuses his work with a powerful energy.

20TH-CENTURY CLASSICS

400 pp.   0-14-018462-7 $12.95

ISAAC BABEL
Collected Stories

FRANCIS BACON
1561 - 1626, BRITISH

The Essays

Edited with an Introduction by
John Pitcher

Including the fifty-eight essays of the 1625 edition, this collection comprises reflections on the successful conduct of life and management of men, as well as reworkings of many of the ideas of

Bacon's philosophical and scientific writings.

288 pp.   0-14-043216-7 $12.95

See *Divine Right and Democracy*.

HONORÉ DE BALZAC
1799 – 1850, FRENCH

The Black Sheep

Translated with an Introduction by Donald Adamson

Two brothers—one a dashing, handsome ex-soldier, the other a sensitive artist—struggle to recover the family inheritance in a novel that explores the devastation that poverty can bring.

344 pp.   0-14-044237-5 $13.95

Cousin Bette

Translated with an Introduction by Marion Ayton Crawford

Vividly bringing to life the rift between the old world and the new, *Cousin Bette* is an incisive study of vengeance, and the culmination of *The Human Comedy*.

448 pp.   0-14-044160-3 $10.95
Penguin Readers Guide Available

Cousin Pons

Translated with an Introduction by Herbert J. Hunt

The companion novel to *Cousin Bette*, *Cousin Pons* offers a diametrically opposite view of the nature of family relationships, focusing on a mild, harmless old man.

336 pp.   0-14-044205-7 $11.95

Eugénie Grandet

Translated with an Introduction by Marion Ayton Crawford

The love of money and the passionate pursuit of it, a major theme in *The Human Comedy*, is brilliantly depicted in the story of Grandet and his obsession with achieving power.

256 pp.   0-14-044050-X $10.95

HONORÉ DE BALZAC

The son of a civil servant, Honoré de Balzac was born in 1799 in Tours, France. After attending boarding school in Vendôme, he gravitated to Paris where he worked as a legal clerk and a hack writer, using various pseudonyms, often in collaboration with other writers. Balzac turned exclusively to fiction at the age of thirty and went on to write a large number of novels and short stories set amid turbulent nineteenth-century France. He entitled his collective works *The Human Comedy*. Along with Victor Hugo and the Dumas, Balzac was one of the pillars of French romantic literature. He died in 1850, shortly after his marriage to the Polish countess Evelina Hanska, his lover of eighteen years.

A Harlot High and Low

*Translated with an Introduction by
Rayner Heppenstall*

Finance, fashionable society, and the
intrigues of the underworld and the
police system form the heart of this
powerful novel, which introduces the
satanic genius Vautrin, one of the greatest villains in world literature.

560 pp.   0-14-044232-4 $13.95

History of the Thirteen

*Translated with an Introduction by
Herbert J. Hunt*

This trilogy of stories—"Ferragus: Chief of
the Companions of Duty," "The Duchesse
De Langeais," and "The Girl with the
Golden Eyes"—purporting to be the history of a secret society, laid the foundation
for Balzac's Scenes of Parisian Life and is a
stunning evocation of all ranks of society.

392 pp.   0-14-044301-0 $13.95

Lost Illusion

*Translated with an Introduction by
Herbert J. Hunt*

This novel of a young man who is
bored with provincial life and tries to
make his way in Parisian society is part
of *The Human Comedy*.

384 pp.   0-14-044251-0 $13.95

Old Goriot

*Translated with an Introduction by
Marion Ayton Crawford*

The intersecting lives of a group of people living in a working-class boarding-
house in nineteenth-century Paris form
the background of this indictment of
the cruelty of city society.

304 pp.   0-14-044017-8 $10.95

Selected Short Stories

*Selected and Translated with an
Introduction by Sylvia Raphael*

This collection includes "El Verdugo,"
"Domestic Peace," "A Study in Feminine
Psychology," "An Incident in the Reign of
Terror," "The Conscript," "The Red Inn,"
"The Purse," "La Grande Bretèche," "A
Tragedy by the Sea," "The Atheist's Mass,"
"Facino Cane," and "Pierre Grassou."

272 pp.   0-14-044325-8 $12.95

The Wild Ass's Skin

*Translated with an Introduction by
Herbert J. Hunt*

Balzac is concerned with the choice
between ruthless self-gratification and
asceticism, and dissipation and restraint,
in a novel that is powerful in its symbolism and realistic depiction of decadence.

288 pp.   0-14-044330-4 $11.95

WILLIAM BARTRAM
1739 – 1823, AMERICAN

Travels

With an Introduction by James Dickey

In April 1773, naturalist William
Bartram set out to explore the southeastern part of what is now the United
States, collecting plant specimens and
making drawings of the region's exotic

flora and fauna. First published in 1791, his exquisite travel diary—enhanced with Bartram's own inimitable line drawings—brings to life the raw beauty of America's southern wilderness as it was more than two hundred years ago.

NATURE CLASSICS

416 pp.   0-14-025300-9 $13.95

"America's conscious reflection on our own natural glory begins with Bartram."

—BILL MCKIBBEN

MATSUO BASHŌ
1644 – 1694, JAPANESE

The Narrow Road to the Deep North and Other Travel Sketches

Translated with an Introduction by Nobuyuki Yuasa

Bashō's haiku are a series of superb pictures in which whole landscapes and seasons are evoked by description of the crucial details.

176 pp.   0-14-044185-9 $11.95

On Love and Barley
Haiku of Bashō

Translated with an Introduction by Lucien Stryk

These 253 selections reveal Bashō's mastery of the genre.

96 pp.   0-14-044459-9 $9.95

CHARLES BAUDELAIRE
1821 – 1867, FRENCH

Baudelaire in English
Edited by Carol Clark and Robert Sykes

This superb anthology brings together the translations of Baudelaire's poetry and prose poems that best reveal the different facets of his personality: the haughtily defiant artist, the tormented bohemian, the savage yet tender lover, and the celebrant of strange, haunted cityscapes.

336 pp.   0-14-044644-3 $14.95

Selected Poems
Translated with an Introduction by Carol Clark

In both his life and his poetry, Baudelaire pushed the accepted limits of his time. His dissolute bohemian life was as shocking to his nineteenth-century readers as was his poetry. Writing in classical style but with brutal honesty, Baudelaire laid bare human suffering, aspirations, and perversions.

256 pp.   0-14-044624-9 $12.95

See The Penguin Book of French Poetry: 1820–1950.

L. FRANK BAUM
1856 – 1919, American

The Wonderful World of Oz
The Wizard of Oz/The Emerald City of Oz/Glinda of Oz

Edited with an Introduction and Notes by Jack Zipes

This fully annotated volume collects three of Baum's fourteen Oz novels in which he developed his utopian vision and which garnered an immense and loyal following. Also included is a selection of the original illustrations by W. W. Denslow and John R. Neill.

20TH-CENTURY CLASSICS
368 pp.   0-14-118085-4 $13.95

PIERRE-AUGUSTIN CARON DE BEAUMARCHAIS
1732 – 1799, French

The Barber of Seville and The Marriage of Figaro

Translated with an Introduction by John Wood

Known to us almost exclusively through the operas of Rossini and Mozart, these two plays, written with a delightfully light touch, marked high points in eighteenth-century comedy.

224 pp.   0-14-044133-6 $9.95

BEDE
c. 673 – 735, Anglo-Saxon

Ecclesiastical History of the English People

Edited with a New Introduction and Notes by D. H. Farmer and Translated by Leo Sherley-Price

Opening with a background sketch of Roman Britain's geography and history, Bede recounts the development of the Anglo-Saxon government and religion during the formative years of the British people.

400 pp.   0-14-044565-X $12.95

BEDE
c. 673 – 735, Anglo-Saxon

BRENDAN
d. 575, Anglo-Saxon

EDDIUS STEPHANUS
c. 8th cent., Anglo-Saxon

The Age of Bede

Edited with an Introduction by D. H. Farmer and Translated by J. F. Webb and D. H. Farmer

Four of the finest medieval hagiographies provide valuable insight into the religious life and thought of the period. This collection includes *The Voyage of St. Brendan, Bede's Life of Cuthbert, Lives of the Abbots of Wearmouth and Jarrow,* and Eddius Stephanus's *Life of Wilfrid.*

256 pp.   0-14-044437-8 $10.95

APHRA BEHN
1640 – 1689, BRITISH

Oroonoko, The Rover, and Other Works

Edited with an Introduction by Janet Todd

This rich collection of works by Aphra Behn—poet, playwright, novelist, feminist, activist, and spy—reveals the talents of the first professional woman writer in English.

400 pp.   0-14-043338-4 $9.95

See *The Penguin Book of Restoration Verse.*

EDWARD BELLAMY
1850 – 1898, AMERICAN

Looking Backward
2000–1887

Edited with an Introduction by Cecelia Tichi

When first published in 1888, *Looking Backward* initiated a national political- and social-reform movement. This profoundly utopian tale addresses the anguish and hope of its age, as well as having lasting value as an American cultural landmark.

240 pp.   0-14-039018-9 $11.9

SAUL BELLOW
B. 1915, AMERICAN (B. CANADA)
NOBEL PRIZE WINNER

"[Bellow's] body of work is more capacious of imagination and language than anyone else's....If there's a candidate for the Great American Novel, I think this is it."
—SALMAN RUSHDIE

The Adventures of Augie March

Ranging from the depths of poverty to the heights of success (and back), this is the sprawling chronicle of a modern-day Columbus in search of reality and fulfillment.

20TH-CENTURY CLASSICS
544 pp.   0-14-018941-6 $12.95
Penguin Readers Guide Available

Dangling Man

Expecting to be inducted into the army, Joseph has given up his job and carefully prepared for his departure to the battle front. When a series of mix-ups delays his induction, he finds himself facing a year of idleness. *Dangling Man* is his journal, a wonderful account of his restless wanderings through Chicago's streets and his musings on the past.

20TH-CENTURY CLASSICS
208 pp.   0-14-018935-1 $12.95

The Dean's December

Switching back and forth between two cities and scenes of humanity struggling within them, *The Dean's December* represents Bellow's "most spirited resistance to the forces of our time" (Malcolm Bradbury).

20TH-CENTURY CLASSICS
320 pp.   0-14-018913-0 $13.95

Henderson the Rain King

Bellow evokes all the rich color and exotic customs of a highly imaginative Africa in this comic novel about a middle-aged American millionaire who, seeking a new, more rewarding life, descends upon an African tribe. Henderson's awesome feats of strength and his unbridled passion for life win him the admiration of the tribe—but it is his gift for making rain that turns him from mere hero into messiah. A hilarious, often ribald story, it is also a profound look at the forces that drive a man through life.

20TH-CENTURY CLASSICS
352 pp.   0-14-018942-4 $13.95

Herzog

Hailed by the *New York Times* as a "masterpiece," *Herzog* is a multifaceted portrait of a modern-day hero. As his life disintegrates around him—he has failed as a writer and teacher, and has lost the affections of his wife to his best friend—Herzog writes unsent letters to friends, enemies, colleagues, and famous people, revealing his wry perceptions of the world and the innermost secrets of his heart.

20TH-CENTURY CLASSICS
352 pp.   0-14-018943-2 $13.95
Penguin Readers Guide Available

Him with His Foot in His Mouth

This dazzling collection of short fiction describes a series of self-awakenings—a suburban divorcée deciding among lovers, a celebrity drawn into his cousin's life of crime, a father remembering bygone Chicago, an artist, and an academic awaiting extradition for some unnamed offense.

20TH-CENTURY CLASSICS
304 pp.   0-14-118023-4 $14.95

Humboldt's Gift

For many years, the great poet Von Humboldt Fleisher and Charlie Citrine, a young man inflamed with a love for literature, were the best of friends. At the time of his death, however, Humboldt is a failure, and Charlie's life has reached a low point. And then Humboldt acts from beyond the grave.

20TH-CENTURY CLASSICS
496 pp.   0-14-018944-0 $14.95

ent, and finds himself intrigued by the possibilities of the future.

20TH-CENTURY CLASSICS

352 pp.   0-14-018936-X $13.95

Mosby's Memoirs and Other Stories

In six darkly comic tales, Saul Bellow presents the human experience in all its preposterousness, poignancy, and pathos. The stories, which include "Leaving the Yellow House," "The Old System," "Looking for Mr. Green," "The Gonzaga Manuscripts," and "A Father-to-Be."

20TH-CENTURY CLASSICS

192 pp.   0-14-018945-9 $11.95

Mr. Sammler's Planet

Introduction by Stanley Crouch

As the country anticipates the first moon shot and visions of Utopia vie with predictions of imminent apocalypse, Sammler, a Holocaust survivor, recalls the horrors of the past while enmeshed in the madness of the pres-

Seize the Day

Introduction by Cynthia Ozick

Deftly interweaving humor and pathos, Bellow evokes in the climactic events of one day the full drama of a man's search to affirm his own worth and humanity.

20TH-CENTURY CLASSICS

144 pp.   0-14-018937-8 $10.95

To Jerusalem and Back
A Personal Account

In this "impassioned and thoughtful book" (*The New York Times*), Bellow records the opinions, passions, and dreams of Israelis of varying viewpoints and adds his own thoughts on being Jewish in the twentieth century.

20TH-CENTURY CLASSICS

192 pp.   0-14-118075-7 $13.95

The Victim

Leventhal is a man uncertain of himself, who believes a down-at-the-heels stranger's accusation enough to find he has become...a victim.

20TH-CENTURY CLASSICS

288 pp.   0-14-018938-6 $12.95

SAUL BELLOW

Saul Bellow was born in Canada of Jewish immigrant parents and reared and educated in Chicago. A winner of numerous prizes, including the Pulitzer Prize (1975), the Nobel Prize in Literature (1976), and three National Book Awards, Bellow often delineates the experiences of the conflicted Jewish American intellectual who struggles to deal with spiritual and humanistic dilemmas in a world that has shed its traditional values and ethics. He has been praised for his vision, his ear for detail, his humor, and the masterful artistry of his prose.

ANDREI BELY
1880 – 1934, RUSSIAN

Petersburg

Translated with an Introduction and Notes by David McDuff

Called by the *New York Times Book Review* the "most important, most influential, and most perfectly realized Russian novel written in the twentieth century," *Petersburg* presaged the dawn of a completely new form of literature when it was published in 1916. History, culture, and politics are blended and juxtaposed; weather reports, current news, fashions, and psychology jostle together with people from Petersburg society in an exhilarating search for the identity of a city.

20TH-CENTURY CLASSICS

624 pp.   0-14-018696-4 $15.95

"My greatest masterpieces of twentieth-century prose are, in order: Joyce's *Ulysses*, Kafka's *Transformation*, Bely's *Petersburg*; and the first half of Proust's fairy tale *In Search of Lost Times* (sic)."

—VLADIMIR NABOKOV

STEPHEN VINCENT BENÉT
1898 – 1943, AMERICAN

The Devil and Daniel Webster and Other Writings

Edited with an Introduction and Notes by Townsend Ludington

Through a versatile array of masterly short stories, the two-time Pulitzer Prize–winner explored such subjects as American society, history, politics, and the supernatural. Sensitively selected and thoughtfully arranged, this vibrant anthology reintroduces readers to an American master.

20TH-CENTURY CLASSICS

400 pp.   0-14-043740-1 $13.95

ARNOLD BENNETT
1867 – 1931, BRITISH

The Old Wives' Tale

Introduction and Notes by John Wain

First published in 1908 and mirroring the achievements of the French realists, this perceptive novel of British provincial life details the affairs of two suffering sisters.

20TH-CENTURY CLASSICS

624 pp.   0-14-018255-1 $11.95

JEREMY BENTHAM

See John Stuart Mill.

GEORGE BERKELEY
1685 – 1753, IRISH

Principles of Human Knowledge and Three Dialogues Between Hylas and Philonius

Edited with an Introduction by Roger Woolhouse

These two masterpieces of empirical thought, whether viewed as extreme skepticism or enlightened common sense, are a major influence on modern philosophy.

224 pp.   0-14-043293-0 $11.95

BÉROUL
C. 12TH CENT., FRENCH

The Romance of Tristan

Translated with an Introduction by Alan S. Fredrick

This edition contains perhaps the earliest and most elemental version of the tragic legend of Tristan and Yseult in a distinguished prose translation. Alan S. Fredrick summarizes missing episodes and includes a translation of "The Tale of Tristan's Madness."

176 pp.   0-14-044230-8 $10.95

AMBROSE BIERCE
1842 – C.1914, AMERICAN

Tales of Soldiers and Civilians and Other Stories

Edited with an Introduction and Notes by Tom Quirk

This new collection gathers three dozen of Bierce's finest tales of war and the supernatural, including "An Occurrence at Owl Creek Ridge" and "The Damned Thing."

256 pp.   0-14-043756-8 $12.95

WILLIAM BLAKE
1757 – 1827, BRITISH

The Complete Poems

Edited by Alicia Ostriker

This edition contains all of Blake's poetry, with more than 150 pages of explanatory notes, including plot outlines of the more difficult poems, a chronology of Blake's life, a supplementary reading list, and a dictionary of proper names.

1,072 pp.   0-14-042215-3 $16.95

See *English Romantic Verse*.

GIOVANNI BOCCACCIO
1313 – 1375, ITALIAN

The Decameron

Translated with a New Introduction and Notes by G. H. McWilliam

Read as a social document of medieval times, as an earthly counterpart of Dante's *Divine Comedy*, or even as an early manifestation of the dawning spirit of the Renaissance, *The Decameron* is a masterpiece of imaginative narrative whose background is the Florentine plague of 1348.

992 pp.   0-14-044629-X $13.95

ANCIUS BOETHIUS
c. 480 – 524, ROMAN

The Consolation of Philosophy
Translated with an Introduction by V. E. Watts

This influential book mingles verse and prose in a sacred dialogue reflecting the doctrines of Plato, Aristotle, the Stoics, and the Neoplatonists.

192 pp.   0-14-044208-1 $13.95

HEINRICH T. BÖLL
1917 – 1985, GERMAN
NOBEL PRIZE WINNER

Billiards at Half-Past Nine
Translated by Leila Vennewitz

Böll's vehement opposition to Fascism and war informs this extraordinary exploration of the legacy of Nazi Germany.

20TH-CENTURY CLASSICS
288 pp.   0-14-018724-3 $13.95

The Clown
Translated by Leila Vennewitz

Through the eyes of a despairing artist Böll draws a revealing portrait of German society under Hitler and in the postwar years.

20TH-CENTURY CLASSICS
272 pp.   0-14-018726-X $13.95

The Lost Honor of Katherina Blum
Translated by Leila Vennewitz

In this masterful journey through a labyrinth of threats, untruths, and violence, a young woman's association with a hunted man makes her the target of an unscrupulous journalist, and she sees only one way out.

20TH-CENTURY CLASSICS
160 pp.   0-14-018728-6 $12.95

TADEUSZ BOROWSKI
1922 – 1951, POLISH (B. UKRAINE)

This Way for the Gas, Ladies and Gentlemen
Selected and Translated by Barbara Vedder with an Introduction by Jan Kott, Introduction Translated by Michael Kandel

Published in Poland after World War II, this collection of concentration camp stories stands as cruel testimony to the depths of inhumanity of which human beings are capable.

20TH-CENTURY CLASSICS
192 pp.   0-14-018624-7 $12.95

JAMES BOSWELL
1740 – 1795, SCOTTISH

The Life of Samuel Johnson
Edited and Abridged with an Introduction and Notes by Christopher Hibbert

This classic biography, completed in 1791, is based on Boswell's conversations with Johnson, documents and letters, and anecdotes from friends, all shaped by Boswell's incomparable wit and originality.

384 pp.   0-14-043116-0 $11.95

See Samuel Johnson.

Lady Audley's Secret

Edited by Jenny Bourne Taylor with an Introduction by Jenny Bourne Taylor with Russell Crofts

Lady Audley's Secret epitomized the scandalous and irresistible "sensation" fiction of the period and established Braddon as the doyenne of the genre. Lady Audley, a beautiful woman with a mysterious past, serves as a commentary on the rise of the middle class and the consumer culture, and her fate reflects the public's fascination with psychological theories about the nature of identity and the definition of madness.

512 pp.   0-14-043584-0 $10.95

See Bede.

The Physiology of Taste

Translated with an Introduction by Anne Drayton

First published in 1825, this book is a brilliant treatise on the pleasures of eating and the rich arts of food, wine, and philosophy, written by a famed French gastronome. Recipes are included.

384 pp.   0-14-044614-1 $13.95

Testament of Youth

Brittain's pacifist and feminist memoir of the First World War, in which she served as a nurse in London, Malta, and in France at the front, is a classic account of an entire generation marked by fatal idealism and changed by war.

20TH-CENTURY CLASSICS

672 pp.   0-14-018844-4 $16.95

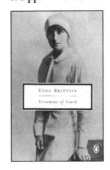

Agnes Grey

Edited with an Introduction and Notes by Angeline Goreau

A young governess experiences disillusionment and discovers love in this elegant novel, which George Moore found the "most perfect prose narrative in English literature."

272 pp.   0-14-043210-8 $8.95

The Tenant of Wildfell Hall

Edited with an Introduction by Stevie Davies

A passionate portrait of a woman's struggle for independence, *The Tenant of Wildfell Hall* is the story of Helen Graham, who flees a disastrous marriage, assumes a false identity, and attempts to make a life for herself and her child in a desolate mansion on the English moors, emerging as a woman of unusual strength and resolve.

576 pp.   0-14-043474-7 $7.95

Jane Eyre

Edited with an Introduction and Notes by Michael Mason

First published in 1847, *Jane Eyre* embodies many of the melodramatic conventions of the Gothic novels of the period. Charlotte Brontë, however, transcends melodrama to create an atypical romantic heroine of independence, intelligence, and integrity.

576 pp.   0-14-043400-3 $7.95

The Professor

Edited with an Introduction by Heather Glen

Published posthumously in 1857, Brontë's first novel is a subtle portrayal of a self-made man and his use of power in an individualistic society that worships property and propriety.

320 pp.   0-14-043311-2 $8.95

Shirley

Edited by Andrew and Judith Hook

Brontë grapples with the social and political issues of the mid–nineteenth century in a sweeping novel that explores the possibilities of reconciling romantic love and the demands of social convention.

624 pp.   0-14-043095-4 $7.95

Villette

Edited by Mark Lilly with an Introduction by Tony Tanner

An autobiographical novel, *Villette* is a moving portrait of the tensions between inner and outer experience and of the anguish of unrequited love.

624 pp.   0-14-043118-7 $10.95

Wuthering Heights

Edited with an Introduction and Notes by Pauline Nestor

The story of the passionate love between Catherine Earnshaw and the wild Heathcliff, told with wholly original emotional and imaginative power, has the depth and simplicity of an ancient tragedy.

400 pp.   0-14-043418-6 $6.95

Penguin Readers Guide Available

Edgar Huntly
Or, Memoirs of a Sleep-Walker

Edited with an Introduction by Norman S. Grabo

One of the first American Gothic novels, *Edgar Huntly* (1787) mirrors the social and political temperaments of the postrevolutionary United States.

288 pp.   0-14-039062-6 $12.95

Wieland and Memoirs of Carwin the Biloquist

Edited with an Introduction and Notes by Jay Fliegelman

A terrifying account of the fallibility of the human mind and, by extension, of democracy itself, *Wieland* brilliantly reflects the psychological, social, and political concerns of the early American republic. In the fragmentary sequel, *Memoirs*, Brown explores Carwin's bizarre history as a manipulated disciple of the charismatic utopian Ludloe.

416 pp.   0-14-039079-0 $10.95

The Power of Sympathy/ The Coquette

Introduction and Notes by Carla Mulford

Written in epistolary form and drawn from actual events, Brown's *The Power of Sympathy* (1789) and Foster's *The Coquette* (1797) were two of the earliest novels published in the United States. Both novels reflect the eighteenth-century preoccupation with the role of women as safekeepers of the young country's morality.

384 pp.   0-14-043468-2 $13.95

The Major Works

Edited with an Introduction and Notes by C. A. Patrides

Author and physician, Sir Thomas Browne,

encapsulates seventeenth-century social, religious, and intellectual concerns in *Religio Medici, Hydriotophia, The Garden of Cyprus, A Letter to a Friend,* and *Christian Morals.*

560 pp.   0-14-043109-8 $14.95

ELIZABETH BARRETT BROWNING
1806 – 1861, BRITISH

Aurora Leigh and Other Poems

Edited by John Robert Glorney Bolton and Julia Bolton Holloway

The romantic story of the making of a woman poet, Elizabeth Barrett Browning's epic novel in blank verse, published in 1856, explores women's issues and the relationship of art to politics and social expression. This volume also contains selections of the author's poetry published from 1826 to 1862, including *Casa Guidi Windows* and the British Library mansucript text of *Sonnets from the Portuguese.*

544 pp.   0-14-043412-7 $11.95

ROBERT BROWNING
1812 – 1889, BRITISH

Selected Poems

Edited with an Introduction and Notes by Daniel Karlin

This edition conveys the intensity, lyric beauty, and vitality of Browning's work through selections from the early *Pippa Passes* (1841), *Dramatic Lyrics* (1842), and *Dramatic Romances and Lyrics* (1845); from the masterpieces *Men and Women* (1855) and *Dramatis Personae* (1864); and from the less familiar works of his later years.

352 pp.   0-14-043726-6 $12.00

(Available in April 2001)

GEORG BÜCHNER
1813 – 1837, GERMAN

Complete Plays, Lenz, and Other Writings

Translated with an Introduction and Notes by John Reddick

Collected in this volume are powerful dramas and psychological fiction by the nineteenth-century iconoclast now recognized as a major figure of world literature. Also included are selections from Büchner's letters and philosophical writings.

368 pp.   0-14-044586-2 $12.95

MIKHAIL BULGAKOV
1891 – 1940, RUSSIAN

The Master and Margarita

Translated by Richard Pevear and Larissa Volokhonsky with an Introduction by Richard Pevear

An artful collage of grotesqueries, dark comedy, and timeless ethical questions, Bulgakov's devastating satire of Soviet life was written during the darkest period of Stalin's regime and remained unpublished for more than twenty-five years after its completion. This brilliant new translation was made from the complete and unabridged Russian text.

20TH-CENTURY CLASSICS

432 pp.   0-14-118014-5 $12.95

IVAN A. BUNIN
1870 – 1953, RUSSIAN
NOBEL PRIZE WINNER

The Gentleman from San Francisco and Other Stories

Translated with an Introduction by David Richards and Sophie Lund

This collection of seventeen stories hails from one of Russia's great realist writers, a modern heir to Chekhov and Turgenev.

20TH-CENTURY CLASSICS

224 pp.   0-14-018552-6 $12.95

JOHN BUNYAN
1628 – 1688, BRITISH

Grace Abounding to the Chief of Sinners

Edited with an Introduction by W. R. Owens

Bunyan's spiritual autobiography relates his religious awakening and eventual triumph over doubt and despair as it charts the experience of his conversion.

144 pp.   0-14-043280-9 $10.95

The Pilgrim's Progress

Edited with an Introduction and Notes by Roger Sharrock

Written in prison, Bunyan's chronicle of Christian's pilgrimage to the Celestial City is a powerful allegory of the conflict between religion and society.

384 pp.   0-14-043004-0 $8.95

MIKHAIL BULGAKOV

Described as "a slanderer of Soviet reality," in the official Big Soviet Encyclopaedia, Mikhail Bulgakov graduated with honors as a doctor from Kiev University in 1916, but only three years later gave up his medical practice to pursue writing. His satirical treatment of government officials in his many plays and stories led to growing political censorship and criticism, which became violent toward the end of his career. Poverty-stricken and in despair, Bulgakov wrote a letter to Stalin begging the government to order him out of the country as "there is no hope for any of my works" in Russia. Instead, Bulgakov was granted his second choice, a position as the assistant director and literary consultant to the Moscow Arts Theater, where he could be closely monitored by government officials. Bulgakov died in disgrace at the age of 49.

The Civilization of the Renaissance in Italy

Translated by S. G. C. Middlemore with a New Introduction by Peter Burke and Notes by Peter Murray

In this influential interpretation of the Italian Renaissance, Burckhardt explores the political and psychological forces that marked the beginning of the modern world.

416 pp.   0-14-044534-X $14.95

A Philosophical Enquiry into the Origin of Our Ideas of the Sublime and Beautiful
And Other Pre-Revolutionary Writings

Edited with an Introduction by David Womersley

Burke is considered by many to be the father of modern political conservatism but his essay on modern aesthetics influenced innumerable writers of the Romantic period. This volume includes his famous text as well as several of his early political writings to reveal the cross-pollination of Burke's aesthetic and political thinking.

528 pp.   0-14-043625-1 $14.95

Reflections on the Revolution in France

Edited with an Introduction by Conor Cruise O'Brien

The great debate on the French Revolution was touched off by *Reflections*, which reveals Burke as a much more radical—even revolutionary—thinker than admitted by those who view him as the father of modern conservatism.

400 pp.   0-14-043204-3 $9.95

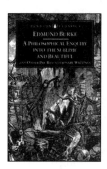

The Secret Garden

Edited with an Introduction and Notes by Alison Lurie

Originally published in 1911, *The Secret Garden* is an extraordinary novel that has influenced writers such as Eliot and Lawrence. The story of the sullen orphan Mary Lennox highlights the transforming powers of love, joy, and nature and of mystical faith and positive thinking.

20TH-CENTURY CLASSICS
288 pp.   0-14-118218-0 $5.95
Penguin Readers Guide Available

"One of the most original and brilliant children's books of the century."

—ALISON LURIE

FRANCES BURNEY
1752 – 1840, BRITISH

Evelina

Edited with an Introduction and Notes by Margaret Anne Doody

This epistolary portrait of female independence and the intrigues of the social classes introduced an entirely new form of novel—the comedy of manners—when it was published anonymously in 1778.

544 pp.   0-14-043347-3 $11.95

ROBERT BURNS
1759 – 1796, SCOTTISH

Selected Poems

Edited by Carol McGuirk

Arranged in probable order of composition, and featuring both lyrics and tunes, this collection of poems and songs written by Burns late in his career reveals his emotional range for modern readers.

368 pp.   0-14-042382-6 $12.95

EDGAR RICE BURROUGHS
1875 – 1950, AMERICAN

Tarzan of the Apes

Introduction and Notes by John Seelye

This 1914 novel gave birth to one of the most legendary characters in fiction, an ideal image of pure animalistic power at odds with the civilized world.

20TH-CENTURY CLASSICS

320 pp.   0-14-018464-3 $8.95

SAMUEL BUTLER
1835 – 1902, BRITISH

Erewhon

Edited with an Introduction by Peter Mudford

Butler's tale of a traveler to a remote island, based on his experiences in New Zealand, combines the elements of traditional utopian fiction and the picaresque novel. The influence of *The Origin of Species* on Butler's writing is apparent.

272 pp.   0-14-043057-1 $10.95

The Way of All Flesh

Edited by James Cochrane with an Introduction by Richard Hoggart

With wit, irony, and, sometimes, rancor, Butler savages the smug values and beliefs of a Victorian family.

448 pp.   0-14-043012-1 $10.95

GEORGE GORDON, LORD BYRON
1788 – 1824, BRITISH

Don Juan

Edited by T. G. Steffan, E. Steffan, and W. W. Pratt with an Introduction by T. G. Steffan

In this rambling, exuberant, conversational poem, the travels of Don Juan are used as a vehicle for some of the most lively and acute commentaries on human societies and behavior in the language. This edition is heavily annotated.

760 pp.   0-14-042216-1 $14.95

Selected Poems

Edited with a Preface by Susan J. Wolfson and Peter J. Manning

Flamboyant, brilliant, and daring, relishing humor and irony, Byron's poetry reflects European Romanticism in an age of revolutions. Among the poems included are "Childe Harold's Pilgrimage" and "Sardanapalus."

832 pp.   0-14-042381-8 $13.95

GEORGE WASHINGTON CABLE
1844 – 1925, American

The Grandissimes

Introduction by Michael Kreyling

Setting forth formidable arguments for racial equality, Cable's novel of feuding Creole families in early nineteenth-century New Orleans blends post–Civil War social dissent and Romanticism.

384 pp.   0-14-043322-8 $14.95

JULIUS CAESAR
100 – 44 b.c., Roman

The Civil War
Together with The Alexandrian War, The African War, and The Spanish War by Other Hands

Translated with an Introduction by Jane F. Gardner

A general of genius, Caesar was also a vivid and powerful writer. These accounts paint a full and surprisingly fair picture of the great struggle that brought Caesar to power and then caused his death.

360 pp.   0-14-044187-5 $10.95

The Conquest of Gaul

Translated by S. A. Hanford and Revised with a New Introduction by Jane F. Gardner

Caesar's account of the Gallic Wars, although based on fact, also served to impress his contemporaries and justify himself to his enemies. The earliest eyewitness account of Britain and its inhabitants appears in these famous memoirs.

272 pp.   0-14-044433-5 $9.95

ABRAHAM CAHAN
1860 – 1951, American
(b. Lithuania)

The Rise of David Levinsky

Edited with an Introduction and Notes by Jules Chametzky

Originally published in 1917, this classic of Jewish American literature tells the story of a young immigrant who works his way to success in the garment industry, but is at a loss in matters of love and identity.

20TH-CENTURY CLASSICS
544 pp.   0-14-018687-5 $13.95

See *American Local Color Writing.*

CAO XUEQIN
c. 1715 – 1763, CHINESE

The Story of the Stone
Also known as The Dream of the Red Chamber

Divided into five volumes, *The Story of the Stone* charts the glory and decline of the illustrious Jia family. This novel re-creates the ritualized hurly-burly of Chinese family life that would otherwise be lost and infuses it with affirming Buddhist belief.

"Indisputably the greatest master-piece...of all the Chinese novels."

—*THE NEW YORK REVIEW OF BOOKS*

The Story of the Stone
Volume 1: The Golden Days
(Chapters 1–26)

Translated with an Introduction by David Hawkes

544 pp.   0-14-044293-6 $15.00

The Story of the Stone
Volume 2: The Crab-Flower Club
(Chapters 27–53)

Translated with an Introduction by David Hawkes

608 pp.   0-14-044326-6 $13.95

The Story of the Stone
Volume 3: The Warning Voice
(Chapters 54–80)

Translated with an Introduction by David Hawkes

640 pp.   0-14-044370-3 $13.95

The Story of the Stone
Volume 4: The Debt of Tears
(Chapters 81–98)

Edited by Gao E and Translated with an Introduction by John Minford

400 pp.   0-14-044371-1 $13.95

The Story of the Stone
Volume 5: The Dreamer Awakes
(Chapters 99–120)

Edited by Gao E and Translated with a Preface by John Minford

384 pp.   0-14-044372-X $13.95

CAO XUEQIN

Cao Xueqin was born in 1715 into a family that for three generations held the office of Commissioner of Imperial Textiles in Nanking. But calamity overtook them and their property was confiscated. Cao Xueqin was living in poverty near Peking when he wrote his famous novel *The Story of the Stone*, the most popular book in all of Chinese literature. It was not published until thirty years after his death in 1763.

THOMAS CARLYLE
1795 – 1881, SCOTTISH

Selected Writings

*Edited with an Introduction by
Alan Shelston*

This representative selection from
Carlyle's writings includes the complete
Chartism, as well as chapters from
*Sartor Resartus, The French Revolution,
On Heroes,* and the *History of Frederick
the Great.*

400 pp.   0-14-043065-2 $14.95

LEWIS CARROLL
1832 – 1898, BRITISH

Alice's Adventures in Wonderland and Through the Looking-Glass

*Edited with an Introduction by
Hugh Haughton*

Lewis Carroll's incomparable tales about
Alice always have intrigued older readers, and the use of puns, parodies, and
absurd arguments about meanings and
manners brilliantly mock—and under-
mine—the rules and social conventions
adults invariably impose on children.

448 pp. 98 b/w drawings
0-14-043317-1 $8.95

Penguin Readers Guide Available

"The two Alices are not books for children, they are the only books in which we become children."
—VIRGINIA WOOLF

The Hunting of the Snark

*Edited with an Introduction by Martin
Gardner and the Original Illustrations of
Henry Holiday*

Inspired by the serendipitous line "For
the Snark was a Boojum, you see," which
occurred to him during a stroll, Lewis
Carroll crafted a classic work of non-
sense poetry that has intrigued readers
for more than a century.

128 pp.   14 b/w illustrations
0-14-043491-7 $9.95

RACHEL L. CARSON
1907 – 1964, AMERICAN

Under the Sea Wind

Illustrated by Rob Hines

The special mystery and beauty of the
sea is the setting for Rachel Carson's
classic portrait of the sea birds and sea
creatures that inhabit the eastern coast
of North America in this seamless series
of riveting adventures along the Atlantic
shore, within the open sea, and down
into its twilight depths.

NATURE CLASSICS
304 pp.   0-14-025380-7 $13.00

ROSARIO CASTELLANOS
1925 – 1974, MEXICAN

The Book of Lamentations

Translated with an Afterword by Esther Allen and an Introduction by Alma Guillermoprieto

A masterpiece of contemporary Latin American fiction by Mexico's greatest twentieth-century woman writer, *The Book of Lamentations* draws on two centuries of struggle among the Maya Indians and the white landowners in the Chiapas region of southern Mexico. The stark clarity of Castellanos's vision is beautifully rendered in Esther Allen's masterful first-ever English translation.

20TH-CENTURY CLASSICS

352 pp.   0-14-118003-X $13.95

BALDESAR CASTIGLIONE
1478 – 1529, MILANESE

The Book of the Courtier

Translated with an Introduction by George Bull

Discretion, decorum, nonchalance, and gracefulness are qualities of the complete and perfect Italian Renaissance courtier that are outlined in this series of imaginary conversations between the principal members of the court of Urbino in 1507.

368 pp.   0-14-044192-1 $13.95

WILLA CATHER
1873 – 1947, AMERICAN

Coming, Aphrodite! and Other Stories

Edited with Notes by Margaret Anne O'Connor and an Introduction by Cynthia Griffin Wolff

Ranging from the simplicity of Cather's first published story, "Peter" (1892), to the extraordinary eroticism of "Coming, Aphrodite!" (1920), this unique selection of short fiction is an engaging and triumphant testament to the genius of an American literary icon.

20TH-CENTURY CLASSICS

352 pp.   0-14-118156-7 $12.95

My Ántonia

Introduction and Notes by John J. Murphy

Cather's portrait of a remembered American girlhood on the Nebraskan prairie at the end of the nineteenth century alternates between insightful lyricism and naturalistic description, as she explores the rich relationship of Ántonia and the narrator, Jim Burden.

20TH-CENTURY CLASSICS

304 pp.   0-14-018764-2 $9.95

Penguin Readers Guide Available

O Pioneers!

Introduction by Blanche H. Gelfant

The first of Cather's renowned prairie novels, *O Pioneers!* established a new voice in American literature—turning the stories of ordinary Midwesterners and immigrants into authentic literary characters.

20TH-CENTURY CLASSICS
224 pp.   0-14-018775-8 $8.95

The Song of the Lark

Edited with an Introduction and Notes by Sherrill Harbison

This moving story about an aspiring musician and singer and her devotion to her art is one of Cather's most autobiographical novels. As is characteristic in Cather's work, the western landscape both eloquently represents the characters' inner lives and regenerates their tired imaginations.

20TH-CENTURY CLASSICS
480 pp.   0-14-118104-4 $9.95
Penguin Readers Guide Available

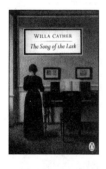

GEORGE CATLIN
1796 – 1872, AMERICAN

North American Indians

Edited with an Introduction by Peter Matthiessen

From 1831 to 1837, George Catlin traveled extensively among the native peoples of North America studying their habits, customs, and mode of life. Catlin's unprecedented fieldwork culminated in more than five hundred oil paintings and his now-legendary journal, collected here in this one-volume edition, and illustrated with more than fifty reproductions of Catlin's incomparable paintings.

NATURE CLASSICS
522 pp.   0-14-025267-3 $12.95

CATULLUS
C. 84 – C. 54 B.C., ROMAN

The Poems of Catullus

Translated with an Introduction by Peter Whigham

These 111 poems introduce the lyric poet Catullus, master of the pungent epigram, who found his inspiration in the glittering Roman society of the late Republic.

256 pp.   0-14-044180-8 $11.95

WILLA CATHER

Born in Virginia in 1873 and raised on a Nebraska ranch, Willa Cather is known for her beautifully evocative short stories and novels about the American West. Cather became the managing editor for *McClure's Magazine* in 1906 and lived for forty years in New York City with her companion, Edith Lewis. In 1922 Cather won the Pulitzer Prize for *One of Ours*, the story of a Western boy in World War I. In 1933 she was awarded the Prix Femina Americaine "for distinguished literary accomplishments." She died in 1947.

MARGARET CAVENDISH
c. 1623 – 1673, British

The Blazing World and Other Writings

Edited with an Introduction by Kate Lilley

These remarkable works of the flamboyant Duchess of Newcastle reveal not only a radical feminist, but a transgressor of every literary and sexual role and code. The title piece is the first work of science fiction ever written, depicting a utopia ruled by a warrior queen.

272 pp.   0-14-043372-4 $12.95

BENVENUTO CELLINI
1500 – 1571, Florentine

Autobiography

Translated with an Introduction and Notes by George Bull

With enviable powers of invective and an irrepressible sense of humor, Cellini provides an unrivaled portrait of the manners and morals of the Italy of Michelangelo and the Medici.

496 pp.   0-14-044718-0 $11.95

MIGUEL DE CERVANTES SAAVEDRA
1547 – 1615, Spanish

Don Quixote

Translated with an Introduction by J. M. Cohen

The adventures of Cervantes's idealistic knight-errant and his simple but astute squire, Sancho Panza, is not only a hilarious parody of the romances of chivalry but an exploration of the relationship between the real and the illusionary.

944 pp.   0-14-044010-0 $8.95

Exemplary Stories

Translated with an Introduction by C. A. Jones

Included in this collection are "The Little Gypsy Girl," "Rinconete and Cortadillo," "The Glass Graduate," "The Jealous Extremaduran," "The Deceitful Marriage," and "The Dog's Colloquy."

256 pp.   0-14-044248-0 $10.95

OWEN CHASE

See Thomas Nickerson.

GEOFFREY CHAUCER
c. 1342 – 1400, British

The Canterbury Tales

Translated into Modern English by Nevill Coghill

The motley members of a five-day pilgrimage from Southwark to Canterbury each tell a story to pass the time. From Knight to Nun and Miller to Monk, these pilgrims from all levels of society reveal a picture of British life in the fourteenth century that is as robust as it is representative. This edition captures the entire body of Chaucer's masterpiece in a thoroughly readable modern translation that preserves much of the freshness and racy vitality of the original text.

528 pp.　　0-14-044022-4　　**$8.95**

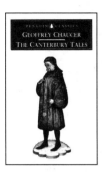

The Canterbury Tales
The First Fragment
Edited with an Introduction and Glosses by Michael Alexander

Comprised of the general Prologue and the prologues and tales of the Knight, Miller, Reeve, and Cook, this is the most widely read portion of Chaucer's masterpiece. This unique edition contains the Middle English text on one page and meticulous glosses of Chaucer's language on the facing page.

320 pp.　　0-14-043409-7　　**$9.95**

Love Visions
Translated into Modern English with an Introduction and Notes by Brian Stone

Spanning Chaucer's working life, these four poems move from the conventional allegorical "love visions" toward realistic storytelling and provide a marvelous self-portrait. This selection includes "The Book of the Duchess," "The House of Fame," "The Parliament of the Birds," and "The Legend of Good Women."

272 pp.　　0-14-044408-4　　**$11.95**

Troilus and Criseyde
Translated into Modern English by Nevill Coghill

Chaucer's depiction of passionate sexual love, his grasp of tragedy, and his sense of the ridiculous hidden in the sublime are all displayed in this poetic retelling of the classical story set during the Trojan War.

336 pp.　　0-14-044239-1　　**$9.95**

ANTON CHEKHOV
1860 – 1904, RUSSIAN

The Duel and Other Stories
Translated with an Introduction by Ronald Wilks

Chekhov's mastery of the short story is illuminated in these examples: "Murderer," "My Wife," "The Black Monk," "Terror," and "The Two Volodyas."

240 pp.　　0-14-044415-7　　**$9.95**

The Fiancée and Other Stories
Translated with an Introduction by Ronald Wilks

The stories in this selection demonstrate his prolific creativity: "The Fiancée," "On Official Business," "Rothschild's Fiddle," "Peasant Women," "Three Years," "With Friends," "The Bet," "New Villa," "At a Country House," "Beauties," "His Wife," and "The Student."

240 pp.　　0-14-044470-X　　**$6.95**

The Kiss and Other Stories

Translated with an Introduction by
Ronald Wilks

As Chekhov's confidence developed, his reputation grew along with his expertise. The stories in this collection represent his mature writings, including "The Man in a Case," "Gooseberries," "Concerning Love," "A Case History," "In the Gully," "Anna Round the Neck," "The Kiss," "Peasants," "The Russian Master," and "The Bishop."

224 pp.   0-14-044336-3 $6.95

Lady with Lapdog and Other Stories

Translated with an Introduction by
David Magarshack

After the 1892 famine, Chekhov moved to a small estate not far from Moscow where he continued his pursuit of realistically characterizing Russian society. "Ward 6," one of the stories in this volume, was written there. Also included are "Grief," "Agafya," "Misfortune," "A Boring Story," "The Grasshopper," "Ariande," "The House with an Attic," "Ionych," and "The Darling."

288 pp.   0-14-044143-3 $9.95

Plays

Translated with an Introduction by
Elisaveta Fen

Chekhov's realistic and sensitive plays revolve around a society on the brink of tremendous change. Included here are *The Cherry Orchard, The Seagull, Uncle Vanya, The Three Sisters, Ivanov, The Bear, The Proposal,* and *A Jubilee.*

464 pp.   0-14-044096-8 $8.95

ANTON CHEKHOV

Anton Chekhov was born in 1860 at Tanganrog in southern Russia. After a harsh childhood he went to Moscow in 1879 and entered the medical faculty of the university, graduating in 1884. In 1886 Chekhov published his first volume of stories. The next year, his first full-length play, *Ivanov,* was produced in Moscow. He continued to practice medicine while writing many of his best stories. In 1898, Stanislavsky produced *The Seagull* at his newly founded Moscow Art Theater. It was for him that Chekhov wrote *Uncle Vanya* (1900), *The Three Sisters* (1901), and *The Cherry Orchard* (1903). After 1900, when his health began to fail, Chekhov moved to Yalta, where he met Tolstoy and Gorky. In 1901 Chekhov married Olga Knipper, one of the Art Theatre's leading actresses. He died in 1904.

CHARLES W. CHESNUTT
1858 – 1932, AMERICAN

Conjure Tales and Stories of the Color Line

Edited with an Introduction by William Andrews

Chesnutt probed psychological depths in black people previously unheard of in Southern regional writing. This important collection brings together all the stories in his two published volumes, *The Conjure Woman* and *The Wife of His Youth*, along with two uncollected works: "Dave's Neckliss" and "Baxter's Procustes."

304 pp.   0-14-118502-3 $10.95

The House Behind the Cedars

Edited with an Introduction by Donald B. Gibson

An early masterwork among American literary treatments of miscegenation, Chesnutt's story is of two young African Americans who decide to pass for white in order to claim their share of the American dream.

20TH-CENTURY CLASSICS
304 pp.   0-14-018685-9 $12.95

The Marrow of Tradition

Edited with an Introduction and Notes by Eric J. Sundquist

This novel is based on a historically accurate account of the Wilmington, North Carolina, "race riot" of 1898, and is a passionate portrait of the betrayal of black culture in America, written by an acclaimed African American writer.

20TH-CENTURY CLASSICS
336 pp.   0-14-018686-7 $13.95

G. K. CHESTERTON
1874 – 1936, BRITISH

The Man Who Was Thursday
A Nightmare

Introduction by Kingsley Amis

Named after the days of the week for security reasons, the seven members of the Central Anarchist Council vow to destroy the world.

20TH-CENTURY CLASSICS
192 pp.   0-14-018388-4 $8.95

ERSKINE CHILDERS
1870 – 1922 IRISH (B. ENGLAND)

The Riddle of the Sands

Foreword by Geoffrey Household

First published in 1903, this gripping tale of espionage is "the first and best of spy stories" (*The Times*, London) and a brilliant forerunner to the work of Graham Greene and John Le Carré.

20TH-CENTURY CLASSICS
336 pp. 4 maps 0-14-118165-6 $7.95

The Awakening and Selected Stories

Edited with an Introduction by Sandra M. Gilbert

First published in 1899, *The Awakening* shows the transformation of Edna Pontellier, who claims for herself moral and erotic freedom. Other selections include "Emancipation," "At the 'Cadian Ball," and "Désirée's Baby."

320 pp.   0-14-039022-7 $7.95

Penguin Readers Guide Available

Bayou Folk and A Night in Acadie

Edited with an Introduction and Notes by Bernard Koloski

Here in one volume are the two short-story collections that established Kate Chopin as one of America's best-loved realist writers. Set in New Orleans and rural Louisiana, they anticipate the modern multi-ethnic, gender-sensitive, and sexually charged world of today.

416 pp.   0-14-043681-2 $11.95

A Vocation and a Voice
Stories

Edited with an Introduction and Notes by Emily Toth

Published for the first time as Chopin intended, this is a collection of her most innovative stories, including "The Story of an Hour," "An Egyptian Cigarette," and "The Kiss."

192 pp.   0-14-039078-2 $10.95

See *American Local Color Writing*.

Arthurian Romances

Translated with an Introduction and Notes by William W. Kibler; Erec and Enide *Translated by Carleton W. Carroll*

Fantastic adventures abound in these courtly romances: *Erec and Enide*, *Cligés*, *The Knight of the Cart*, *The Knight with the Lion*, and *The Story of the Grail*.

528 pp.   0-14-044521-8 $12.95

Murder Trials

Translated with an Introduction by Michael Grant

Cicero's speeches "In Defence of Sextus Roscius of Amerina," "In Defence of Aulus Cluentius Habitus," "In Defence of Gaius Rabirius," "Note on the Speeches in Defence of Caelius and Milo," and "In Defence of King Deiotarus" provide insight into Roman life, law, and history.

368 pp.   0-14-044288-X $13.95

The Nature of the Gods

Translated by Horace C. P. McGregor with an Introduction by J. M. Ross

In *De natura deorum,* Cicero sets out the ancient Greeks' conclusions about the existence and nature of deities and the extent of their involvement in human affairs.

288 pp.   0-14-044265-0 $11.95

On Government

Translated with an Introduction by Michael Grant

These pioneering writings on the mechanics, tactics, and strategies of government were devised by the Roman Republic's most enlightened thinker.

432 pp.   0-14-044595-1 $13.95

On the Good Life

Translated with an Introduction by Michael Grant

This collection of Cicero's writings discusses duty, friendship, the training of a statesman, and the importance of moral integrity in the search for happiness.

384 pp.   0-14-044244-8 $11.95

Selected Political Speeches

Translated with an Introduction by Michael Grant

The seven speeches in this volume, annotated to supply the relevant political history of the period, include the speeches against the Catiline conspiracy as well as the first "Philippic" against Mark Antony.

336 pp.   0-14-044214-6 $12.95

Selected Works

Translated with an Introduction by Michael Grant

Divided into two parts—"Against Tyranny" and "How to Live"—this selection of Cicero's work reveals the private and public sides of his liberal personality and his opposition to oppressive and unparliamentary methods of government.

272 pp.   0-14-044099-2 $12.95

WILLIAM CLARK

See Meriwether Lewis.

CARL VON CLAUSEWITZ
1780 – 1831, Prussian

On War

Edited with an Introduction by Anatol Rapoport and Translated by Col. J. J. Graham

This treatise presents the great Prussian soldier's views both on total war and on war as a continuation of foreign policy.

464 pp.   0-14-044427-0 $12.95

Fanny Hill
Or, Memoirs of a Woman of Pleasure
Edited with an Introduction by Peter Wagner

This infamous story of a prostitute's rise to respectability holds a place in the history of the English novel alongside the works of Richardson, Fielding, and Smollett.

240 pp.   0-14-043249-3 $8.95

Belle du Seigneur

Set largely in the elegant city of Geneva in the mid-1930s, *Belle du Seigneur* is a hilarious and powerful mock-epic concerning the mental world of the cuckold. Winner of the French Academy's highest honor and Britain's prestigious prize for literature.

20TH-CENTURY CLASSICS
320 pp.   0-14-018871-1 $15.95

The Complete Poems
Edited by William Keach

Endowed with a surfeit of imagination and creativity, Coleridge endlessly revised his poetry, changing passages, adding new lines, and even writing several variations of the same poem. Faced with the challenge of putting together an authoritative collection, William Keach presents the final texts of all the poems published during Coleridge's lifetime and a substantial selection from the verse still in manuscript at his death, together with comprehensive, informative notes on significant variants.

672 pp.   0-14-042353-2 $15.95

Selected Poems
Edited with an Introduction by Richard Holmes

This collection—divided into eight categories of theme and genre, including Conversation Poems, Ballads, Hill Walking Poems, and Confessional Poems—rediscovers Coleridge as a Romantic autobiographer of tremendous power, daring, and range.

400 pp.   0-14-042429-6 $12.00

Chéri and The Last of Chéri
Translated by Roger Senhouse with an Introduction by Raymond Mortimer

Earthy, sensuous, and daring, this classic portrait of the ill-fated affair between a very young man and a middle-aged woman is a wonderful introduction to Colette's extravagant, imaginative imagery —and her profound understanding of the human heart.

20TH-CENTURY CLASSICS
256 pp.   0-14-018317-5 $11.95

The Claudine Novels
Translated by Antonia White

The four Claudine novels constitute Colette's first series of books. Written between 1900 and 1903, they chronicle the experiences of a young girl growing to maturity and display a lyricism and candor that mark the author's later works.

20TH-CENTURY CLASSICS

560 pp.   0-14-018322-1 $14.00

Gigi and The Cat

Translated by Roger Senhouse and Antonia White

In these two superb stories, Colette reveals her grasp of the politics of sex.

20TH-CENTURY CLASSICS

160 pp.   0-14-018319-1 $12.00

The Ripening Seed

Translated by Roger Senhouse

In this novel, Colette captures that precious, painful moment when childhood innocence gives way to the birth of knowledge and desire.

20TH-CENTURY CLASSICS

128 pp.   0-14-018321-3 $11.95

The Vagabond

Translated by Enid McLeod

This tender and poetic tale of unrequited love and lonliness reflects on the essential fragility of human emotions.

20TH-CENTURY CLASSICS

192 pp.   0-14-018325-6 $10.95

WILKIE COLLINS
1824 – 1889, BRITISH

Armadale

Edited with an Introduction and Notes by John Sutherland

This intricately plotted Victorian melodrama draws on the substance and style of the popular press of the day: fraud, bigamy, drug addiction, and domestic poisonings all make appearances as Collins chronicles the evil ways of a spectacularly beautiful but unscrupulous woman.

752 pp.   0-14-043411-9 $11.95

The Law and the Lady

Edited with an Introduction by David Skilton

Here Collins introduced one of English literature's earliest woman detectives, Valeria Woodville, who investigates the murder of her husband's first wife in an attempt to prove his innocence.

432 pp.   0-14-043607-3 $10.95

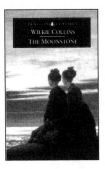

*The Moonstone

Edited with an Introduction by Sandra Kemp

The Moonstone, a priceless yellow diamond, is looted from an Indian temple and given to Rachel Verinder on her eighteen birthday, only to be stolen again that very night.

528pp.   0-14-043408-9 $6.95

Penguin Readers Guide Available

"The first, the longest, and the best of modern English detective novels."

—T. S. ELIOT

No Name

Edited with an Introduction and Notes by Mark Ford

A tale of courage and confrontation in the world of rigid Victorian society, Collins's novel creates a vivid and disturbing view of the hypocrisy inherent in the upper class.

640 pp.   0-14-043397-X $12.95

*The Woman in White

Edited with an Introduction by Matthew Sweet

This thriller, revolving around the identities of two mysterious women, caused great excitement when it was published in 1860 and continues to enthrall.

720 pp.   0-14-043731-2 $7.95

Penguin Readers Guide Available

CHRISTOPHER COLUMBUS
1451 – 1506, ITALIAN

The Four Voyages

Edited and Translated with an Introduction by J. M. Cohen

This volume includes Columbus's letters and logbook and remains the definitive primary source on his voyages to Cuba, Hispaniola, Jamaica, Trinidad, and Central America.

320 pp.   0-14-044217-0 $10.95

CONFUCIUS
551 – 479 B.C., CHINESE

The Analects

Translated with an Introduction by D. C. Lau

The only reliable account of the philosophy of the legendary Chinese sage, the *Lun-yü* (*Analects*) constitute a collection of Confucius's sayings compiled by his pupils shortly after his death.

256 pp.   0-14-044348-7 $10.95

JOSEPH CONRAD
1857 – 1924, BRITISH
(B. POLAND)

Almayer's Folly

Set in Malaya, Conrad's first novel charts the decline of a Dutch merchant after twenty-five years of hard struggle against overwhelming odds.

20TH-CENTURY CLASSICS

176 pp.   0-14-018030-3 $9.95

Chance

Neglected by her bankrupt father and rejected by her governess, Flora, desperate, takes refuge at sea on Captain Anthony's ship in this unrelenting novel of emotional isolation.

20TH-CENTURY CLASSICS

368 pp.   0-14-018654-9 $6.95

JOSEPH CONRAD
Heart of Darkness

Heart of Darkness

Edited with an Introduction and Notes by Robert Hampson

Marlow, a seaman and wanderer, travels to the heart of the African continent in search of a corrupt man named Kurtz. Instead he discovers a horrible secret in this exploration of the subconscious and the grim reality of imperialism. This edition includes more than seventy pages of critical commentary, together with Conrad's "The Congo Diary," the record of his 1890 journey upon which the novel is based.

20TH-CENTURY CLASSICS

224 pp.   0-14-018652-2 $7.95

Lord Jim

Edited by Cedric Watts and Robert Hampson with an Introduction and Notes by Cedric Watts

Conrad's powerful portrait of a young idealist whose one moment of weakness marks his life forever probes the nature of innocence and experience, heroism and cowardice.

20TH-CENTURY CLASSICS

384 pp.   0-14-018092-3 $5.95

The Nigger of the "Narcissus"

Edited with an Introduction and Notes by Cedric Watts

In his third novel and first major work, Conrad explores the themes of political and psychological subversion when the "closed society" on a ship is threatened by a storm and by mutiny.

20TH-CENTURY CLASSICS

208 pp.   0-14-018094-X $12.95

Nostromo

Edited with an Introduction and Notes by Martin Seymour-Smith

Conrad's pessimistic worldview colors this novel depicting the brutality of Latin American politics and the tragedies that inevitably ensue.

20TH-CENTURY CLASSICS

480 pp.   0-14-018371-X $8.95

A Personal Record and A Mirror of the Sea

Edited with an Introduction and Notes by Mara Kainins

This volume brings together two collections of Conrad's most autobiographical essays. Although a largely enigmatic presence in his novels, here, Conrad shares personal anecdotes and adventures that reveal both the great novelist and the young man who broke with his Polish background to become a British citizen.

20TH-CENTURY CLASSICS

384 pp.   0-14-018966-1 $9.95

The Rescue

When Captain Tom Lingard sets sail toward the islands of the Eastern Archipelago, he expects an adventurous sea voyage. Instead he finds Mrs. Travels, a woman from an entirely different world with an independence of spirit that strikes a chord in Lingard's heart.

20TH-CENTURY CLASSICS
384 pp.   0-14-018034-6 $9.95

The Secret Agent

Edited with an Introduction and Notes by Martin Seymour-Smith

A black satire of British society, this chilling tale features amoral characters on both sides of the law—fatuous civil servants and corrupt policemen, bomb-carrying terrorists and sleazy pornographers.

20TH-CENTURY CLASSICS
272 pp.   0-14-018096-6 $9.95

The Shadow-Line

A young captain in crisis at sea must wrestle with his isolation and his conscience to cross the "shadow-line" between youth and adulthood. Written at the beginning of World War I, this is Conrad's attempt to open people's eyes to the meaning of war.

20TH-CENTURY CLASSICS
160 pp.   0-14-018097-4 $10.95

Tales of Unrest

Conrad exhibits his tenacious grasp of expression and hard experience gained from years at sea in this collection, which includes "Karain: A Memory," "The Idiots," "An Outpost of Progress," "The Return," and "The Lagoon."

20TH-CENTURY CLASSICS
208 pp.   0-14-018036-2 $8.95

Typhoon and Other Stories

Edited with an Introduction, Notes, and Appendix by Paul Kirschner

Originally published in 1903, this vol-

JOSEPH CONRAD

Born in Poland as Józef Teodor Konrad Korzeniowski in 1857, Joseph Conrad led an itinerant life until the mid-1890s, first in exile in Russia with his family and then as a seaman. During the course of his maritime career, he worked as a gunrunner, tried to commit suicide by shooting himself in the chest, and sailed throughout Asia and on the Congo River. Subsequently, he used these experiences in many of his stories. Ending his career as a seaman in 1894, he married Jessie George in 1896 and retired to Kent. Known particularly for his masterpieces *Heart of Darkness*, *Nostromo*, and *Lord Jim*, many of his works concern men struggling with their consciences in exotic and dangerous locales.

ume, written as Conrad bids farewell to his life as a seaman, contains "Typhoon," "Falk: A Remembrance," "Amy Foster," and "Tomorrow."

20TH-CENTURY CLASSICS

320 pp.   0-14-018257-8 $7.95

Under Western Eyes

Edited with an Introduction and Notes by Paul Kirschner

Conrad deftly depicts the political turmoil in Russia in 1911 and its psychological repercussions in this novel about a student unwittingly caught in revolutionary intrigue.

20TH-CENTURY CLASSICS

400 pp.   0-14-018849-5 $9.95

Victory

Edited with an Introduction by Robert Hampson

A story of rescue and violent tragedy set in the Malayan archipelago, *Victory* combines high adventure with a sensitive portrayal of three drifters.

20TH-CENTURY CLASSICS

416 pp.   0-14-018978-5 $10.00

Youth/Heart of Darkness/ The End of the Tether

Edited with an Introduction and Notes by John Lyon

These three novels, originally published together, form a subtle, somewhat skeptical portrait of the "ages of man." Combining the traditional elements of adventure stories with psychological insights, these works demonstrate why Conrad has been hailed as a vital link between Victorian literature and the birth of the modern novel.

20TH-CENTURY CLASSICS

384 pp.   0-14-018513-5 $7.95

BENJAMIN CONSTANT
1767 – 1830, FRENCH

Adolphe

Translated with an Introduction by Leonard Tancock

This chronicle of the love affair between a young man and an older woman is based on the author's own stormy affair with Madame de Staël.

128 pp.   0-14-044134-4 $11.95

CAPTAIN JAMES COOK
1728 – 1779, BRITISH

The Journals of Captain Cook

Selected and Edited with Introductions by Philip Edwards

In three expeditions between 1768 and 1779, Captain Cook charted the entire coast of New Zealand and the east coast of Australia, and brought back detailed descriptions of Tahiti, Tonga, and a host of previously unknown islands in the Pacific including the Hawaiian islands. This selection preserves the spirit and rhythm of the full narrative, as well as Cook's idiosyncratic spelling.

672 pp. 17 maps 0-14-043647-2 $9.95

The Deerslayer

Introduction by Donald E. Pease

In this acclaimed depiction of life during America's westward movement, part of *The Leatherstocking Tales*, Cooper describes the young manhood of Natty Bumppo, his mythical hero who remains one of the most significant characters in American literature.

384 pp.   0-14-039061-8 $10.95

The Last of the Mohicans

Introduction by Richard Slotkin

Tragic, fast-paced, and stocked with the elements of a classic Western adventure, this novel takes Natty Bumppo and his Indian friend Chingachgook through hostile Indian territory during the French and Indian War.

688 pp.   0-14-039024-3 $9.95

The Pathfinder

Introduction and Notes by Kay Seymour House

The fourth novel in *The Leatherstocking Tales* is a "romance," the story of Natty

Bumppo's unsuccessful courtship of a young woman during the French and Indian War.

496 pp.   0-14-039071-5 $9.95

The Pioneers

Introduction and Notes by Donald A. Ringe

The first of *The Leatherstocking Tales* introduces the mythical hero Natty Bumppo in a portrait that contrasts the natural codes of Bumppo to the rigid legal and social structures of a new settlement.

448 pp.   0-14-039007-3 $9.95

The Prairie

Introduction by Blake Nevius

The final novel in Cooper's epic, *The Prairie* depicts Natty Bumppo at the end of his life, still displaying his indomitable strength and dignity.

384 pp.   0-14-039026-X $11.95

The Spy

Introduction and Notes by Wayne Franklin

An historical adventure reminiscent of Sir Walter Scott's Waverley romances, Cooper's novel centers on Harvey Birch, a common man wrongly suspected of being a spy for the British.

464 pp.   0-14-043628-6 $12.95

The Cid/Cinna/ The Theatrical Illusion

Translated with an Introduction by John Cairncross

The Cid, Corneille's masterpiece set in

medieval Spain, was the first great work of French classical drama; *Cinna*, written three years later in 1641, is a tense political drama, while *The Theatrical Illusion*, an earlier work, is reminiscent of Shakespeare's exuberant comedies.

288 pp.   0-14-044312-6 $11.95

MALCOLM COWLEY
1898 – 1989, AMERICAN

Exile's Return
A Literary Odyssey of the 1920s

Introduction by Donald W. Faulkner

Hemingway, Fitzgerald, Dos Passos, and their Lost Generation confrères are memorably brought to life in Cowley's classic memoir.

20TH-CENTURY CLASSICS

352 pp.   0-14-018776-6 $14.95

"Far and away the best book about this generation."

—*THE NEW YORK TIMES*

STEPHEN CRANE
1871 – 1900, AMERICAN

Maggie: A Girl of the Streets
And Other Tales of New York

Edited with an Introduction by Larzer Ziff

This unflinching portrayal of the squalor and brutality of turn-of-the-century New York caused a scandal upon its initial publication in 1893. This volume also includes twelve other tales and sketches written between 1892 and 1896.

288 pp.   0-14-043797-5 $8.95

The Red Badge of Courage and Other Stories

Edited with an Introduction by Pascal Covici, Jr.

Here is one of the greatest novels ever written about war and its psychological effects on the individual soldier. This edition also includes the short stories "The Open Boat," "The Bride Comes to Yellow Sky," "The Blue Hotel," "A Poker Game," and "The Veteran."

304 pp.   0-14-039081-2 $8.95

J. HECTOR ST. JOHN DE CRÈVECOEUR
1735 – 1813, AMERICAN (B. FRANCE)

Letters from an American Farmer and Sketches of Eighteenth-Century America

Edited with an Introduction by Albert E. Stone

America's physical and cultural landscape is captured in these two classics of American history. *Letters* provides an invaluable view of the pre-Revolutionary and Revolutionary eras; *Sketches* details in vivid prose the physical setting in which American settlers created their history.

496 pp.   0-14-039006-5 $13.95

QUENTIN CRISP
1908 – 1999, AMERICAN
(B. ENGLAND)

The Naked Civil Servant
Preface by Michael Holroyd

Crisp describes his life with uninhibited exuberance in this classic autobiography. He came out as a gay man in 1931, when the slightest sign of homosexuality shocked public sensibilities, and he did so with provocative flamboyance, determined to spread the message that homosexuality did not exclude him or anyone else from the human race.

20TH-CENTURY CLASSICS

224 pp.   0-14-118053-6 $12.95

SOR JUANA INÉS
DE LA CRUZ
1648 – 1695, MEXICAN

Poems, Protest, and a Dream
Selected Writings
Translated with Notes by Margaret Sayers Peden and an Introduction by Ilan Stavans

La Respuesta a Sor Filotea, the most famous prose work of Sor Juana Inés de la Cruz, is a passionate defense of the rights of women to study, teach, and write, and is one of the world's earliest treatises on these subjects. Also included in this wide-ranging bilingual collection by Latin America's finest baroque poet is a new translation of her masterpiece, the epistemological poem "Primero Sueño," as well as autobiographical sonnets, religious poetry, secular love poems, playful verses, and lyrical tributes to New World culture.

304 pp.   0-14-044703-2 $12.95

QUOBNA OTTOBAH
CUGOANO
C.1757 – UNKNOWN, AFRICAN

Thoughts and Sentiments
on the Evil of Slavery
Edited with an Introduction and Notes by Vincent Carretta

Thoughts and Sentiments, the most rad-

SOR JUANA INÉS DE LA CRUZ

Juana Inés de Asbaje was born out of wedlock to a criolla mother and a Basque father in 1648 in San Miguel Nepantla, Mexico. In 1664 she entered the court of the viceroy's wife, the Marquise of Mancera, as a lady-in-waiting and several years later became a nun in the Order of St. Jerome. Known for her vast library, Sor Juana Inés de la Cruz wrote five plays, the best known being *El Divino Narciso* (*The Divine Narcissus*), as well as poems, lyrics, and sonnets, including "Primero Sueño" ("First I Dream"). Considered Latin America's finest baroque poet and, like Sappho, nicknamed "the tenth muse," she received both acclaim and the censure of the church for her work.

ical assault published by a writer of African descent on slavery, was Cugoano's response to the hypocrisy of Enlightenment Europe's attitude toward slavery. This is the only available edition of a neglected classic and includes Cugoano's correspondence with Edmund Burke, King George III, and William Pitt.

224 pp.   0-14-044750-4 $11.95

"A masterful achievement... Carretta's edition restores this important, but little known, author to his rightful place as a central figure in the Black Atlantic tradition of the eighteenth century."

—HENRY LOUIS GATES, JR

E. E. CUMMINGS
1894 – 1962, AMERICAN

The Enormous Room
Edited with an Introduction and Glossary by Samuel Hynes

Drawing from Cummings's unexpected confinement in a French concentration camp, this rambunctious modern story reflects the essential paradox of his experience: to lose everything—all comforts, possessions, all rights and privileges—is to become free, and so to be saved.

20TH-CENTURY CLASSICS

384pp.   0-14-118124-9 $11.95

"When a book like *The Enormous Room* manages to emerge from the morass of print we flounder in, it is time to take off your new straw hat and jump on it."

—JOHN DOS PASSOS

QUINTUS CURTIUS RUFUS
C. 1ST CENT. A.D., ROMAN

The History of Alexander
Translated by John Yardley with an Introduction and Notes by Waldemar Heckel

Although no other human being has attracted so much speculation, Alexander has remained an enigma. This history of his life provides by far the most plausible and haunting portrait of Alexander: a brilliantly realized image of a man ruined by constant good fortune in his youth.

352 pp.   0-14-044412-2 $11.95

RICHARD HENRY DANA, JR.
1815 – 1882, AMERICAN

Two Years Before the Mast
A Personal Narrative of Life at Sea
Edited with an Introduction and Notes by Thomas Philbrick

Dana's account of his passage as a common seaman from Boston around Cape Horn to California, and back, is a remarkable portrait of the seagoing life.

Bringing to the public's attention for the first time the plight of the most exploited segment of the American working class, he forever changed readers' romanticized perceptions of life at sea.

576 pp.   0-14-039008-1 $11.95

DANTE
1265 – 1321, FLORENTINE

The Divine Comedy
Volume 1: Inferno

Translated with an Introduction, Notes, and Commentary by Mark Musa

This vigorous new blank-verse translation of the poet's journey through the circles of Hell recreates for the modern reader the rich meanings that Dante's poem had for his contemporaries while preserving his simple, natural style and capturing the swift movement of the original Italian verse.

432 pp.   0-14-044441-6 $10.95

The Divine Comedy
Volume 2: Purgatory

Translated with an Introduction, Notes, and Commentary by Mark Musa

400 pp.   0-14-044442-4 $10.95

The Divine Comedy
Volume 3: Paradise

Translated with an Introduction, Notes, and Commentary by Mark Musa

456 pp.   0-14-044443-2 $10.95

The Divine Comedy
Volume 1: Hell

Translated with an Introduction by Dorothy L. Sayers

DANTE ALIGHIERI

Dante Alighieri was born in Florence in 1265 to a noble but impoverished family. At twenty, he married Gemma Donati, by whom he had four children. He had first met his muse Bice Portinari, whom he immortalized as Beatrice, in 1274, and when she died in 1290 he sought distraction by studying philosophy and theology and by writing *La Vita Nuova*. During this time he became involved in the strife between the Guelfs and the Ghibellines, becoming a prominent White Guelf. When the Black Guelfs came to power in 1302 Dante was condemned to exile. He took refuge first in Verona and after wandering from place to place, as far as Paris, he settled in Ravenna. There he completed the *Divine Comedy*, which he had begun in about 1308, if not later. Dante died in Ravenna in 1321.

Sayer's revered translation that attempts to reveal Dante through his classic work as a poet of vivid personality: sublime, intellectual, humorous, simple, and tender.

352 pp.   0-14-044006-2 $10.95

The Divine Comedy
Volume 2: Purgatory

Translated with an Introduction by Dorothy L. Sayers

392 pp.   0-14-044046-1 $10.95

The Divine Comedy
Volume 3: Paradise

Translated by Dorothy L. Sayers and Barbara Reynolds with an Introduction by Barbara Reynolds

400 pp.   0-14-044105-0 $11.95

La Vita Nuova

Translated with an Introduction by Barbara Reynolds

This series of astonishing and tender love poems to Beatrice is interspersed with Dante's own explanations of their sources and detailed analyses of their structure.

128 pp.   0-14-044216-2 $9.95

CHARLES DARWIN
1809 – 1882, BRITISH

The Origin of Species

Edited with an Introduction by J. W. Burrow

The foundation of our current understanding about the place of humanity in the universe, this scientific account of Darwin's evolutionary view of the world challenged contemporary beliefs about Divine Providence and the fixity of species.

480 pp.   0-14-043205-1 $10.95

The Voyage of the Beagle
Charles Darwin's Journal of Researches

Edited and Abridged with an Introduction by Janet Browne and Michael Neve

This shortened version of Darwin's journal of his five-year voyage on the HMS *Beagle* provides a profusion of detail about natural history and geology and illuminates the local people, politics, and customs of the places he visited.

448 pp.   0-14-043268-X $11.95

ELIZABETH DAVID
1914 – 1992, BRITISH

"Probably the greatest food writer we have."
—JAMES BEARD

French Provincial Cooking
Foreword by Julia Child

First published in 1962, David's culinary odyssey through provincial France forever changed the way we think about food. This delightful exploration of the traditions of French cooking includes recipes.

20TH-CENTURY CLASSICS

**544 pp. 28 pp. b/w illustrations
0-14-118153-2 $14.95**

Italian Food

Foreword by Julia Child

One of the first books to demonstrate the range of Italian cuisine, this volume distinguishes the complex traditions of Tuscany, Sicily, Lombardy, Umbria, and many other regions.

20TH-CENTURY CLASSICS

**384 pp. 20 pp. b/w illustrations
0-14-118155-9 $13.95**

ROBERTSON DAVIES
1913 – 1995, CANADIAN

Fifth Business

With an Introduction by Gail Godwin

The first novel of Davies' celebrated Deptford Trilogy, *Fifth Business* stands alone as a remarkable story told by a rational man who discovers that the marvelous is only another aspect of the real.

20TH-CENTURY CLASSICS

288 pp. 0-14-118615-1 $14.00

Penguin Readers Guide Available
(Available in January 2001)

"A mature, accomplished, and altogether remarkable book, one of the best...it simply cannot be ignored."

—THE WASHINGTON POST BOOK WORLD

DANIEL DEFOE
1660 – 1731, BRITISH

A Journal of the Plague Year

Edited by Anthony Burgess and Christopher Bristow with an Introduction by Anthony Burgess

The shocking immediacy of Defoe's description of plague-racked London makes this one of the most convincing accounts of the Great Plague of 1665 ever written.

256 pp. 0-14-043015-6 $8.95

Moll Flanders

Edited with an Introduction by David Blewett

This tale of Moll Flanders's glorious, picaresque progress through vice, poverty, mishaps, and strange coincidences is an exuberant panorama of eighteenth-century England.

464 pp. 0-14-043313-9 $8.95

Robinson Crusoe

Edited with an Introduction by Angus Ross

Robinson Crusoe runs away to sea and after a number of adventures is shipwrecked on an uninhabited island.

There he remains for twenty years with his friendly cannibal servant, Man Friday, until he is rescued and returned to England. This tale is of considerable moral significance; it sets up tension between God's purpose and Crusoe's very human impulses.

320 pp.   0-14-043007-5 $7.95

Roxana
Edited by David Blewett

Defoe's last novel, *Roxana,* depicts the decline and defeat of a woman tempted by the glamour of immortality.

416 pp.   0-14-043149-7 $11.95

JOHN W. DE FOREST
1826 – 1906, AMERICAN

Miss Ravenel's Conversion from Secession to Loyalty
Edited with an Introduction and Notes by Gary Scharnhorst

Drawing on his own combat experience with the Union forces, De Forest crafted a riveting war novel whose honesty and gritty realism surpassed its contemporaries and anticipated the realistic war writings of Hemingway, Mailer, and Tim O'Brien.

544 pp.   0-14-043757-6 $14.95

"One of the best American novels ever written."
—WILLIAM DEAN HOWELLS

THOMAS DE QUINCEY
1785 – 1859, BRITISH

Confessions of an English Opium Eater
Edited with an Introduction by Alethea Hayter

De Quincey's powerful evocation of his constant and bitter struggle against the incapacity and torpor of opium use brings to life the "celestial" dreams and terrifying nightmares that transport and destroy the addict.

232 pp.   0-14-043061-X $10.95

RENÉ DESCARTES
1596 – 1650, FRENCH

*Discourse on Method and Related Writings
Translated with an Introduction and Notes by Desmond M. Clarke

This superb translation of Descates' seminal contribution to modern philosophy and science puts the work in context by including extracts from his correspondence, the *Rules for Guiding One's Intelligence,* and *The World.*

256 pp.   0-14-044699-0 $7.95

*Meditations and Other Metaphysical Writings
Translated with an Introduction by Desmond M. Clarke

Descartes' definitive statement on the foundations of his whole philosophy is brought together with extensive selections from the *Objections and Replies,* relevant correspondence, and other metaphysical writings from the period—all in new translations.

256 pp.   0-14-044701-6 $9.95

BERNAL DÍAZ DEL CASTILLO
1492 – C. 1581, SPANISH

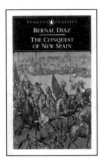

The Conquest of New Spain

Translated with an Introduction by J. M. Cohen

Fifty years after the startling defeat of the Aztecs by Hernán Cortés and his small band of adventurers, Díaz writes a magnificent account of his experience as a soldier in Cortés's army.

416 pp.   0-14-044123-9 $11.95

CHARLES DICKENS
1812 – 1870, BRITISH

American Notes for General Circulation

Edited with an Introduction by John S. Whitley and Arnold Goldman

The youthful, still-rough United States of 1842 is vividly recalled in this journal of Dickens's famous tour, offering a fascinating view of the New World by one of the Old World's greatest writers and social thinkers.

368 pp.   0-14-043077-6 $10.95

Barnaby Rudge

Edited with an Introduction and Notes by Gordon W. Spence

In this superb novel about individuals caught in the horrors of the rebellion of apprentices against their masters, Dickens dramatizes his fascination with private murder and public violence.

768 pp.   0-14-043090-3 $9.95

Bleak House

Edited with an Introduction and Notes by Nicola Bradbury and Original Illustrations by Hablot K. Browne ("Phiz")

Part romance, part melodrama, part detective story, this novel centers around the interminable land inheritance suit of Sarndyce and Sarndyce and spreads out among a web of relationships in every level of society from the simple-minded but self-important Sir Leicester Dedlock to Jo the street sweeper. Its story is a metaphor for the decay and corruption at the heart of British society.

1,088 pp.   0-14-043496-8 $10.95

The Christmas Books
Volume 1: A Christmas Carol/ The Chimes

Edited with an Introduction and Notes by Michael Slater

A Christmas Carol, with its unique blend of comedy and horror and the delightful grotesque, Scrooge, continues to mark our celebrations of Christmas. *The Chimes* is a provocative satire of how the wealthy celebrate New Year's Eve.

272 pp.   0-14-043068-7 $7.95

The Christmas Books
Volume 2: The Cricket on the Hearth/ The Battle of Life/The Haunted Man

Edited with an Introduction and Notes by Michael Slater

The Cricket on the Hearth is a delightful comedy set in a world of toys; *The Battle of Life* and *The Haunted Man* share the theme of the morally beneficial effects of memory.

368 pp.   0-14-043069-5 $9.95

David Copperfield

Edited with an Introduction and Notes by Jeremy Tambling

Written in the form of an autobiography and intimately rooted in Dickens's own life, this is the evergreen story of a young man growing to maturity in both affairs of the world and affairs of the heart.

912 pp.   0-14-043494-1 $7.95

Penguin Readers Guide Available

Dombey and Son

Edited by Peter Fairclough with an Introduction by Raymond Williams

Against the teeming streets of mid-Victorian London, Dickens examines Britain's new industrial power and its potential for creation and destruction.

992 pp.   0-14-043048-2 $8.95

Great Expectations

Edited with an Introduction by David Trotter and Notes by Charlotte Mitchell

With its rich array of characters and a narrative that moves from comedy to pathos to tragedy, *Great Expectations* is one of Dickens's most entertaining novels.

544 pp.   0-14-043489-5 $7.95

Penguin Readers Guide Available

CHARLES DICKENS

Charles Dickens was born in Portsmouth on February 7, 1812, the second of eight children. His father, a government clerk, was imprisoned for debt and Dickens was sent to work at the age of twelve. He became a reporter of parliamentary debates for the *Morning Chronicle* and began to publish sketches in various periodicals. *The Pickwick Papers* were published in 1836–37 and became a publishing phenomenon and Dickens's characters the center of a popular cult. He died on June 9, 1870. Dickens's popularity during his lifetime was exceptional but, as the distinguished literary critic Walter Allen said, his influence continues to be felt and "his work has become part of the literary climate within which Western man lives."

Hard Times

Edited with an Introduction by Kate Flint

With its vivid depiction of Coketown's tall chimneys trailing "interminable serpents of smoke" and its evocations of the dismal conditions of oppressed workers, *Hard Times* is certainly an "industrial novel." While it conveys deep concern for children, family, and home life, it is a heartfelt satire as well, targeting utilitarianism, self-help doctrines, and the mechanization of the mid-Victorian soul.

384 pp.   0-14-043398-8 $6.95

*Little Dorrit

Edited with an Introduction and Notes by Stephen Wall and Helen Small

In one of the supreme masterpieces of his maturity, Dickens portrays a world of hypocrisy and shame, of exploiters and parasites, in a penetrating study of the psychology of imprisonment.

928 pp.   40 line drawings   1 map
0-14-043492-5 $8.95

*Martin Chuzzlewit

Edited with an Introduction and Notes by Patricia Ingham and Original Illustrations by Hablot K. Browne ("Phiz")

Moving from sunny farce to the grimmest reaches of criminal psychology, this study of selfishness and hypocrisy follows the lives of two brothers with very different fates.

864 pp.   38 b/w illustrations
0-14-043614-6 $10.95

The Mystery of Edwin Drood

Edited by Arthur J. Cox with an Introduction by Angus Wilson

Unfinished at the time of Dickens's death, this novel explores the dark opium underworld and the uneasy and violent fantasies of its inhabitants.

320 pp.   0-14-043092-X $7.95

*Nicholas Nickleby

Edited with an Introduction by Mark Ford

Around the central story of Nicholas Nickleby and the misfortunes of his family, Dickens creates a gallery of colorful characters: the muddle-headed Mrs. Nickleby, the gloriously theatrical Crummles, their protégée Miss Petowker, the pretentious Mantalinis, and the mindlessly cruel Squeers and his wife. *Nicholas Nickleby* endures as one of the touchstones of the English comic novel.

864 pp.   39 b/w illustrations
0-14-043512-3 $7.95

The Old Curiosity Shop

Edited by Angus Easson with an Introduction by Malcolm Andrews

This novel contains some of Dickens's most bizarre characters, including the lecherous dwarf Quilp, as well as his most sentimental creation, the innocent

Little Nell, who is destroyed by an evil world.

720 pp.   0-14-043075-X $8.95

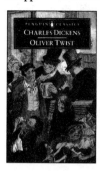

Oliver Twist

Edited by Peter Fairclough with an Introduction by Angus Wilson

This story of Oliver, a boy of unknown parentage who escapes a workhouse and embarks on a life of crime, shows how the lack of compassion in privileged society helps to make poverty a nursery of crime.

496 pp.   0-14-043017-2 $6.95

Our Mutual Friend

Edited with an Introduction and Notes by Adrian Poole and Illustrations by Marcus Stone

With a cast that embraces the "accumulated scum of humanity," this novel, the last Dickens completed before his death, probes into the crimes and guilt of dead fathers and its impact on a generation of sons and daughters.

928 pp.   0-14-043497-6 $10.95

*The Pickwick Papers

Edited with an Introduction by Mark Wormald

The story of the adventures of the charming, portly Sam Weller and his Pickwick Club catapulted the twenty-four-year-old Dickens to fame. This edition contains the original 1837 illustrations.

848 pp.   44 b/w illustrations   2 maps
0-14-043611-1 $9.95

Pictures from Italy
1850–1870

Edited with an Introduction and Notes by Kate Flint

This thrilling travelogue—with Dickens's prolific powers of description—is the result of encounters with Italy's colorful street life, the visible signs of its richly textured past, and its urban desolation.

272 pp.   0-14-043431-3 $11.95

Selected Journalism
1850–1870

Edited with an Introduction and Notes by David Pascoe

This collection showcases Dickens's much-admired talent for bringing touches of imagination and entertaining insights to factual accounts of life in London.

688 pp.   0-14-043580-8 $15.95

Selected Short Fiction

Edited with an Introduction and Notes by Deborah A. Thomas

Divided into three sections—"Tales of the Supernatural," "Impressionistic Sketches," and "Dramatic Monologues" —this volume reveals Dickens's recurring concerns and places them clearly in the context of related elements in his novels.

368 pp.   0-14-043103-9 $8.95

Sketches by Boz

Edited with an Introduction by Dennis Walder and Original Illustrations by George Cruikshank

Dickens's first book, published when he was twenty-four, *Sketches by Boz* is a wonderful miscellany of reportage, observation, fancy, and fiction—all centering on the teeming metropolis of London. With its episodic structure, improvisational flourishes, comic invention, and cast of odd and eccentric characters, it introduces all the elements characteristic of Dickens's great novels.

688 pp.   0-14-043345-7 $13.95

*A Tale of Two Cities

Edited with an Introduction and Notes by Richard Maxwell

In this stirring tale of the French Revolution, Dickens reveals much about his own "psychological revolution," examining his fears and innermost conflicts through the actions of Charles Darnay, Sydney Carton, and Lucie Manette.

528 pp.   17 b/w illustrations
0-14-043730-4 $6.95

DENIS DIDEROT
1713 – 1784, FRENCH

Jacques the Fatalist and His Master

Translated by Michael Henry with an Introduction and Notes by Martin Hall

In this revolutionary novel, a leading figure of the Enlightenment celebrates the unpredictable nature of man and the world as he considers the behavior of the moral being and the philosophical dilemma of free will and determinism.

264 pp.   0-14-044472-6 $12.95

The Nun

Translated with an Introduction by Leonard Tancock

Conventional Christianity is sharply criticized in a tale about a woman confined to a convent against her will.

192 pp.   0-14-044300-2 $10.95

Rameau's Nephew and D'Alembert's Dream

Translated with Introductions by Leonard Tancock

In the form of dialogues, Diderot attacks stale conventions and offers a surprisingly modern view of life, sex, and morals.

240 pp.   0-14-044173-5 $12.95

CASSIUS DIO
c. 163 – 235, ROMAN

The Roman History
The Reign of Augustus

Translated by Ian Scott-Kilvert with an Introduction by John Carter

Following Rome's long road to peace after decades of civil war, Cassius Dio provides the fullest account of the reign of the first emperor in Books 50 through 60 of his *Roman History*.

368 pp.   0-14-044448-3 $14.95

The Complete English Poems
Edited by A. J. Smith

Written in the natural rhythms of the speaking voice, John Donne's love poetry is considered some of the greatest of all time.

680 pp.   0-14-042209-9 $15.00

JOHN DOS PASSOS
1896 – 1970, AMERICAN

Three Soldiers
Introduction and Notes by Townsend Ludington

Based on his personal experiences in France during the First World War, Dos Passos's novel is a fierce denunciation of the military.

20TH-CENTURY CLASSICS
400 pp.   0-14-118027-7 $9.95

FYODOR DOSTOYEVSKY
1821 – 1881, RUSSIAN

The Brothers Karamazov
Translated with an Introduction and Notes by David McDuff

This striking new translation of Dostoyevsky's masterful drama of parricide and family rivalry chronicles the murder of Fyodor Karamazov and the subsequent investigation and trial. This excellent translation recaptures the sound, tone, and rough humor of the

original, and includes extensive notes.
960 pp.   0-14-044527-7 $11.95

Crime and Punishment
Translated with an Introduction and Notes by David McDuff

Dostoyevsky's masterpiece of modern literature is a study in the psychology of the criminal mind, an indictment of social conditions, and an engrossing portrait of Raskolnikov's Russia.

656 pp.   0-14-044528-5 $11.95
Penguin Readers Guide Available

The Devils
Translated with an Introduction by David Magarshack

Denounced by radical critics as the work of a reactionary, this powerful story of Russian terrorists who plot destruction only to murder one of their own seethes with provocative political opinions.

704 pp.   0-14-044035-6 $10.95

The Gambler/Bobok/A Nasty Story
Translated with an Introduction by Jessie Coulson

Conveying all the intensity and futility of an obsession, *The Gambler* is based on Dostoyevsky's firsthand experience;

"Bobok" and "A Nasty Story" are two of the author's best darkly comic stories.

240 pp.   0-14-044179-4 $10.95

The House of the Dead

Translated with an Introduction by David McDuff

The four years Dostoyevsky spent in a Siberian prison inform this portrait of convicts, their diverse stories, and prison life, rendered in almost documentary detail.

368 pp.   0-14-044456-4 $10.95

The Idiot

Translated with an Introduction by David Magarshack

At the center of a novel that has the plot of a thriller, Dostoyevsky portrays the Christlike figure of Prince Myshkin, bringing readers face-to-face with human suffering and spiritual compassion.

624 pp.   0-14-044054-2 $10.95

Netochka Nezvanova

Translated with an Introduction by Jane Kentish

Written as a serial, this never-complet-ed first publication treats many of the themes that dominate Dostoyevsky's later great novels.

176 pp.   0-14-044455-6 $10.95

Notes from the Underground/ The Double

Translated with an Introduction by Jessie Coulson

In *Notes from the Underground*, Dostoyevsky portrays a nihilist who probes into the dark underside of man's nature; *The Double* is Dostoyevsky's classic study of a psychological breakdown.

288 pp.   0-14-044252-9 $8.95

Poor Folk and Other Stories

Translated with an Introduction and Notes by David McDuff

Dostoyevsky's first great literary triumph, the novella *Poor Folk* is presented here, along with "The Landlady," "Mr. Prokharchin," and "Polzunkov."

288 pp.   0-14-044505-6 $9.95

Uncle's Dream and Other Stories

Translated with an Introduction by David McDuff

FYODOR DOSTOYEVSKY

Fyodor Mikhaylovich Dostoyevsky was born in Moscow in 1821, the second of eight children. When he was eighteen, his father, a doctor, was murdered by the family's serfs. His acclaimed first novel, *Poor Folk*, was published in 1846 and was followed quickly by less-admired stories. Three years later he was arrested for associating with radicals and sentenced to be executed. Though reprieved at the last moment, he was sent into exile at a labor camp in Siberia for four years, where the only book he was allowed to have was the New Testament. As a master of the psychological novel and as a profoundly Christian and Russian writer, Dostoyevsky examined the spiritual dimensions of suffering in the epic novels *Crime and Punishment* and *The Brothers Karamazov*, as well as in other distinguished novels, short stories, and diaries. He died in St. Petersburg in 1881.

Completed after four years of Siberian exile, *Uncle's Dream* is remarkable for its uncharacteristic objectivity, satire, and even farce, revealing a profound transformation in the author's worldview. In addition, this edition includes the stories "A Weak Heart," "White Nights," and "The Meek Girl."

304 pp.   0-14-044518-8 $10.95

The Village of Stepanchikovo

Translated with an Introduction by Ignat Avsey

This work introduces a Dostoyevsky unfamiliar to most readers, revealing his unexpected talents as a humorist and satirist. While its lighthearted tone and amusing plot make it a joy to read, it also contains the prototypes of characters who appear in his later works.

224 pp.   0-14-044658-3 $10.95

FREDERICK DOUGLASS
1818 – 1895, AMERICAN

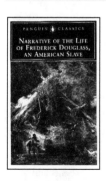

Narrative of the Life of Frederick Douglass, an American Slave

Edited with an Introduction by Houston A. Baker, Jr.

The preeminent example of the American slave narrative, Douglass's personal account of life in the pre–Civil War American South is a telling indictment of the institution of slavery and of the people and the country that allowed it to flourish.

160 pp.   0-14-039012-X $8.95

THEODORE DREISER
1871 – 1945, AMERICAN

Jennie Gerhardt

Edited with an Introduction and Notes by James L. W. West III

This unexpurgated edition of Dreiser's 1911 novel about a woman compromised by birth and fate not only restores passages critical of society but offers a stronger heroine and a clearer picture of the immigrant milieu into which she—and Dreiser—were born.

20TH-CENTURY CLASSICS
432 pp.   0-14-018710-3 $11.95

Sister Carrie

Introduction by Alfred Kazin

This subversive landmark novel, restored and unexpurgated, portrays the social world of turn-of-the-century United States through the story of a woman who becomes the mistress of a wealthy man.

20TH-CENTURY CLASSICS
496 pp.   0-14-018828-2 $12.95

W. E. B. DU BOIS
1868 – 1963, AMERICAN

The Souls of Black Folk

Introduction by Donald B. Gibson and Notes by Monica M. Elbert

Social reformer and activist W. E. B. Du Bois expresses his passionate concern for the future of his race in this 1903 collection of essays depicting the psychological effects of segregation on American society. This classic exploration of the moral and intellectual issues surrounding the perception of blacks within American society remains an important document of our social and political history.

20TH-CENTURY CLASSICS

288 pp.   0-14-018998-X $9.95

ALEXANDER DUMAS
1802 – 1870, French

The Count of Monte Cristo

Translated with an Introduction and Notes by Robin Buss

This is the quintessential novel of revenge, complete with a mysterious and implacable hero who will stop at nothing to punish the men who betrayed him and brought about his unjust imprisonment. It is a tale of nonstop adventure, intrigue, and excitement.

1,136 pp.   0-14-044615-X $12.95

The Three Musketeers

Translated with an Introduction by Lord Sudley

Based on historic fact, this is the stirring, romantic story of d'Artagnan, Athos, Porthos, and Aramis, and their fight to preserve the honor of their Queen.

720 pp.   0-14-044025-9 $9.95

GERALD DURRELL
1925 – 1994, British

My Family and Other Animals

When the Durrell family can no longer endure the damp, gray English climate, they do what any sensible family would do: sell their house and relocate to the sun-soaked Greek island of Corfu. There, ten-year-old Gerry pursues his interest in natural history with a joyful passion, revealing the engrossing, hidden world of the island's fauna.

NATURE CLASSICS

272 pp.   0-14-028902-X $12.95

MEISTER ECKHART
c. 1260 – 1327, German

Selected Writings

Edited and Translated with an Introduction by Oliver Davies

Including some works translated into English for the first time, *Selected Writings* illuminates the German Dominican Meister Eckhart's synthesis of traditional Christian belief and Greek metaphysics, yielding a boldly speculative philosophy founded on "oneness" of the universe and on a God at once personal and transcendent.

336 pp.   0-14-043343-0 $13.95

MARIA EDGEWORTH
1768 – 1849, IRISH

The Absentee

*Edited with an Introduction
by Heidi Thompson*

Maria Edgeworth's sparkling satire
about an Anglo-Irish family—more
concerned with London society than
their duties and responsibilities to those
who live and work on their Irish
estates—is also a landmark novel of
morality and social realism.

320 pp.   0-14-043645-6 $10.95

Castle Rackrent and Ennui

*Edited with an Introduction by
Marilyn Butler*

These are two stylish novels of Anglo-
Irish relations: *Castle Rackrent* is an
Irish family history unreliably narrated
by a loyal servant; *Ennui* is a "confession" by an aristocrat caught up in Ireland's 1798 revolution.

368 pp.   0-14-043320-1 $11.95

Ormond

*Edited with an Introduction and Notes by
Claire Connolly*

Blending issues of moral development
with questions about the shape of Ireland's political future, Edgeworth
emphasizes the importance of education and upbringing, as opposed to
inheritance and lineage in the tale of
Harry Ormond, a handsome orphan
determined to make his way in the
world.

352 pp.   0-14-043644-8 $12.00

(Available in March 2001)

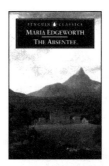

EINHARD
c. 770 – 840, FRANKISH-SWISS

NOTKER THE STAMMERER
c. 840 – 912, SWISS

Two Lives of Charlemagne

*Translated with an Introduction by
Lewis Thorpe*

Einhard offers a factual account of
Charlemagne's personal life and his
achievements in warfare, learning, art,
and statesmanship, while Notker's anec-
dotal approach presents Charlemagne
as a near-legendary figure.

240 pp.   0-14-044213-8 $13.00

GEORGE ELIOT
1819 – 1880, BRITISH

Adam Bede

*Edited with an Introduction by
Stephen Gill*

The story of a beautiful country girl's
seduction by a local squire and the bitter consequences is told with Eliot's
peculiar, haunting power.

608 pp.   0-14-043121-7 $8.95

Daniel Deronda

Edited with an Introduction and Notes by Terence Cave

In *Daniel Deronda*, her remarkable final novel, Eliot set out to come to terms with the British Jews, a society-within-a-society of which her contemporaries seemed to be either oblivious or contemptuous. Eliot weaves her plot strands intimately, infusing them with her insights about human nature and daring the readers of *Middlemarch* and *Adam Bede* to consider realms of experience completely new to the Victorian novel.

848 pp.   0-14-043427-5 $9.95

Felix Holt: The Radical

Edited with an Introduction and Notes by Lynda Mugglestone

Esther Lyon, the heroine, must choose between two men—one of independent wealth and one who is a political rascal — while also deciding her fate as a woman.

576 pp.   0-14-043435-6 $11.95

Middlemarch

Edited with an Introduction and Notes by Rosemary Ashton

This superb novel, Eliot's finest achievement, portrays the shape and texture of a rising provincial town of the 1830s through the remarkable story of determined heroine Dorothea Brooke—an idealist and a woman of conviction trapped in an agonizing marriage to the egotistical Mr. Casaubon.

880 pp.   0-14-043388-0 $9.95

The Mill on the Floss

Edited with an Introduction and Notes by A. S. Byatt

This affectionate and perceptive portrayal of childhood and adolescence in rural England features an imaginative heroine whose spirit closely resembles Eliot's own.

696 pp.   0-14-043120-9 $8.95

Romola

Edited with an Introduction by Dorothea Barrett

Published in 1863, *Romola* probes into the issues of gender and learning and of desire and scholarship.

688 pp.   0-14-043470-4 $10.95

*Scenes of Clerical Life

Edited with an Introduction and Notes by Jennifer Gribble

These stories constitute Eliot's fictional debut and contain what became her enduring themes: the impact of religious controversy and social change in provincial life, and the power of love to transform the lives of individual men and women.

416 pp. 1 map 0-14-043638-3 $8.95

"The exquisite truth and delicacy, both of the humour and the pathos of those stories, I have never seen the like of."

—CHARLES DICKENS

Selected Essays, Poems, and Other Writings

Edited by A. S. Byatt and Nicholas Warren with an Introduction by A. S. Byatt

Rich in wit and energy dissimilar from that of her novels, this collection of Eliot's shorter works includes contributions to the *Westminster Review*, selections from *Impressions of Theophrastus Such*, passages from her translations of Feuerbach and Strauss, the "Notes on Form in Art," and other major essays.

544 pp.   0-14-043148-9 $12.95

Silas Marner

Edited with an Introduction and Notes by David Carroll

In a novel that combines the emotional and moral satisfaction of a fairy tale with the realism and intelligence that are her hallmarks, Eliot counterpoints Silas's experiences with those of Godfrey Cass, the rich squire who is Eppie's father. Godfrey's refusal to claim Eppie, the offspring of his secret marriage to a woman far beneath him in social class, condemns him to a life filled with guilt and fear of disclosure.

240 pp.   0-14-043480-1 $6.95

T. S. ELIOT
1888 – 1965, BRITISH
(B. AMERICA)
NOBEL PRIZE WINNER

The Waste Land and Other Poems

Edited with an Introduction and Notes by Frank Kermode

This new edition collects all of the poems published in Eliot's first three volumes of verse, including "The Love Song of J. Alfred Prufrock," "Portrait of a Lady," "Gerontion," "Sweeney Among the Nightingales," and "Whispers of Immortality." Along with *The Waste Land*, as Frank Kermode writes in his Introduction, "the early poems establish what the later poems confirm: taken together, they constitute a strong claim for Eliot's primacy among twentieth-century poets in English."

20TH-CENTURY CLASSICS

96 pp.   0-14-118072-2 $7.95

RALPH WALDO EMERSON
1803 – 1882, AMERICAN

Selected Essays

Edited with an Introduction by Larzer Ziff

This sampling includes fifteen essays that highlight the formative and significant ideas of this central American thinker: "Nature," "The American Scholar," "An Address Delivered Before the Senior Class in Divinity College, Cambridge," "Man the Reformer," "History," "Self-Reliance," "The Over-Soul," "Circles," "The Transcendentalist," "The Poet," "Experience," "Montaigne: Or, the Skeptic," "Napoleon: Or, the Man of the World," "Fate," and "Thoreau."

360 pp.   0-14-039013-8 $11.95

See *Nineteenth-Century American Poetry*.

FRIEDRICH ENGELS
1820 – 1895, GERMAN

The Condition of the Working Class in England

Edited with a Foreword by Victor Kiernan

Introducing ideas further developed in *The Communist Manifesto*, this savage indictment of the bourgeoisie studies British factory, mine, and farm workers—graphically portraying the human suffering born of the Industrial Revolution.

304 pp.   0-14-044486-6 $13.95

See Karl Marx.

OLAUDAH EQUIANO
c. 1735 – 1797, BRITISH
(B. WEST AFRICA)

The Interesting Narrative and Other Writings

Edited with an Introduction and Notes by Vincent Carretta

An account of the slave trade by a native African, former slave, and loyal British subject, *The Interesting Narrative* is both an exciting, often ter-

rifying, adventure story and an important precursor to such famous nineteenth-century slave narratives as Frederick Douglass's autobiography.

368 pp.   0-14-043485-2 $10.95

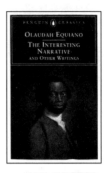

ERASMUS
c. 1469 – 1536, DUTCH

Praise of Folly

Translated by Betty Radice with an Introduction and Notes by A. H. T. Levi

The best introduction to the work of Erasmus, this is one of the finest masterpieces of the sixteenth century, updated and superbly translated to reflect the latest scholarly research.

256 pp.   0-14-044608-7 $10.95

OLAUDAH EQUIANO

Born in 1745, Olaudah Equiano was kidnapped at the age of ten in what is now southeastern Nigeria and sold to English slave traders. Within a few weeks, he was sold to Michael Henry Pascal, an officer in the British Navy. With Pascal, Equiano saw military action during the Seven Years War, but when the war ended, Pascal reneged on his promise to free Equiano, instead selling him back into slavery. Equiano, a clever businessman, managed to save enough money to buy his freedom in 1766. Returning to London, he became an outspoken opponent of the slave trade with *The Interesting Narrative*, published in 1789. He married an Englishwoman in 1792, and left a sizable estate at his death on March 31, 1797.

Parzival

Translated by A. T. Hatto

A prose translation of Wolfram von Eschenbach's thirteenth-century narrative poem recreates and completes the story of the Holy Grail, left unfinished by Chrétien de Troyes.

448 pp.   0-14-044361-4 $14.00

Alcestis and Other Plays

Translated by John Davie with an Introduction and Notes by Richard Rutherford

Euripides was the first of the great Greek tragedians to depict the figures of ancient mythology as fallible human beings. Shocking to his contemporaries, the four plays in this collection—*Alcestis, Medea, The Children of Heracles,* and *Hippolytus*—are uncannily modern not only in their insights but also in their realistic portraits of women, both good and evil.

240 pp.   0-14-044643-5 $9.95

The Bacchae and Other Plays

Translated with an Introduction by Philip Vellacott

Four plays—*Ion* and *Helen* in prose and *The Bacchae* and *The Women of Troy* with dialogue rewritten in verse—depict the guilt and suffering of war, and the subsequent loss of faith.

256 pp.   0-14-044044-5 $9.95

Electra and Other Plays

Translated by John Davie with an Introduction by Richard Rutherford

Written in the period from 426 to 415 B.C., during the fierce struggle for supremacy between Athens and Sparta, these five plays are haunted by the horrors of war, and in particular its impact on women. Included are: *Andromache, Electra, Hecabe, Suppliant Women,* and *Trojan Women.*

220 pp.   0-14-044668-0 $9.95

Medea and Other Plays

Translated with an Introduction by Philip Vellacott

Euripides was the first playwright to use the chorus as commentator, to put contemporary language into the mouths of heroes, and to interpret human suffering without reference to the gods. These verse translations of *Medea, Hecuba, Electra,* and *Mad Heracles* capture all the brilliance of his work.

208 pp.   0-14-044129-8 $8.95

Orestes and Other Plays

Translated with an Introduction by Philip Vellacott

Spanning the last twenty-four years of Euripides's career, this volume includes

The Children of Heracles, Andromache, The Suppliant Women, The Phoenician Women, Orestes, and *Iphigenia in Aulis.*

448 pp.   0-14-044259-6 $9.95

EUSEBIUS
c. 260 – c. 339, PALESTINIAN

The History of the Church

Edited and Revised with an Introduction by Andrew Louth and Translated by G. A. Williamson

A clear, readable translation of the ten books of Bishop Eusebius's *Ecclesiastical History*—the only surviving record of the Church during its crucial first three hundred years—this edition recounts the martyrdoms, heresies, schisms, and proceedings that led to Nicaea and other great church councils.

440 pp.   0-14-044535-8 $15.95

RICHARD FARIÑA
1937 – 1966, AMERICAN

Been Down So Long It Looks Like Up to Me

Introduction by Thomas Pynchon

In this classic novel of the 1960s—an unerring, corrosively comic depiction of a campus in revolt—Fariña evokes

the period as precisely, wittily, and poignantly as F. Scott Fitzgerald captured the Jazz Age.

20TH-CENTURY CLASSICS

352 pp.   0-14-018930-0 $13.95

FANNY FERN
1811 – 1872, AMERICAN

Ruth Hall
A Domestic Tale of the Present Time

Introduction and Notes by Susan Belasco Smith

In *Ruth Hall*, one of the bestselling novels of the 1850s, Fanny Fern drew heavily on her own experiences: the death of her first child and her beloved husband, a bitter estrangement from her family, and her struggle to make a living as a writer. Written as a series of short vignettes and snatches of overheard conversations, it is as unconventional in style as in substance and strikingly modern in its impact.

384 pp.   0-14-043640-5 $10.95

HENRY FIELDING
1707 – 1754, BRITISH

*Joseph Andrews/Shamela

Edited with an Introduction by Judith Hawley

With both these comic novels Fielding took aim at the conventional morals and mores found in the novels of his contemporary, Samuel Richardson. *Joseph Andrews* spoofs the rollicking and colorful adventures of *Tom Jones* and *Shamela* is a brilliant parody of *Pamela,* in which a virtuous servant girl long resists her master's advances and is eventually "rewarded" with marriage.

432 pp.   0-14-043386-4 $9.95

Tom Jones

Edited with an Introduction by
R. P. C. Mutter

A novel rich in incident and coincidence, this picaresque tale of a lusty, handsome young man and his amorous adventures mocks the literary—and moral—conventions of Fielding's time.

912 pp.   0-14-043009-1 $8.95

F. SCOTT FITZGERALD
1896 – 1940, AMERICAN

The Beautiful and Damned

Introduction by Kermit Vanderbilt

It is the vivid depiction of life amid the glitter of Jazz Age New York that transforms the now-familiar stories about F. Scott and Zelda Fitzgerald's early marriage—as well as Fitzgerald's impressions of several well-known literary figures—into a captivating work of fiction.

20TH-CENTURY CLASSICS

448 pp.   0-14-118087-0 $8.95

Jazz Age Stories

Edited with an Introduction and Notes by Patrick O'Donnell

An original collection of Fitzgerald's greatest tales from the "Roaring '20s," *Jazz Age Stories* includes "Bernice Bobs Her Hair," "The Ice Palace," and "A Diamond as Big as the Ritz."

20TH-CENTURY CLASSICS

400 pp.   0-14-118048-X $9.95

This Side of Paradise

Edited with an Introduction and Notes by Patrick O'Donnell

The story of Amory Blaine's adoles-

HENRY FIELDING

Henry Fielding was born at Sharpham Park in Somerset in 1707. In London, between 1729 and 1739, he wrote some twenty-five dramatic pieces, including a series of topical satires that lampooned Sir Robert Walpole and his government. In reaction to these plays, Walpole introduced the Stage Licensing Act in 1737, which effectively ended Fielding's career as a dramatist. His novel-writing career began in 1741 with *Shamela*, a burlesque written in reaction to what he saw as the smug morality propounded by Samuel Richardson's *Pamela*. Fielding then published his own alternative conception of the art and purpose of the novel, *Joseph Andrews*, which achieved immediate popularity. His masterpiece *Tom Jones*, one of the great comic novels in English literature, was published in 1749. Commissioned as a justice of the peace for Westminster, he devoted the last years of his life to the field of criminal justice.

cence and undergraduate days at Princeton, *This Side of Paradise* captures the essence of an American generation struggling to define itself in the aftermath of World War I and the destruction of the "old order."

20TH-CENTURY CLASSICS

320 pp.   0-14-018976-9 $9.95

GUSTAVE FLAUBERT
1821 – 1880, FRENCH

Bouvard and Pécuchet
with The Dictionary of Accepted Ideas

Translated with an Introduction by A. J. Krailsheimer

Unfinished at the time of Flaubert's death in 1880, *Bouvard and Pécuchet* features two Chaplinesque figures in a farce that mocks bourgeois stupidity and the banality of intellectual life in France.

336 pp.   0-14-044320-7 $14.00

Flaubert in Egypt

Edited and Translated with an Introduction by Francis Steegmuller

At once a classic of travel literature and a penetrating portrait of a "sensibility on tour," *Flaubert in Egypt* wonderfully captures the young writer's impressions during his 1849 voyages. Using diaries, letters, travel notes, and the evidence of Flaubert's traveling companion, Maxime Du Camp, Francis Steegmuller reconstructs his journey through the bazaars and brothels of Cairo and down the Nile to the Red Sea.

240 pp.   0-14-043582-4 $12.95

Madame Bovary

Translated with an Introduction and Notes by Geoffrey Wall

Flaubert's landmark story unfolds the desperate love affair of Emma Bovary, the bored provincial housewife who abandons her husband in defiance of bourgeois values.

320 pp.   0-14-044526-9 $8.95

GUSTAVE FLAUBERT

Born in Rouen in 1821, Gustave Flaubert was the son of a brilliant surgeon and grew to be strongly critical of bourgeois society. He quit law school in 1841 after being diagnosed with epilepsy and devoted himself to writing. His stormy affair with the poet Louise Colet ended after nine years in 1855. His masterpiece *Madame Bovary*, based on two different true stories, was published the next year, and Flaubert narrowly escaped being convicted for immorality due to its daring content. His work reflects his passion for poetic prose and, at the same time, relentless objectivity. Flaubert counted among his friends George Sand, Turgenev, Zola, and his protégé Maupassant.

Salammbô

*Translated with an Introduction by
A. J. Krailsheimer*

An epic story of lust, cruelty, and sensuality, this historical novel is set in
Carthage in the days following the First
Punic War with Rome.

288 pp.   0-14-044328-2 $12.95

Selected Letters

*Translated with an Introduction by
Geoffrey Wall*

Spanning Flaubert's life from adolescence to his years of fame as a writer,
this collection of letters is a compelling
portrait of the artist.

464 pp.   0-14-044607-9 $13.95

Sentimental Education

*Translated with an Introduction by
Robert Baldick*

Flaubert skillfully recreates the fiber of
his times and society in this novel of a
young man's romantic attachment to an
older woman.

432 pp.   0-14-044141-7 $5.95

Three Tales

*Translated with an Introduction by
Robert Baldick*

In *A Simple Life*, Flaubert recounts the
life of a pious servant girl; in *The
Legend of St. Julian*, Hospitaller gives
insight into medieval mysticism; and
Hérodias is a powerful story of the
martyrdom of St. John the Baptist.

128 pp.   0-14-044106-9 $9.95

THEODOR FONTANE
1819 – 1898, GERMAN

Effi Briest

*Translated with an Introduction by
Douglas Parmée*

This story of a woman's adultery and its
consequences is a stunning portrait of
the rigidity of the Prussian aristocracy
in the mid–nineteenth century.

272 pp.   0-14-044190-5 $11.95

FORD MADOX FORD
1873 – 1939, BRITISH

The Fifth Queen

With an Introduction by A. S. Byatt

This masterful example of historical
fiction is Ford's acclaimed portrait of
Henry VIII's controversial fifth Queen,
the beautiful, clever, and outspoken
Katherine Howard.

20TH-CENTURY CLASSICS

608 pp.   0-14-118130-3 $12.95

Penguin Readers Guide Available

"A magnificent bravura piece."
—GRAHAM GREENE

The Good Soldier

Ford explores the deceptions of Edward Ashburnham, an impeccable British gentleman and soldier with an overbearing ruthlessness in affairs of the heart.

20TH-CENTURY CLASSICS
240 pp.   0-14-018081-8 $9.95

JOHN FORD
1568 – C. 1639, BRITISH

Three Plays

Edited with an Introduction and Commentary by Keith Sturgess

Sexual tragedy and political failure are uncompromisingly examined in *'Tis Pity She's a Whore*, *The Broken Heart*, and *Perkin Warbeck*, all written during the first half of the seventeenth century.

416 pp.   0-14-043059-8 $10.95

E. M. FORSTER
1879 – 1970, BRITISH

"One of the wisest and the warmest, one of the gentlest and yet one of the most sharp-edged, of the great modern English writers."

—MALCOLM BRADBURY

Howards End

Edited with an Introduction and Notes by David Lodge

A chance acquaintance bringing together the prosperous bourgeois Wilcox family and the clever, cultured, and idealistic Schlegel sisters sets in motion a chain of events that will entangle three families and their aspirations for personal and social harmony.

20TH-CENTURY CLASSICS
352 pp.   0-14-118213-X $9.95
Penguin Readers Guide Available

A Room with a View

Edited with an Introduction and Notes by Malcolm Bradbury

Lucy Honeychurch is torn between the expectations of her world and the passionate yearnings of her heart. Within this sparkling love story, Forster has couched a perceptive examination of class structure and a penetrating social comedy.

20TH-CENTURY CLASSICS
256 pp.   0-14-118329-2 $9.95
Penguin Readers Guide Available

Selected Stories

Edited with an Introduction and Notes by David Leavitt and Mark Mitchell

The twelve stories in this collection are rich in irony and often feature violent events, discomforting coincidences, and other disruptive happenings that throw the characters' perceptions and beliefs off balance. Included are "The Story of a Panic," "The Machine Stops," "The Eternal Moment," and others.

20TH-CENTURY CLASSICS
224 pp.   0-14-118619-4 $13.00
(Available in March 2001)

HANNAH WEBSTER FOSTER

See William Hill Brown.

GEORGE FOX
1624 – 1691, BRITISH

The Journal

Edited with an Introduction and Notes by Nigel Smith

The fascinating autobiographical account of struggles, hardships, and successes from the father of Quakerism is presented in an edition that enhances the coherence of the main narrative while retaining the immediacy and excitement of the original. Extracts from Fox's letters and travelogues and William Penn's Preface to the first printed edition supplement the main text.

576 pp.   0-14-043399-6 $14.95

ANATOLE FRANCE
1844 – 1924, FRENCH
NOBEL PRIZE WINNER

The Gods Will Have Blood

Translated with an Introduction by Frederick Davies

Set during the French Revolution in the fifteen months preceding the fall of Robespierre, this novel by Nobel Prize winner Anatole France powerfully re-creates the Terror—a period of intense and virtually indiscriminate violence.

20TH-CENTURY CLASSICS

256 pp.   0-14-018457-0 $12.95

BENJAMIN FRANKLIN
1706 – 1790, AMERICAN

The Autobiography and Other Writings

Edited with an Introduction by Kenneth A. Silverman

Tracing his rise from a printer's apprentice to an internationally famous scientist, inventor, statesman, legislator, and diplomat, Franklin distills the complex and passionate intellectual strivings of his life into a persona extolling industry and sober virtue. Also included here are selections from Franklin's essays and letters.

320 pp.   0-14-039052-9 $6.95

SIR JAMES FRAZER
1854 – 1941, SCOTTISH

The Golden Bough
Abridged Edition

Introduction by George W. Stocking, Jr.

A monumental study of magic, folklore, and religion, *The Golden Bough* draws on the myths, rites and rituals, totems and taboos, and customs of ancient European civilizations and primitive cultures throughout the world. Frazer's ideas had a far-reaching impact on the course of modern anthropology, philosophy, and psychology, and on the writing of literary figures such as D. H. Lawrence, Ezra Pound, and T. S. Eliot.

20TH-CENTURY CLASSICS
944 pp.   0-14-018931-9 $14.95

"Perhaps no book has had so decisive an effect upon modern literature."

—LIONEL TRILLING

HAROLD FREDERIC
1856 – 1898, AMERICAN

The Damnation of Theron Ware
Introduction by Scott Donaldson

A candid inquiry into the intertwining of religious and sexual fervor, and a telling portrait of the United States at the end of the nineteenth century, this novel foreshadows the rise of naturalism in American literature.

512 pp.   0-14-039025-1 $13.95

MARY E. WILKINS FREEMAN
1852 – 1930, AMERICAN

A New England Nun and Other Stories
Edited with an Introduction and Notes by Sandra A. Zagarell

"Regionalist" writer Freeman began her career when writing was becoming the first culture industry and her work appeared in many popular magazines. This collection showcases her many modes—romantic, gothic, and psychologically symbolic—as well as her use

of humor and irony and comprises fifteen stories and the novella, *The Jamesons.*

320 pp.   0-14-043739-8 $12.95

JEAN FROISSART
C. 1337 – C. 1410, FRENCH

Chronicles
Selected and Translated with an Introduction by Geoffrey Brereton

This selection from Froissart's *Chronicles* forms a vast panorama of Europe, from the deposition of Edward II to the downfall of Richard II.

496 pp.   0-14-044200-6 $12.95

ROBERT FROST
1874 – 1963, AMERICAN

Early Poems
A Boy's Will, North of Boston, Mountain Interval, and Other Poems
Edited with an Introduction and Notes by Robert Faggen

This volume presents Frost's first three books, masterful and innovative collections that contain some of his best-known poems, including "Mowing," "Mending Wall," "After Apple-Picking,"

"Home Burial," "The Oven Bird," "Birches," and "The Road Not Taken."

20TH-CENTURY CLASSICS
288 pp.   0-14-118017-X $9.95

WILLIAM GADDIS
1922 – 1998, AMERICAN

Carpenter's Gothic

This story of raging comedy and despair centers on the tempestuous marriage of an heiress and a Vietnam veteran.

20TH-CENTURY CLASSICS
272 pp.   0-14-118222-9 $13.95

"Everything in this compelling and brilliant vision of America—the packaged sleaze, the incipient violence, the fundamentalist furor, the constricted sexuality—is charged with the force of a volcanic eruption."

—WALTER ABISH

JR

Introduction by Frederick R. Karl

The hero of this novel of epic comedy and satire is an eleven-year-old capitalist who parlays Navy surplus forks and some defaulted bonds into a vast empire of free enterprise. Winner of the National Book Award in 1976.

20TH-CENTURY CLASSICS
752 pp.   0-14-018707-3 $18.95

The Recognitions

Introduction by William H. Gass

First published in 1955 and considered one of the most profound works of fiction of this century, *The Recognitions* tells the story of a painter-counterfeiter who forges out of love, not larceny, in an age when the fakes have become indistinguishable from the real.

20TH-CENTURY CLASSICS
976 pp.   0-14-018708-1 $21.95

HAMLIN GARLAND
1860 – 1940, AMERICAN

A Son of the Middle Border

Edited with an Introduction and Notes by Joseph B. McCullough

Mining the history of his own family, Garland's bittersweet narrative about growing up on a Wisconsin farm is an epic of America's immigration toward new frontiers in the nineteenth century and of the gradual disillusionment with the pioneer ideal.

20TH-CENTURY CLASSICS
416 pp.   0-14-018796-0 $11.95

Cranford/Cousin Phillis

Edited with an Introduction and Notes by Peter J. Keating

Both *Cranford*, an affectionately ironic and understated depiction of an early Victorian country town, and *Cousin Phillis*, the story of an unfulfilled love affair, are concerned with the transition from old values to new.

368 pp.   0-14-043104-7 $10.95

Gothic Tales

Edited by Laura Kranzler

In these nine strange and wonderful tales, Gaskell—best known for books about middle-class life in country villages—used spine-tingling, supernatural elements to explore human frailties and the dualities in everyday life.

416 pp.   0-14-043741-X $12.00

(Available in February 2001)

The Life of Charlotte Brontë

Edited with an Introduction and Notes by Elisabeth Jay

Novelist Elizabeth Gaskell drew on her friendship with the author of *Jane Eyre*, *Shirley*, and *Villette* to write this compelling psychological portrait of Brontë, whose controversial works belied the reclusive life she led.

544 pp.   0-14-043493-3 $10.95

Mary Barton

Edited with an Introduction and Notes by Macdonald Daly

A powerful depiction of industrial strife and class conflict in Manchester in the 1840s, Elizabeth Gaskell's first novel won widespread attention and established her reputation as a writer concerned with social and political issues.

464 pp.   0-14-043464-X $7.95

North and South

Edited with an Introduction and Notes by Patricia Ingham

Gaskell's great portrait of vastly differing conditions in England's industrial north and rural south explores the exploitation of the working class and links the plight of workers with that of women.

480 pp.   0-14-043424-0 $8.95

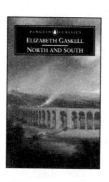

Ruth

Edited with an Introduction by Angus Easson

Overturning the conventional assumption that a woman once seduced is condemned to exclusion from respectable society, Gaskell draws a heroine whose emotional honesty, innate morality, and the love she shares with her illegitimate son are sufficient for redemption.

432 pp.   0-14-043430-5 $8.95

Wives and Daughters

Edited with an Introduction and Notes by Pam Morris

This is Gaskell's comic tale of the coming-of-age of two very different stepsisters and of men and women constantly, if unintentionally, at cross-purposes. Beneath the nostalgic domesticity of *Wives and Daughters* readers will discover the same acute insights that have won Gaskell's earlier, more controversial novels new readership.

720 pp.   0-14-043478-X $13.95

WILLIAM H. GASS
B. 1924, AMERICAN

Omensetter's Luck

With an Afterword by the Author

The quirky, impressionistic, and breathtakingly original story of an ordinary community galvanized by the presence of an extraordinary man, *Omensetter's Luck* (1966) has been called the "most important work of fiction by an American in this literary generation" (Richard Gilman, *The New Republic*).

20TH-CENTURY CLASSICS

320 pp.   0-14-118010-2 $12.95

JOHN GAY
1685 – 1732, BRITISH

The Beggar's Opera

Edited by Bryan Loughrey and T. O. Treadwell with an Introduction by Bryan Loughrey

This witty parody of Italian opera, featuring the denizens of the British underworld, was performed more than any other play during the eighteenth century.

128 pp.   0-14-043220-5 $8.95

GEOFFREY OF MONMOUTH
C. 1100 – 1155, WELSH

The History of the Kings of Britain

Translated with an Introduction by Lewis Thorpe

This heroic epic of the twelfth century, describing such half-legendary kings as Cymbeline, Arthur, and Lear inspired Malory, Spenser, Shakespeare, and many other writers.

384 pp.   0-14-044170-0 $13.95

GERALD OF WALES
C. 1146 – 1223, NORMAN/WELSH

The History and Topography of Ireland

Translated with an Introduction and Notes by John O'Meara

Arguably the most authoritative primary source for what is known about medieval Ireland, this lively history by a twelfth-century Norman describes the land's topography, natural resources, and inhabitants in vivid detail.

144 pp.   maps   0-14-044423-8 $12.95

The Journey Through Wales/ The Description of Wales

Translated with an Introduction by Lewis Thorpe

The Journey, an accurate and comprehensive history of twelfth-century Wales, is filled with lively anecdotes and folklore; *The Description* offers a fascinating picture of the life of ordinary Welshmen.

336 pp.   0-14-044339-8 $13.95

EDWARD GIBBON
1737 – 1794, BRITISH

The History of the Decline and Fall of the Roman Empire

Edited with an Introduction and Appendices by David Womersley

Inspired by a visit to Rome in 1764, Edward Gibbon spent twenty years weaving together his epic chronicle. This definitive three-volume edition presents a complete unmodernized text, the author's own comments and notes, and his famous *Vindication*.

The History of the Decline and Fall of the Roman Empire
Volume I

Edited with an Introduction and Appendices by David Womersley

Launches the history by describing the Empire during the Age of Trajan and the Antonines.

1,120 pp.   0-14-043393-7 $24.95

The History of the Decline and Fall of the Roman Empire
Volume II

Edited with an Introduction and Appendices by David Womersley

Includes two of Gibbon's most subtle portraits, those of Constantine and Julian the Apostate.

1,008 pp.   0-14-043394-5 $24.95

The History of the Decline and Fall of the Roman Empire
Volume III

Edited with an Introduction and Appendices by David Womersley

Examines the enfeebled state of the Byzantine Empire and the spread of Islam.

1,184 pp.   0-14-043395-3 $24.95

EDWARD GIBBON

Edward Gibbon was born in 1737, in Putney, and was the only child of his parents to survive infancy. Although his education was frequently interrupted by ill health he was finally able to study Greek and French in Lausanne, Switzerland. It was while he was in Rome in 1764 that he first conceived the work that was to become *The History of the Decline and Fall of the Roman Empire*. The first volume of his famous *History* was published in 1776, the second and third appeared in 1781, and the final three in 1788. He died while on a visit to his friend, Lord Sheffield, who later edited Gibbon's autobiographical papers and published them in 1796.

*The History of the Decline and Fall of the Roman Empire

Abridged with a New Introduction by David Womersley

Based on Womersley's three-volume Penguin Classics edition, this new abridgement contains complete chapters from all three volumes, linked by extended bridging passages, vividly capturing the architecture of Gibbon's masterwork.

848 pp.   0-14-043764-9 $15.00

(Available in January 2001)

"Womersley has produced a wholly new edition...which is a fitting monument to the greatest of all English historians."

—NIALL FERGUSON

STELLA GIBBONS
1902 – 1989, BRITISH

Cold Comfort Farm

First published to great acclaim in 1932, and now recognized as one of the funniest books ever written, this witty parody mocks the melodrama, earthly sensuality, and use of symbolism found in the works of Thomas Hardy,

D. H. Lawrence, and other popular "country-life" novels of the period.

20TH-CENTURY CLASSICS

240 pp.   0-14-018869-X $11.95

CHARLOTTE PERKINS GILMAN
1860 – 1935, AMERICAN

Herland, The Yellow Wall-Paper, and Selected Writings

Edited with an Introduction by Denise D. Knight

Gilman used the utopian form, satire, and fantasy powerfully to critique women's place in society. This volume collects her classic story, "The Yellow Wall-Paper," her most famous novel, *Herland*, and a selection of her poetry and other short fiction.

20TH-CENTURY CLASSICS

384 pp.   0-14-118062-5 $9.95

See *Four Stories by American Women.*

GEORGE GISSING
1857 – 1903, BRITISH

New Grub Street

Edited with an Introduction by Bernard Bergonzi

Through Edwin Reardon, a struggling

novelist, and his friends on Grub Street—Milvain, a journalist, and Yule, an embittered critic—Gissing brings to life the literary climate of 1880s London.

560 pp.   0-14-043032-6 $13.95

The Odd Women

Introduction by Elaine Showalter

A refreshing antidote to Victorian novels celebrating romantic love and marriage, *The Odd Women* is a dramatic look at the actual circumstances, options, and desires of women, told with psychological and political realities that are astonishingly contemporary.

416 pp.   0-14-043379-1 $11.95

WILLIAM GODWIN
1756 – 1836, BRITISH

Caleb Williams

Edited with an Introduction and Notes by Maurice Hindle

A psychological detective novel about power, *Caleb Williams* was an imaginative contribution to the radical cause in the British debate on the French Revolution.

448 pp.   0-14-043256-6 $11.95

See Mary Wollstonecraft.

JOHANN WOLFGANG VON GOETHE
1749 – 1832, GERMAN

Elective Affinities

Translated with an Introduction by R. J. Hollingdale

Condemned as immoral when it was first published, this novel reflects the conflict Goethe felt between his respect for the conventions of marriage and the possibility of spontaneous passion.

304 pp.   0-14-044242-1 $11.95

Faust, Part 1

Translated with an Introduction by Philip Wayne

Goethe's masterpiece dramatizes the struggle of modern man to solve the mysteries of energy, pleasure, and the creation of life.

208 pp.   0-14-044012-7 $8.95

Faust, Part 2

Translated with an Introduction by Philip Wayne

Rich in allusion and allegory, *Faust, Part 2* explores philosophical themes that obsessed Goethe throughout his life.

288 pp.   0-14-044093-3 $10.95

Italian Journey

Translated with an Introduction by W. H. Auden and Elizabeth Mayer

Goethe's account of his passage through Italy from 1786 to 1788 is a great travel chronicle as well as a candid self-portrait of a genius in the grip of spiritual crisis.

512 pp.   0-14-044233-2 $13.95

Maxims and Reflections

Translated by Elizabeth Stopp and Edited with an Introduction by Peter Hutchinson

An essential introduction to Goethe, these 1,413 maxims and reflections reveal not only some of his deepest thoughts on art, ethics, literature, and natural science but also his immediate reactions to books, chance encounters, and his administrative work.

208 pp.   0-14-044720-2 $11.95

Selected Verse

Translated with an Introduction by David Luke

This dual-language edition of nearly three hundred poems draws from every period of Goethe's work, and includes substantial portions of *Faust*.

368 pp.   0-14-042074-6 $12.95

The Sorrows of Young Werther

Translated with an Introduction and Notes by Michael Hulse

Based partly on Goethe's unrequited love for Charlotte Buff, this novel of pathological sensibility strikes a powerful blow against Enlightenment rationalism.

144 pp.   0-14-044503-X $10.95

See *Romantic Fairy Tales*.

VINCENT VAN GOGH
1853 – 1890, Dutch

The Letters of Vincent van Gogh

Edited and Selected with an Introduction by Ronald de Leeuw and Translated by Arnold Pomerans

This volume reinstates passages omitted from early editions of van Gogh's letters and includes, whenever possible, the wonderful pen-and-ink sketches he added to his written messages. Winner of the 1997 PEN/Book-of-the-Month Club Translation Prize.

560 pp.   0-14-044674-5 $14.95

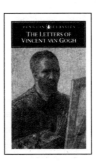

NIKOLAI GOGOL
1809 – 1852, Russian

Dead Souls

Translated with an Introduction by David Magarshack

The hero of this satiric masterpiece is Gogol's most beguiling and devilish creation, a man who buys dead serfs. Gogol's attempts to continue the story in two more books obsessed him, eventually driving him to madness and death.

384 pp.   0-14-044113-1 $10.95

Diary of a Madman and Other Stories

Translated with an Introduction by Ronald Wilks

These five stories, "Diary of a Madman," "The Overcoat," "How Ivan Ivanovich Quarrelled with Ivan Nikiforovich," "Ivan Fyodorovich Shponka and His Aunt," and "The

Nose," demonstrate Gogol's peculiar and strikingly original imagination.

192 pp.   0-14-044273-1 $9.95

OLIVER GOLDSMITH
1728 – 1774, BRITISH

The Vicar of Wakefield

Edited with an Introduction and Notes by Stephen Coote

This charming comedy is an artful send-up of the literary conventions of Goldsmith's time—the pastoral scene, the artificial romance, the stoic bravery of the hero—culminating in a highly improbable denouement.

224 pp.   0-14-043159-4 $7.95

IVAN GONCHAROV
1812 – 1891, RUSSIAN

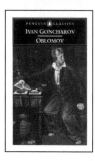

Oblomov

Translated with an Introduction by David Magarshack

Goncharov's detached yet sympathetic portrait of the humdrum life of his ineffectual and slothful hero is a tragicomedy created through painstaking accumulation of seemingly insignificant details alongside a sympathetic analysis of his character.

496 pp.   0-14-044040-2 $12.95

MAXIM GORKY
1868 – 1936, RUSSIAN

My Childhood

Translated with an Introduction by Ronald Wilks

The first part of Gorky's celebrated autobiography, this volume records with charm and poignancy the childhood of extreme poverty and brutality that deepened Gorky's understanding of the "ordinary Russian," an experience that would influence some of his greatest works.

20TH-CENTURY CLASSICS

240 pp.   0-14-018285-3 $12.95

SIR EDMUND GOSSE
1849 – 1928, BRITISH

Father and Son

Edited with an Introduction and Notes by Peter Abbs

An account of the religious fanaticism surrounding his upbringing, Gosse's novel also serves as a brilliant and moving document of Victorian social and intellectual history.

20TH-CENTURY CLASSICS

224 pp.   0-14-018276-4 $11.95

GOTTFRIED VON STRASSBURG
C. 12TH – 13TH CENT., GERMAN

Tristan

Translated with an Introduction by A. T. Hatto

This medieval version of the legendary romance between Tristan and Isolde portrays Tristan as a sophisticated pre-Renaissance man.

384 pp.   0-14-044098-4 $13.95

ULYSSES S. GRANT
1822 – 1885, American

Personal Memoirs

With an Introduction and Notes by James M. McPherson

Grant's memoirs demonstrate the intelligence, intense determination, and laconic modesty that made him the Union's foremost commander.

320 pp.   0-14-043701-0 $14.95

"Perhaps the most revelatory autobiography of high command to exist in any language."

—JOHN KEEGAN

HENRY GREEN
1905 – 1973, British

"Green's remains the most interesting and vital imagination in English fiction in our time."

—EUDORA WELTY

Loving/Living/Party Going

Introduction by John Updike

This volume brings together three of Henry Green's intensely original novels: *Loving* brilliantly contrasts the lives of servants and masters in an Irish castle during World War II; *Living* those of workers and owners in a Birmingham iron foundry; *Party Going* presents a party of wealthy travelers stranded by fog in a London railway hotel while throngs of workers await trains in the station below.

20TH-CENTURY CLASSICS
528 pp.   0-14-018691-3 $14.95

GRAHAM GREENE
1904 – 1991, British

"Graham Greene was in a class by himself....He will be read and remembered as the ultimate chronicler of twentieth-century man's consciousness and anxiety."

—WILLIAM GOLDING

Brighton Rock

Greene's chilling exposé of violence and gang warfare in the prewar British underworld features Pinkie, a protagonist who is the embodiment of evil.

20TH-CENTURY CLASSICS
256 pp.   0-14-018492-9 $12.95

A Burnt-Out Case

A world-famous architect, who has lost interest in his life and art, anonymously begins work at a leper colony in order to cure his "disease of the mind."

20TH-CENTURY CLASSICS
200 pp.   0-14-018539-9 $11.95

The Captain and the Enemy

Greene's last novel is a fascinating tale of adventure and intrigue that follows an Englishman from his boyhood with an odd surrogate family to Panama where he becomes involved in gun smuggling and betrayal.

20TH-CENTURY CLASSICS

208 pp.   0-14-018855-X $11.95

Collected Essays

Collected Essays contains nearly eighty essays, reviews, and occasional pieces composed between novels, plays, and travel books over four prolific decades.

20TH-CENTURY CLASSICS

352 pp.   0-14-018576-3 $12.95

Collected Short Stories

Previously published in three volumes —*May We Borrow Your Husband?*, *A Sense of Reality*, and *Twenty-one Stories*—these thirty-seven stories reveal Greene in a range of contrasting moods, sometimes cynical and witty, sometimes searching and philosophical.

20TH-CENTURY CLASSICS

368 pp.   0-14-018612-3 $13.95

The Comedians

Three men meet on a ship bound for Haiti, a world in the grip of the corrupt "Papa Doc" and his sinister secret police, the Tontons Macoute.

20TH-CENTURY CLASSICS

288 pp.   0-14-018494-5 $12.95

The End of the Affair

A love affair, abruptly and inexplicably broken off, prompts the grief-stricken novelist Maurice Bendrix to hire a private detective to discover the cause.

20TH-CENTURY CLASSICS

192 pp.   0-14-018495-3 $11.95

England Made Me

A tour de force of moral suspense, this is the story of a confirmed liar and cheat whose untimely discovery of decency may cost him not only his job but also his life.

20TH-CENTURY CLASSICS

208 pp.   0-14-018551-8 $11.95

A Gun for Sale

Raven's cold-blooded killing of the Minister of War is an act of violence with chilling repercussions, not just for Raven himself but for the nation as a whole.

20TH-CENTURY CLASSICS

208 pp.   0-14-018540-2 $12.95

The Heart of the Matter

The terrifying depiction of a man's awe of the Church and Greene's ability to portray human motive and to convey such a depth of suffering make *The Heart of the Matter* one of his most enduring and tragic novels.

20TH-CENTURY CLASSICS

272 pp.   0-14-018496-1 $12.95

Journey Without Maps

This chronicle of Greene's journey through Liberia in the 1930s is at once vivid reportage and a powerful document of spiritual hunger and renewal.

20TH-CENTURY CLASSICS

256 pp.   0-14-018579-8 $12.95

The Last Word and Other Stories

These twelve stories, spanning from 1923 to 1989, represent the quintessential Graham Greene. Rich in gallows humor, they have the power both to move and to entertain.

20TH-CENTURY CLASSICS

160 pp.   0-14-118157-5 $11.95

The Lawless Roads

This story of Greene's visit to Mexico emerged after he was commissioned to find out how ordinary people had reacted to the brutal anticlerical purges of President Calles.

20TH-CENTURY CLASSICS

224 pp.   0-14-018580-1 $12.95

Loser Takes All

This superb story offers up a tale of an unsuccessful accountant's second try at luck and love.

20TH-CENTURY CLASSICS

128 pp.   0-14-018542-9 $9.95

The Man Within

The themes of betrayal, pursuit, and the search for peace run through Greene's first published novel about a smuggler who takes refuge from his avengers.

20TH-CENTURY CLASSICS

224 pp.   0-14-018530-5 $11.95

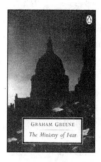

The Ministry of Fear

This is a complex portrait of the shadowy inner landscape of Arthur Rowe—torn apart with guilt over mercifully murdering his sick wife—and the terrifying and phantasmagoric landscape of England during the Blitz.

20TH-CENTURY CLASSICS

224 pp.   0-14-018536-4 $12.00

GRAHAM GREENE

Graham Greene was born in England in 1904 and died in 1991 in Switzerland. He studied at the Berkhamsted School, where his father was headmaster, before entering Balliol College, Oxford. In 1926 Greene became a journalist for the *Nottingham Journal* and converted to Catholicism to be closer to his future wife, Vivien Dayrell-Browning. His first novel, *The Man Within*, was published three years later. *The Quiet American*, *Our Man in Havana*, and *Orient Express* are among his numerous provocative, exotically suspenseful, and often hilarious explorations of the corruption of the human spirit. Many of his novels have been adapted successfully to the screen.

Our Man in Havana

In this comic novel, Wormwold tries to keep his job as a secret agent in Havana by filing bogus reports based on Lamb's *Tales from Shakespeare* and dreaming up military installations from vacuum-cleaner designs.

20TH-CENTURY CLASSICS

224 pp.   0-14-018493-7 $12.95

The Power and the Glory

Introduction by John Updike

Set in a terror-ridden Mexican state, Greene's masterpiece is a compelling depiction of a "whisky priest" struggling to overcome physical and moral cowardice and find redemption.

20TH-CENTURY CLASSICS

224 pp.   0-14-018499-6 $12.95

The Quiet American

While the French Army in Indo-China grapples with the Vietminh, a young and high-minded American based in Saigon begins to channel economic aid to a "Third Force"—leading him to blunder into a complex political and cultural world he seems not to understand fully, with disastrous and violent results.

20TH-CENTURY CLASSICS

192 pp.   0-14-018500-3 $11.95

Stamboul Train

Set on the Orient Express, this suspense thriller involves the desperate affair between a pragmatic Jew and a naïve chorus girl entangled in lust, duplicity, and murder.

20TH-CENTURY CLASSICS

224 pp.   0-14-018532-1 $12.95

The Third Man and The Fallen Idol

This edition pairs two thrillers: Greene's legendary *The Third Man* and *The Fallen Idol*, in which a small boy discovers the deadly truths of the adult world.

20TH-CENTURY CLASSICS

160 pp.   0-14-018533-X $10.95

Travels with My Aunt

Henry Pulling's dull suburban life is interrupted when his septuagenarian Aunt Augusta persuades him to travel the world with her in her own inimitable style.

20TH-CENTURY CLASSICS

272 pp.   0-14-018501-1 $12.95

Twenty-one Stories

Some of the stories included here are comic, others are wryly sad. They can be deeply shocking or hauntingly tragic. Whatever the mood, each one is compellingly entertaining.

20TH-CENTURY CLASSICS

224 pp.   0-14-018534-8 $10.95

LADY ISABELLA GREGORY
1852 – 1932, IRISH

Selected Writings

Edited with an Introduction and Notes by Lucy McDiarmid and Maureen Waters

This volume, the first comprehensive collection of Lady Gregory's enormously varied writings, includes the influential Irish play *Kathleen ni Houlihan*, which she wrote with Yeats, and selections from Gregory's journals, autobiography, and essays, as well as her plays and little-known love poems.

20TH-CENTURY CLASSICS
624 pp.   0-14-018955-6 $14.95

GREGORY OF TOURS
539 – 594, FRANKISH

A History of the Franks

Translated with an Introduction by Lewis Thorpe

This colorful narrative of French history in the sixth century is a dramatic and detailed portrait of a period of political and religious turmoil.

720 pp.   0-14-044295-2 $15.95

ZANE GREY
1872 – 1939, AMERICAN

Riders of the Purple Sage

Introduction by Jane Tompkins

A great drama of psyche and landscape, Zane Grey's bestselling 1912 adventure romance is the definitive Western novel, with popular appeal and distinct codes of chivalry and toughness.

20TH-CENTURY CLASSICS
304 pp.   0-14-018440-6 $9.95

JACOB GRIMM
1785 – 1863, GERMAN

WILHELM GRIMM
1786 – 1859, GERMAN

Selected Tales

Translated with an Introduction and Notes by David Luke

Sixty-five selections from *Kinder-und Hausmärchen* provide a representative sample of the folktale motifs that have fascinated children and adults around the world for centuries.

432 pp.   0-14-044401-7 $12.95

RICHARD HAKLUYT
C. 1552 – 1616, BRITISH

Voyages and Discoveries

Edited and Abridged with an Introduction by Jack Beeching

In this work of Hakluyt—a Renaissance diplomat, scholar, and spy—lies the beginnings of geography, economics, ethnography, and the modern world itself.

448 pp.   0-14-043073-3 $12.95

ALEXANDER HAMILTON

See James Madison.

KNUT HAMSUN
1859 - 1952, NORWEGIAN
NOBEL PRIZE WINNER

Hunger

Translated with an Introduction and Notes by Sverre Lyngstad

First published in Norway in 1890, *Hunger* probes into the depths of consciousness with frightening and gripping power. Like the works of Dostoyevsky, it marks an extraordinary break with Western literary and humanistic traditions.

20TH-CENTURY CLASSICS

224 pp.   0-14-118064-1 $10.95

"The classic novel of humiliation, even beyond Dostoyevsky... Lyngstad's translation restores to the English-speaking reader one of the cold summits in modern prose literature."

—GEORGE STEINER

Mysteries

Translated with an Introduction and Notes by Sverre Lyngstad

Johan Nilsen Nagel is a mysterious stranger who suddenly turns up in a small Norwegian town one summer—and just as suddenly disappears. The novel creates a powerful sense of Nagel's stream-of-thought as he increasingly withdraws into the torture chamber of his own subconscious psyche.

20TH-CENTURY CLASSICS

352 pp.   0-14-118618-6 $14.00

(Available in January 2001)

Pan

From Lieutenant Thomas Glahn's Papers

Translated with an Introduction and Notes by Sverre Lyngstad

A remarkable new translation of Hamsun's portrait of a man rejecting the

KNUT HAMSUN

Knut Hamsun was born in 1859 to a poor peasant family in central Norway. Based on his experiences as a struggling writer, Hamsun's first novel, *Hunger* (1890), was an immediate critical success. Best known as a novelist, Hamsun found the contemporary novel plot-ridden and psychologically unsophisticated and aimed to transform it to accommodate the nuances of conscious and unconscious life as well as the vagaries of human behavior. Hamsun's innovative aesthetic is exemplified in his most successful novels of the decade—*Mysteries* (1892) and *Pan* (1894). Perhaps his best known work is *The Growth of the Soil* (1917), which earned him a Nobel Prize in 1920. A Nazi sympathizer during World War II, Hamsun was later forced to forfeit his considerable fortune to the state. He died in poverty in 1952.

claims of bourgeois society for a Rousseauian embrace of Nature and Eros.

20TH-CENTURY CLASSICS

224 pp.   0-14-118067-6 $9.95

THOMAS HARDY
1840 – 1928, BRITISH

Desperate Remedies

Edited with an Introduction and Notes by Mary Rimmer

Blackmail, murder, and romance are among the ingredients of Hardy's first published novel, which appeared anonymously in 1871. In its depiction of country life and insight into psychology and sexuality, it already bears the unmistakeable imprint of Hardy's genius.

512 pp. 1 map 0-14-043523-9 $13.95

The Distracted Preacher and Other Tales

Edited with an Introduction and Notes by Susan Hill

Hardy captures the provincial experiences of his native Dorset and environs in eleven of his best and most representative stories, including "The Withered Arm," "Barbara of the House of Grebe," "The Son's Veto," and "A Tragedy of Two Ambitions."

368 pp.   0-14-043124-1 $9.95

*Far from the Madding Crowd

Edited with an Introduction and Notes by Rosemarie Morgan with Shannon Russell

In this tale of rural romance—and Hardy's most humorous novel—the capricious and willful Bathsheba Everdene is wooed by three very different men and comes to comprehend the true nature of generosity, humility, and, ultimately, love.

480 pp.   0-14-043521-2 $7.95

The Hand of Ethelberta

Edited with an Introduction and Notes by Tim Dolin and Illustrations by George du Maurier

This tale of an opportunistic yet ultimately loyal adventuress, who begins life humbly and ends as the wife of a rakish aristocrat, will surprise readers of Hardy's more familiar, and darker, Wessex novels.

512 pp.   0-14-043502-6 $13.95

*Jude the Obscure

Edited with an Introduction and Notes by Dennis Taylor

In this haunting love story, the stonemason Jude Fawley and Sue Brideshead, both having left earlier marriages, find happiness in their relationship. Ironically, when tragedy tests their union, it is Sue, the modern emancipated woman, who proves unequal to the challenge. This edition reprints the 1895 text with Hardy's Postscript of 1912.

528 pp. 1 map 0-14-043538-7 $7.95

Penguin Readers Guide Available

A Laodicean

*Edited with an Introduction and Notes by
John Schad*

Hardy's experience as a professional
architect shines through in the meticulous, highly visual descriptions of towns
and buildings in this novel. Using the
restoration of a castle as a framework,
Hardy considers the ancient analogy
between architecture and philosophy.

512 pp.   0-14-043506-9 $9.95

The Mayor of Casterbridge

*Edited with an Introduction and Notes by
Keith Wilson*

Thomas Hardy's fascination with the
dualities inherent in human nature is
at the root of this depiction of a man
who overreaches the limits allowed by
society. Using the device of classic
tragedy—the downfall of a man caused
by the whims of chance and his own
fatal flaws—Hardy took the British
novel in a new direction and emerged as
not only the last Victorian novelist but
the first modern one.

448 pp.   20 b/w illustrations   2 maps
0-14-043513-1 $7.95

A Pair of Blue Eyes

*Edited with an Introduction and Notes by
Pamela Dalziel*

Clearly based on Hardy's relationships
with his family, his fiancée, and his
closet male friend, this story of a classic
love triangle between Elfride Swan-
court, Stephen Smith, and Henry
Knight explores how lovers fall victim,
in different ways, to society's assump-
tions about class and gender.

448 pp.   0-14-043529-8 $8.95

The Pursuit of the Well-Beloved and The Well-Beloved

*Edited with an Introduction by
Patricia Ingham*

Containing the 1892 serial version and
the version that appeared in book form
in 1897, this volume not only brings one
of Hardy's lesser-known works to the
public but also sheds light on Hardy's
tendency to interweave either/or variations in his plots and fashion a "series of
screenings," as he himself described in
Jude the Obscure.

416 pp.   3 maps   0-14-043519-0 $9.95

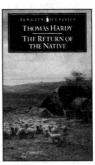

*The Return of the Native

*Edited with Notes by Tony Slade and an
Introduction by Penny Boumelha*

One of Hardy's classic statements about
modern love, courtship, and marriage,
The Return of the Native explores the
impersonal forces and eternal verities
that control the lives of Eustacia Vye and
Clym Yeobright, the returning "native."

496 pp.   2 b/w illustrations   2 maps
0-14-043518-2 $8.95

Selected Poems

Edited with an Introduction and Notes by Robert Mezey

This generous selection of nearly two hundred poems will help readers recognize Hardy as one of the greatest poets of the twentieth century.

192 pp.   0-14-043699-5 $8.95

"Hardy is among the greatest poets, and this authoritative selection represents him wonderfully."

—JOHN HOLLANDER

Tess of the D'Urbervilles

Edited with Notes by Tim Dolin and an Introduction by Margaret R. Higonnet

Tess's seduction, hopeful marriage, and cruel abandonment compose an unforgettable novel that exhibits the hallmarks of Hardy's best art: a keen sense of tragedy and a sharp critique of social hypocrisy. This edition of Hardy's most moving and poetic novel includes as appendices Hardy's Prefaces, a map, illustrations, and episodes censored from the *Graphic* periodical version.

512 pp.   3 b/w illustrations   2 maps
0-14-043514-X $7.95

The Trumpet-Major

Edited with an Introduction and Notes by Linda M. Shires

Set against the background of the Napoleonic Wars, this is a fascinating story of love and desire. By a sophisticated shuffling of the literary modes of comedy, romance, and history, Hardy depicts the incongruities of individual experience and social values.

416 pp.   0-14-043540-9 $7.95

Two on a Tower

Edited with an Introduction and Notes by Sally Shuttleworth

Hardy's most complete treatment of the theme of love across the divides of age and class, *Two on a Tower* was first published in 1882 and charts the tragic romance of Lady Viviette Constantine and Swithin St. Cleve.

336 pp.   0-14-043536-0 $10.95

*Under the Greenwood Tree

Edited with an Introduction and Notes by Tim Dolin

In the first of his Wessex novels, Hardy interweaves the lingering courtship of Dick Dewy and Fancy Day with the battle for survival of the old string choir— the last in the country—against the new vicar's mechanical church organ.

288 pp. 1 map 0-14-043553-0 $5.95

The Withered Arm and Other Stories

Edited with an Introduction by Kristen Brady

These nine short stories constitute some of Hardy's finest early work and foreshadow his later novels in their controversial sexual politics, their refusal of romantic structures, and their elegiac pursuit of past, lost loves.

464 pp.   0-14-043532-8 $11.95

The Woodlanders

Edited with an Introduction and Notes by Patricia Ingham

In this portrait of four people caught up in a web of intense, often unrequited passion, Hardy explores the complexity of sexual feelings and the roles of social class, gender, and evolutionary survival.

464 pp. 1 map 0-14-043547-6 $7.95

See *The Penguin Book of First World War Poetry.*

JAROSLAV HAŠEK
1883 – 1923, CZECH

The Good Soldier Švejk

Translated with an Introduction by Cecil Parrott and Illustrations by Josef Lada

This novel portrays the "little man" fighting officialdom and bureaucracy with the only weapons available to him—passive resistance, subterfuge, native wit, and dumb insolence.

20TH-CENTURY CLASSICS

784 pp.   0-14-018274-8 $14.95

JOEL CHANDLER HARRIS
1848 – 1908, AMERICAN

Uncle Remus
His Songs and His Sayings

Edited with an Introduction by Robert Hemenway

The dialect, lore, and flavor of black life in the nineteenth-century South is portrayed as it appeared to Georgia-born Joel Chandler Harris in Uncle Remus's "Legends of the Old Plantation."

288 pp.   0-14-039014-6 $10.95

See *American Local Color Writing.*

JOHN HAWKES
1925 – 1998, AMERICAN

The Lime Twig/Second Skin/ Travesty

Introduction by Patrick McGrath with a Preface by Robert Coover

Bringing together early novels by Hawkes, this volume displays his mastery as a prose stylist and the range and power of his imagination.

20TH-CENTURY CLASSICS

320 pp.   0-14-018982-3 $14.95

NATHANIEL HAWTHORNE
1804 – 1864, AMERICAN

The Blithedale Romance

Introduction and Notes by Annette Kolodny

In language that is suggestive and often erotic, Hawthorne offers a superb depiction of a utopian community that cannot survive the individual passions of its members.

304 pp. 0-14-039028-6 $7.95

The House of the Seven Gables

Edited with an Introduction and Notes by Milton R. Stern

This enduring novel of crime and retribution is a psychological drama that vividly reflects the social and moral values of New England in the 1840s.

352 pp. 0-14-039005-7 $8.95

The Marble Faun

Introduction and Notes by Richard H. Brodhead

Set in Rome, Hawthorne's tale of the influence of European culture on American morality echoes *The Scarlet Letter* in its concern with the nature of transgression and guilt.

480 pp. 0-14-039077-4 $9.95

The Scarlet Letter

Introduction by Nina Baym with Notes by Thomas E. Connolly

Hawthorne's novel of guilt and redemption in pre-Revolutionary Massachussetts provides vivid insight into the social and religious forces that shaped early America.

256 pp. 0-14-039019-7 $5.95

Selected Tales and Sketches

Selected with an Introduction by Michael J. Colacurcio

Displaying Hawthorne's understanding of the distinctly American consciousness, these thirty-one short fictions of the early nineteenth century include "Young Goodman Brown," "The Minister's Black Veil," and "Rappaccini's Daughter."

488 pp. 0-14-039057-X $10.95

GEORG WILHELM FRIEDRICH HEGEL
1770 – 1831, GERMAN

Introductory Lectures on Aesthetics

Translated by Bernard Bosanquet with an Introduction and Commentary by Michael Inwood

Hegel's writings on art—and his profound conclusion that art was in terminal decline—have had a broad impact on our culture.

240 pp. 0-14-043335-X $12.95

See *German Idealist Philosophy*.

HÉLOÏSE

See Abélard.

O. HENRY
1862 – 1910, AMERICAN

Selected Stories
*Edited with an Introduction by
Guy Davenport*

Compiled here are eighty classic stories
—about con men, tricksters, and innocent deceivers, about fate, luck, and
coincidence—by one of the great masters of American literary comedy and
the short-story form. Included are "The
Ransom of Red Chief," "A Retrieved
Reformation," and "The Rose of Dixie."

20TH-CENTURY CLASSICS

384 pp.   0-14-018688-3 $13.95

GEORGE HERBERT
1593 – 1633, BRITISH

The Complete English Poems
*Edited with an Introduction and Notes by
John Tobin*

The Temple, Herbert's masterpiece of
worldly anguish and divine transcen-
dence; his uncollected English verse; *A
Priest to the Temple* (prose); and selections from Herbert's Latin poetry with
translations form the basis of this volume.

496 pp.   0-14-042348-6 $14.95

See *The Metaphysical Poets*.

HERODOTUS
C. 490 – C. 425 B.C., GREEK

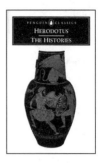

The Histories
*Translated by Aubrey de Sélincourt and
Revised with an Introduction and Notes
by John M. Marincola*

Written during a period of increasing
conflict between Sparta and Athens,
these compelling descriptions of great
battles, rulers, and political upheavals
attempt to recapture the glorious past of
a unified Greece.

672 pp.   0-14-044638-9 $10.95

HESIOD
C. 8TH CENT. B.C., GREEK

THEOGNIS
C.6TH CENT. – 5TH CENT. B.C., GREEK

Hesiod and Theognis
*Translated with Introductions and Notes
by Dorothea Wender*

Together these two poets—Hesiod, the
epic poet, and Theognis, the elegist—
offer a superb introduction to the life
and thought of ancient Greece.

176 pp.   0-14-044283-9 $10.95

Siddhartha

Translated by Joachim Neugroschel with an Introduction by Ralph Freedman

Set in India, *Siddhartha* is the story of a young Brahmin's search for ultimate reality after meeting with the Buddha.

20TH-CENTURY CLASSICS

176 pp.   0-14-118123-0 $5.95

Army Life in a Black Regiment and Other Writings

Edited with an Introduction and Notes by R. D. Madison

Colonel Higginson's stirring account of his wartime experiences as the leader of the first regiment of emancipated slaves "has some claim to be the best written narrative to come from the Union during the Civil War" (Henry Steele Commager). This edition of *Army Life* features a selection of Higginson's essays, including "Nat Turner's Insurrection" and "Emily Dickinson's Letters."

352 pp.   0-14-043621-9 $10.95

Leviathan

Edited with an Introduction by C. B. Macpherson

Written amid the turmoil of the English civil war, Hobbes's apologia for the emergent seventeenth-century mercantile society speaks directly to twentieth-century minds in its concern for peace, systematic analysis of power, and elevation of politics to the status of a science.

736 pp.   0-14-043195-0 $9.95

The Life and Opinions of the Tomcat Murr

Translated and Annotated by Anthea Bell with an Introduction by Jeremy Adler

Hoffman was a follower of Cervantes and Sterne, a pioneering "magical realist," fascinated by Gothic horror. This bizarre double narrative is a supreme example of literary bravado that reveals Hoffman as the greatest of German storytellers.

384 pp.   0-14-044631-1 $12.95

The Tales of Hoffmann

Selected and Translated with an Introduction by R. J. Hollingdale

Eight of Hoffmann's best and best-known tales are retold in this collection —among them "Mademoiselle de Scudery," "Doge and Dogeressa," and "The Sandman," which forms the basis for the first half of Offenbach's opera.

416 pp.   0-14-044392-4 $10.95

FRIEDRICH HÖLDERLIN
1770 – 1843, GERMAN

Selected Poems and Fragments

Edited by Jeremy Adler and Translated with a New Preface and Introduction by Michael Hamburger

Though his literary talents were scarcely known to his contemporaries, Friedrich Hölderlin has emerged today as one of Europe's supreme poets. In this superb bilingual selection, Michael Hamburger has produced the definitive English version of a giant of German literature.

240 pp.   0-14-042416-4 $14.95

HOMER
C. 8TH CENT. B.C., GREEK

The Iliad

Translated by Robert Fagles with an Introduction and Notes by Bernard Knox

Fagles combines his talents as poet and scholar to present this masterful, elegant translation of the stirring story of the Trojan War and the rage of Achilles.

672 pp.   0-14-044592-7 $9.95

"An astonishing performance. There is no modern version of the whole *Iliad* which is better or as good, and this should now become the standard translation for a new generation."

—PETER LEVI

The Iliad
A New Prose Translation

Translated with an Introduction by Martin Hammond

This prose translation captures the emotional power and the dramatic

HOMER

The Greeks believed that *The Iliad* and *The Odyssey* were composed by a single poet whom they named Homer. Nothing is known of his life. While seven Greek cities claim the honor of being his birthplace, ancient tradition and the dialect and locational knowledge of the poems place him in Ionia, located in the eastern Aegean. His birthdate is undocumented as well, though most modern scholars now place the composition of *The Iliad* and *The Odyssey* between 725 and 675 B.C. The subject of Homer's epics involves the Trojan War, generally dated around 1200 B.C., but they actually reflect the eighth-century world of the Eastern Mediterranean; a world of dramatic growth and expansion, emerging out of the Dark Ages that followed the collapse of the Mycenaen civilization in the twelfth century.

tension of the first and greatest literary achievement of Greek civilization.

416 pp.   0-14-044444-0 $10.95

The Iliad

Translated by E. V. Rieu

The original highly-acclaimed translation by E. V. Rieu, editor of Penguin Classics from 1944 to 1964.

480 pp.   0-14-044014-3 $9.95

The Odyssey

Translated by E. V. Rieu with a Revised Translation by D. C. H. Rieu and a New Introduction by Peter Jones

Odysseus's perilous ten-year voyage from Troy to his home in Ithaca is recounted in a revised translation that captures the swiftness, drama, and worldview of the Greek original.

448 pp.   0-14-044556-0 $9.95

See *Greek Literature.*

ANTHONY HOPE
1863 – 1933, BRITISH

The Prisoner of Zenda and Rupert of Hentzau

With an Introduction and Notes by Gary Hoppenstand

The ever-popular *The Prisoner of Zenda* and the darker, more dramatic *Rupert of Hentzau* are full of swash-buckling feats of heroism as well as witty ironies that brilliantly satirize late nineteenth-century European politics.

400 pp.   0-14-043755-X $7.95

GERARD MANLEY HOPKINS
1844 – 1889, BRITISH

Poems and Prose

Edited and Selected by W. H. Gardner

This edition contains verse wrought from the creative tensions and para-doxes of a poet-priest who strove to evoke the spiritual essence of nature sensuously. Besides such poems as "The Wreck of the Deutschland," "The Wind-hover," and "God's Grandeur," this collection includes the "terrible sonnets," numerous journal entries, and Hopkins's letters to Robert Bridges.

272 pp.   0-14-042015-0 $14.95

HORACE
65 – 8 B.C., ROMAN

The Complete Odes and Epodes

Translated with Notes by W. G. Shepherd and an Introduction by Betty Radice

The elusive personality and ironic philosophy of Horace are exemplified in seventeen epodes, 103 odes, and *The Centennial Hymn.*

256 pp.   0-14-044422-X $12.95

The Satires of Horace and Persius

Translated with an Introduction and Notes by Niall Rudd

The broad range of the controversial Roman poetic form the satura is illustrated in eighteen satires and twenty-three epistles of Horace and six metaphorical essays of the Stoic critic Persius, presented in modern verse translation.

304 pp.   0-14-044279-0 $11.95

WILLIAM DEAN
HOWELLS
1837 – 1920, AMERICAN

A Modern Instance

Introduction by Edwin H. Cady

The story of a philandering, dishonest Boston journalist and the woman who divorces him, this is the first serious treatment of divorce in American writing and a powerful example of realism in literature.

480 pp.   0-14-039027-8 $12.95

The Rise of Silas Lapham

Introduction by Kermit Vanderbilt

The social and moral questions posed by the Gilded Age of American business are chronicled in this tale of a newly rich New England family.

352 pp.   0-14-039030-8 $10.95

VICTOR HUGO
1802 – 1885, FRENCH

Les Misérables

Translated with an Introduction by Norman Denny

Including unforgettable descriptions of the Paris sewers, the Battle of Waterloo, and the fighting at the barricades during the July Revolution, this is at once a thrilling narrative and a vivid social document.

1,248 pp.   0-14-044430-0 $11.95
Penguin Readers Guide Available

Nôtre-Dame of Paris

Translated with an Introduction by John Sturrock

Hugo's powerful evocation of Paris in 1482 and the tragic tale of Quasimodo, the hunchback of Notre-Dame, has become a classic example of French romanticism.

496 pp.   0-14-044353-3 $11.95

ALEXANDER VON HUMBOLDT
1769 – 1859, German

Personal Narrative of a Journey to the Equinoctial Regions of the New Continent

Abridged and Translated with an Introduction and Notes by Jason Wilson and a Historical Introduction by Malcolm Nicolson

With *Personal Narrative*, the German scientist and explorer Alexander von Humboldt invented the art of travel writing. Translated into English for the first time since 1851, this edition demonstrates Humboldt's extraordinary ability to present scientific observations and information in an entertaining, engaging style. His book, imbued with the spirit of nineteenth-century romanticism, profoundly influenced Charles Darwin and other Victorian scientists.

400 pp.   0-14-044553-6 $12.95

DAVID HUME
1711 – 1776, Scottish

Dialogues Concerning Natural Religion

Edited with an Introduction and Notes by Martin Bell

Modeled on Cicero's *De natura deorum*, this classic treatise on natural religion portrays the eighteenth-century conflict between scientific theism and philosophical skepticism. Hume savages the traditional arguments for the existence of God and suggests that the only religion that can stand up to serious scrutiny is one that is rationally and philosophically derived by the human mind.

160 pp.   0-14-044536-6 $10.95

A Treatise of Human Nature

Edited with an Introduction by Ernest C. Mossner

The first work of this influential philosopher is an unprecedented extension of the Copernican revolution in science to the realm of philosophy.

688 pp.   0-14-043244-2 $12.95

ELSPETH HUXLEY
1907 – 1997, Kenyan

The Flame Trees of Thika
Memories of an African Childhood

Huxley's eloquent 1959 memoir ranks in beauty and power with Isak Dinesen's *Out of Africa*. As pioneering settlers in Kenya, Huxley's family discovered—the hard way—the world of the African. With an extraordinary gift for detail and a keen sense of humor,

Huxley recalls her childhood in a land that was as harsh as it was beautiful.

20TH-CENTURY CLASSICS

288 pp.   0-14-118378-0 $12.95

"The secret of this book's compulsive attraction is the meeting of the fresh field and the innocent eye."

—MARY RENAULT

Red Strangers

Introduction by Richard Dawkins

Epic in its scale, *Red Strangers* is the thoroughly engrossing novel of four generations of a Kikuyu family whose lifestyle and culture were dramatically and damagingly transformed by the forces of colonization in Africa.

20TH-CENTURY CLASSICS

432 pp.   0-14-118205-9 $13.95

J. K. HUYSMANS
1848 – 1907, FRENCH

Against Nature

Translated by Robert Baldick

This chronicle of the exotic practices and perverse pleasures of a hero, who is a thinly disguised version of the author, was condemned by the public as a work of alarming depravity—and was much admired by Oscar Wilde.

224 pp.   0-14-044086-0 $12.95

HENRIK IBSEN
1828 – 1906, NORWEGIAN

Brand

A Version for the Stage by Geoffrey Hill

The story of a minister driven by faith to risk the death of his wife and child, *Brand* pits a man of vision against the forces of ignorance and venality.

176 pp.   0-14-044676-1 $9.95

A Doll's House and Other Plays

Translated with an Introduction by Peter Watts

From *The League of Youth*, his first venture into realistic social drama, to *A Doll's House*, a provocative portrait of a woman's struggle for freedom, to the family tensions depicted in *The Lady from the Sea*, Ibsen is concerned with the individual's conflicts with society.

336 pp.   0-14-044146-8 $8.95

HENRIK IBSEN

Henrik Ibsen was born at Skien, Norway, in 1828. His family went bankrupt when he was a child, and he struggled with poverty for many years. His first ambition was medicine, but he abandoned this to write and to work in theater. A scholarship enabled him to travel to Rome in 1864. In Italy he wrote *Brand* (1866), which earned him a state pension, and *Peer Gynt* (1867), for which Grieg later wrote the incidental music. These plays established his reputation. From *The League of Youth* (1869) onward, Ibsen renounced poetry and wrote prose drama. He supported in his plays many crucial issues of his day, such as the emancipation of women. Plays like *Ghosts* (1881) and *A Doll's House* (1879) caused a critical uproar.

Ghosts and Other Plays

Translated with an Introduction and Notes by Peter Watts

Incisive, critical, and controversial, *Ghosts* and *A Public Enemy* depict the negative effects of social rigidity on individual lives; *When We Dead Awaken*, Ibsen's last play, is a story of internal turmoil that can be read as the dramatist's comments on his lifework.

304 pp.   0-14-044135-2 $9.95

Hedda Gabler and Other Plays

Translated with an Introduction and Notes by Una Ellis-Fermor

The Pillars of the Community and *The Wild Duck* show Ibsen's preoccupation with problems of personal and social morality; *Hedda Gabler*, the latest of these plays, is both a drama of individual conflict and a partial return to social themes.

368 pp.   0-14-044016-X $8.95

The Master Builder and Other Plays

Translated with an Introduction by Una Ellis-Fermor

The four plays collected here—*The Master Builder, Rosmersholm, Little Eyolf*, and *John Gabriel Borkman*—

were written late in Ibsen's career and reflect his then growing interests in internal conflicts and the dangers of self-deception.

384 pp.   0-14-044053-4 $7.95

Peer Gynt

Translated with an Introduction by Peter Watts

This high-spirited poetical fantasy, based on Norwegian folklore, is the story of an irresponsible, lovable hero. After its publication, Ibsen abandoned the verse form for more realistic prose plays.

224 pp.   0-14-044167-0 $8.95

SAINT IGNATIUS OF LOYOLA
1491 – 1556, SPAIN

Personal Writings

Translated with Introductions and Notes by Joseph A. Munitiz and Philip Endean

The founder of the Jesuit order, Ignatius Loyola was one of the most influential figures of the Counter-Reformation. The works in this volume—*Reminiscences, The Spiritual Diary, The Spiritual Exercises*, and selected letters—shed light on the more private aspects of Ignatius's life and beliefs.

464 pp.   0-14-043385-6 $13.95

GILBERT IMLAY
1754 – 1828, AMERICAN

The Emigrants

*Edited with an Introduction by
W. M. Verhoeven and Amanda Gilroy*

Imlay's delightful epistolary adventure of 1793, set on the American frontier, was one of the first American novels. The trials of an emigrant family in the Ohio River Valley of Kentucky contrast the decadence of Europe with the utopian promise of the American West. Its sensational love plots also dramatize the novel's surprising feminist allegiances.

400 pp.   0-14-043672-3 $12.95

ELIZABETH INCHBALD
1753 – 1821, BRITISH

A Simple Story

*Edited with an Introduction by
Pamela Clemit*

In scenes charged with understated erotic tension, this novel tells the stories of the flirtatious Miss Milner who falls in love with her guardian, a Catholic priest and aristocrat, and of their daughter who, banished from her father's sight, desperately craves his love.

368 pp.   0-14-043473-9 $9.95

WASHINGTON IRVING
1783 – 1859, AMERICAN

The Legend of Sleepy Hollow and Other Stories

*With an Introduction and Notes by
William L. Hedges*

Irving's delightful 1819 miscellany of essays, and sketches includes the two classic tales "The Legend of Sleepy Hollow" and "Rip Van Winkle."

368 pp.   0-14-043769-X $8.95

HARRIET JACOBS

Harriet Jacobs was born into slavery in about 1813 in North Carolina. Jacobs became the slave of Dr. James Norcom, who tried to force her into a relationship with him. Instead, she became involved with another white man, Samuel Tredwell Sawyer, with whom she had two children. Eventually Jacobs ran away, hiding in the crawl space in her grandmother's house for seven years. She finally escaped to the North in 1842, and lived and worked in New York City and Boston until her freedom was purchased in 1852. In the meantime, Sawyer had managed to purchase their two children as well as Jacobs's brother John, who went on to work for the abolitionist cause. In 1861, Jacobs published *Incidents in the Life of a Slave Girl* under the pseudonym Linda Brent. She died in 1897.

Incidents in the Life of a Slave Girl
Written by Herself

Edited with an Introduction and Notes by Nell Irvin Painter

Jacobs's haunting, evocative memoir of her life as a slave in North Carolina and her final escape and emancipation is one of the most important books ever written documenting the traumas and horrors of slavery—and the particular experiences of female slaves—in the antebellum South. This edition also includes "A True Tale of Slavery," written by Jacobs's brother John, for a London periodical.

240 pp.   0-14-043795-9 $10.95

The Ambassadors

Introduction and Notes by Harry Levin

One of Henry James's three final novels, this tale, set in Paris, is a finely drawn portrait of a man's late awakening to the importance of morality.

520 pp.   0-14-043233-7 $5.95

The American

Introduction and Notes by William Spengemann

This story of an American millionaire rejected by the family of the European aristocrat he loves is James's first novel to dramatize the social relationship between the Old World and the New.

392 pp.   0-14-039082-0 $11.95

The American Scene

Introduction and Notes by John F. Sears

The American Scene is a haunting, brilliant journal by one of America's greatest literary observers, published in 1907 after James's final journey through this country after living abroad for twenty years.

400 pp.   0-14-043416-X $12.95

The Aspern Papers and The Turn of the Screw

Introduction and Notes by Anthony Curtis

Set in a palazzo in Venice, *The Aspern Papers* tells of the confrontation between an elderly woman and a charming young man; in *The Turn of the Screw*, the story of a governess and her charges, James conjures up inexplicable terrors.

272 pp.   0-14-043224-8 $5.95

The Awkward Age

Introduction and Notes by Ronald Blythe

This study of innocence exposed to corrupting influences has been praised for its natural dialogue and the delicacy of feeling it conveys.

328 pp.   0-14-043297-3 $8.95

*The Bostonians

Edited by Richard Lansdown

In this story of a Mississippi lawyer and a radical feminist vying for exclusive possession of a beautiful woman, James explores what it means to be fully human, for both men and women.

480 pp.   0-14-043766-5 $9.00

(Available in March 2001)

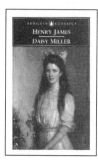

Daisy Miller

Edited with an Introduction by Geoffrey Moore and Notes by Patricia Crick

James's first novel to reach great popularity, this is also the first of his timeless portraits of American women.

128 pp.   0-14-043262-0 $5.95

The Europeans

Edited with an Introduction by Tony Tanner and Notes by Patricia Crick

This subtle examination of the effect of two slightly raffish Europeans upon their cousins in rural Boston in 1830 was published the year after James's *The American*.

576 pp.   0-14-043232-9 $7.95

The Figure in the Carpet and Other Stories

Edited with an Introduction and Notes by Frank Kermode

James's first short story, launched in 1864, was followed, throughout his varied literary career, by nearly a hundred more. This sampling includes "The Author of Beltraffio," "The Lesson of the Master," "The Private Life," "The Middle Years," "The Death of the Lion," "The New Time," "The Figure in the Carpet," and "John Delavoy."

464 pp.   0-14-043255-8 $11.95

The Golden Bowl

Introduction by Gore Vidal and Notes by Patricia Crick

A work unique among James's novels in that things come out happily for the characters, this is the story of the alliance between Italian aristocracy and American millionaires.

576 pp.   0-14-043235-3 $8.95

Italian Hours

Edited with an Introduction and Notes by John Auchard

In these essays on travels in Italy, written from 1872 to 1909, Henry James explores art and religion, political shifts and cultural revolutions, his own ambivalent reactions to the transformations of nineteenth-century Europe, and the nature of travel itself.

416 pp.   0-14-043507-7 $13.95

The Jolly Corner and Other Tales

Edited with an Introduction by Roger Gard

All written after 1900, these stories share the themes and moods that best illustrate James's late style. The selection includes "The Third Person," "Broken Wings," "The Beast in the Jungle," "The Birthplace," "The Jolly Corner," "The Velvet Glove," "Crapy Cornelia," and "The Bench of Desolation."

320 pp.   0-14-043328-7 $10.95

The Portrait of a Lady

Edited with an Introduction by Geoffrey Moore and Notes by Patricia Crick

Regarded by many critics as James's masterpiece, this is the story of Isabel Archer, an independent American heiress captivated by the languid charms of an Englishman.

688 pp.   0-14-043223-X $9.95
Penguin Readers Guide Available

The Princess Casamassima

Edited with an Introduction by Derek Brewer and Notes by Patricia Crick

A young man involved in the world of revolutionary politics falls in love with the beautiful Princess Casamassima and finds he must make a choice between his honor and his desires.

608 pp.   0-14-043254-X $10.95

Roderick Hudson

Edited with an Introduction by Geoffrey Moore and Notes by Patricia Crick

In his first full-length novel James writes with verve and passion about an egotistical young sculptor and the mentor who tries to help him develop his talents.

400 pp.   0-14-043264-7 $9.95

The Spoils of Poynton

Edited with an Introduction by David Lodge and Notes by Patricia Crick

In this study of irreducible ambiguity, a family quarrel unfolds when a mother and son disagree on whom he should marry, and one of the potential brides will not make her true feelings known.

256 pp.   0-14-043288-4 $10.95

HENRY JAMES

Henry James was born into a brilliant family in New York City in 1843. In 1875, James moved to Europe, eventually settling in England. His fourth novel, *Daisy Miller*—a story about a naïve American girl visiting the Continent— became a runaway bestseller when it was published in 1879. His tale of the supernatural, *The Turn of the Screw*, created a sensation when it appeared in 1898 in *Collier's Weekly*. In it, as in his other works, James explored the interaction between innocence and corrupt experience. He was one of the first writers in the English language to embrace stream-of-consciousness writing and greatly influenced the works of writers such as James Joyce, Virginia Woolf, Joseph Conrad, and Edith Wharton. James died in 1916.

The Tragic Muse

Introduction and Notes by Philip Horne

James explores the tensions between the artistic life and worldly temptations in a novel that is at once satiric and serious. He muses on the concept of "art for art's sake," on the vagaries of society's infatuation with the artist, and, as he writes in his Preface, on "the personal consequences of the art-appetite raised to intensity, swollen to voracity."

576 pp.   0-14-043389-9 $14.95

Washington Square

Introduction and Notes by Brian Lee

This early novel, set in New York, is a spare and intensely moving story of divided loyalties and innocence betrayed.

224 pp.   0-14-043226-4 $7.95

What Maisie Knew

Edited with an Introduction and Notes by Paul Theroux and Additional Notes by Patricia Crick

In creating a portrait of a young girl raised in a world of intrigue and betrayal, James sketches with subtle irony the actions and motives of her corrupt adult companions.

288 pp.   0-14-043248-5 $9.95

The Wings of the Dove

Edited with an Introduction by John Bayley and Notes by Patricia Crick

The story of Milly Theale, a rich, lonely, and gravely ill young woman searching for happiness, this beautifully written novel deals with human greed and human tragedy.

520 pp.   0-14-043263-9 $9.95

Pragmatism and Other Writings

Edited with an Introduction and Notes by Giles Gunn

This volume presents in its entirety James's seminal set of lectures in which he argues for the "reasonableness of ordinary experience" and selections from his other formative works, *The Meaning of Truth, Psychology, The Will to Believe,* and *Talks to Teachers on Psychology.*

368 pp.   0-14-043735-5 $14.95

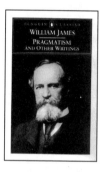

The Varieties of Religious Experience
A Study in Human Nature

Edited with an Introduction by Martin E. Marty

In this synthesis of religion and psychology, James discusses conversion, repentance, and other religious experiences in terms of the individual experience rather than the precepts of organized religion.

576 pp.   0-14-039034-0 $11.95

JOHN JAY

See James Madison.

THOMAS JEFFERSON
1743 – 1826, American

Notes on the State of Virginia

Edited with an Introduction and Notes by Frank Shuffelton

Jefferson's chronicle of the natural, social, and political history of Virginia is at once a scientific discourse, an attempt to define America, and a brilliant examination of the idea of freedom.

400 pp.   0-14-043667-7 $12.95

JEROME K. JEROME
1859 – 1927, British

Three Men in a Boat and Three Men on the Bummel

Edited with an Introduction and Notes by Jeremy Lewis

Three Men in a Boat is the beloved comic account of three friends and a dog as they experience misadventures on a "relaxing" river jaunt. Jerome's heroes proved so popular that he brought them back for an equally

picaresque bicycle tour of Germany in *Three Men on the Bummell.*

400 pp.   0-14-043750-9 $9.95

SARAH ORNE JEWETT
1849 – 1909, American

The Country of the Pointed Firs and Other Stories

Edited with an Introduction by Alison Easton

Modeled in part on Flaubert's sketches of life in provincial France, *The Country of the Pointed Firs* is a richly detailed portrait of a seaport on the Maine coast as seen through the eyes of a summer visitor. Jewett celebrates the friendships shared by the town's women, interweaving conversations and stories about poor fishermen and retired sea captains, thus capturing the spirit of community that sustains the declining town.

304 pp.   0-14-043476-3 $8.95

See *American Local Color Writing* and *Four Stories by American Women.*

JAMES WELDON JOHNSON
1871 – 1938, American

"James Weldon Johnson's name stirs up emotions which are contained only by tremendous control....Aptly, deeply, with love and humor and a powerful rhyming tongue, he has told our story and sung our song."

—MAYA ANGELOU

The Autobiography of an Ex-Colored Man

Edited with an Introduction and Notes by William L. Andrews

First published in 1912, Johnson's pioneering fictional "memoir" is an unprecedented analysis of the social causes and artistic consequences of a black man's denial of his heritage.

20TH-CENTURY CLASSICS
304 pp.   0-14-018402-3 $9.95

Complete Poems

Edited with an Introduction by Sondra Kathryn Wilson

This volume brings together all of Johnson's published works, a number of previously unpublished poems, and reflections on his pioneering contributions to recording and celebrating the African-American experience.

20TH-CENTURY CLASSICS
352 pp.   0-14-118545-7 $14.00

God's Trombones
Seven Negro Sermons in Verse

Illustrated by Aaron Douglas

The inspirational sermons of the old Negro preachers are set down as poetry in this classic collection.

20TH-CENTURY CLASSICS
64 pp.   0-14-018403-1 $8.95

Lift Every Voice and Sing
Selected Poems

This selection brings together more than forty poems including "Lift Every Voice and Sing"—Johnson's most famous lyric and now embraced as the African-American National Anthem.

20TH-CENTURY CLASSICS
112 pp.   0-14-118387-X $9.95

JAMES WELDON JOHNSON

James Weldon Johnson, born to a middle-class family in Jacksonville, Florida, in 1871, was a major figure in the creation and development of African American literature and culture. A twentieth-century Renaissance man, Johnson was the first African American lawyer admitted to the Florida bar. In his public service and as a poet, songwriter, essayist, and novelist, Johnson dedicated himself to honoring his roots, championing the artistic achievements of the black community that expressed the "racial spirit by symbols from within rather than by symbols from without." From his pioneering collection of spirituals in *God's Trombones* to his autobiographical works, to his lyrical poetry of *Saint Peter Relates an Incident*, Johnson brought to life—and celebrated with humor and dignity—the African American experience.

The History of Rasselas, Prince of Abissinia

Edited with an Introduction by D. J. Enright

The pilgrimage of Rasselas from Abissinia to Egypt is used as a vehicle for Johnson's musings on such wide-ranging subjects as flying machines, poetry, marriage, and madness.

160 pp. 0-14-043108-X $9.95

Selected Writings

Edited with an Introduction and Notes by Patrick Crutwell

Generous selections from Johnson's major works include *A Journey to the Western Islands of Scotland*, *The Dictionary of the English Language*, and *The Lives of the English Poets*, as well as portions of his journals, letters, and papers.

576 pp. 0-14-043033-4 $14.95

A Journey to the Western Islands of Scotland/ The Journal of a Tour to the Hebrides

Edited with an Introduction and Notes by Peter Levi

The remarkable friendship between Johnson and Boswell is celebrated in these complementary journals written during their tour of Scotland in 1773. Abridged.

272 pp. 0-14-043221-3 $14.95

See James Boswell.

Chronicles of the Crusades

Translated with an Introduction by M. R. B. Shaw

These two famous Old French chronicles were composed by soldiers who took part in the Holy Wars and offer both eyewitness accounts of the battles and pictures of life in the East.

368 pp. 0-14-044124-7 $13.95

The Complete Poems

Edited with a Preface and Notes by George Parfitt

Nearly 400 works display the characteristic blend of classical and contemporary ideals that imbues Jonson's work, including *Epigrams*, *The Forest*, *Underwoods: Miscellaneous Poems*, *Horace, The Art of Poetry,* and *Timber: Or Discoveries.*

640 pp. 0-14-042277-3 $14.95

Three Comedies

Edited by Michael Jameison

Shakespeare's nearest rival created in *Volpone* and *The Alchemist* hilarious portraits of cupidity and chicanery, while in *Bartholomew Fair* he portrays his fellow Londoners at their most festive—and most bawdy.

496 pp. 0-14-043013-X $11.95

See *The Metaphysical Poets.*

FLAVIUS JOSEPHUS
C. 37 – C. 100, ROMAN

The Jewish War
Revised Edition

Translated by G. A. Williamson and Revised with an Introduction, Notes, and Appendices by E. Mary Smallwood

Josephus depicts in vivid detail the Jewish rebellion of A.D. 66, supplying much of the available information on first-century Palestine.

512 pp.   0-14-044420-3 $14.95

JAMES JOYCE
1882 – 1941, IRISH

Dubliners

Introduction and Notes by Terence Brown

In these stories about the men and women of the struggling lower middle class and their anxious desires for respectability, Joyce creates an exacting portrait of and a lament for his native city and Irish culture.

20TH-CENTURY CLASSICS
368 pp.   0-14-018647-6 $9.95

Finnegans Wake
With an Introduction by John Bishop

Written in a fantastic dream-language, forged from polyglot puns and portmanteau words, the *Wake* features some of Joyce's most inventive writing.

20TH-CENTURY CLASSICS
672 pp.   0-14-118126-5 $16.95

> "Joyce's masterpiece...if aesthetic merit were ever again to center the canon *Finnegans Wake* would be as close as our chaos could come to the heights of Shakespeare and Dante."
>
> —HAROLD BLOOM

JAMES JOYCE

Born in Dublin in 1882 and educated by Jesuits, James Joyce moved to the Continent after graduating from the University of Dublin. While he was teaching English abroad, many of his closest friends were among the more than 500 Irish patriots killed by the British in the Easter Rebellion. Although he would never live in Ireland again, his works describe and reflect his homeland in both dialect and setting. His epic novel *Ulysses*, one of the supreme masterpieces of twentieth-century literature, was published in Paris in 1922 and banned as obscene in the United States until 1933. In 1940, Joyce fled Paris to Zurich, where he died the following year.

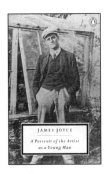

A Portrait of the Artist as a Young Man

Introduction and Notes by Seamus Deane

Joyce's rich and complex coming-of-age story of the artist Stephen Dedalus— one of the great portraits of modern "Irishness"— is a tour de force of style and technique.

20TH-CENTURY CLASSICS

384 pp.   0-14-018683-2 $8.95

JULIAN OF NORWICH
C. 1342 – C. AFTER 1416, BRITISH

*Revelations of Divine Love

Translated by Elizabeth Spearing with an Introduction and Notes by A. C. Spearing

The first known woman writing in English, Julian of Norwich identified the female nature of Christ's suffering, the motherhood of God, and, using images from domestic daily life, emphasized the homeliness of God's love. Including both the long and short versions of the *Revelations*, this new translation from the Middle English preserves Julian's directness of expression and the rich complexity of her thoughts.

240 pp.   0-14-044673-7 $11.95

JUSTINIAN I
483 – 565, ROMAN

The Digest of Roman Law
Theft, Rapine, Damage, and Insult

Translated with an Introduction by C. F. Kolbert

Codified by Justinian I and published under his aegis in A.D. 533, this celebrated work of legal history forms a fascinating picture of ordinary life in Rome.

192 pp.   0-14-044343-6 $11.95

JUVENAL
C. 55 – 138, ITALIAN

*Sixteen Satires
Third Edition

Translated with an Introduction and Notes by Peter Green

Whores, fortune-tellers, shameless sycophants, aging flirts, and debauched officials populate Juvenal's Rome and he sternly puts into exquisite relief the splendor and squalor of his infamous times. In this edition, Green substantially revises and updates his celebrated translation.

320 pp.   0-14-044704-0 $10.95

FRANZ KAFKA
1883 – 1924, CZECH
(B. AUSTRO-HUNGARY)

The Transformation ("Metamorphosis") and Other Stories

Translated from the German and Edited by Malcolm Pasley

This collection of all the works published during Kafka's lifetime includes "The Transformation," Kafka's famous story of a man who wakes to find himself trapped in the body of an insect; "The Meditation"; "The Stoker," a fragment from a novel set in America; "Before the Law," the only part of *The Trial* published during Kafka's lifetime; "In the Penal Colony"; and "A Fasting Artist."

20TH-CENTURY CLASSICS
256 pp.   0-14-018478-3 $10.95

BANNA KANUTE
D. 1994, GAMBIAN

See Bamba Suso.

JOHN KEATS
1795 – 1821, BRITISH

The Complete Poems
Second Edition

Edited by John Barnard

In addition to all the poems and plays known to be written by the archetypal romantic poet, this edition includes long extracts from Keats's letters, his annotations to *Paradise Lost*, and two poems and a play fragment that have been attributed to him.

760 pp.   0-14-042210-2 $13.95

Selected Poems

Edited with an Introduction and Notes by John Barnard

This beautifully repackaged edition of Keats's most treasured poems illustrates both the rapid development of his poetic skills and his preoccupying themes of love, art, sorrow, the natural world, and the nature of the imagination. *Selected Poems* includes "On First Looking into

Chapman's Homer," "Endymion," and "La Belle Dame Sans Merci."

256 pp.   0-14-043725-8 $9.95

MARGERY KEMPE
C. 1373 – C. 1438, BRITISH

The Book of Margery Kempe

Translated with an Introduction by Barry Windeatt

This earliest-known British autobiography is a remarkable and touching record of the author's difficult pilgrimage from madness to Christian faith.

336 pp.   0-14-043251-5 $12.95

JACK KEROUAC
1922 – 1969, AMERICAN

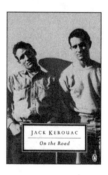

On the Road

Introduction by Ann Charters

The novel that defined the Beat generation, this exuberant tale of Sal Paradise and Dean Moriarty traversing the United States swings to the rhythms of the 1950s.

20TH-CENTURY CLASSICS
320 pp.   0-14-018521-6 $12.95
Penguin Readers Guide Available

> "Just as, more than any other novel of the Twenties, *The Sun Also Rises* came to be regarded as the testament of the Lost Generation, so it seems certain that *On the Road* will come to be known as that of the Beat Generation."
>
> —GILBERT MILSTEIN, *THE NEW YORK TIMES*

JOHN MAYNARD KEYNES
1883 – 1946, BRITISH

The Economic Consequences of the Peace
Introduction by Robert Lekachman

One of the great economic and political works of our time, Keynes's brilliant and prescient analysis of the economic effects of the Treaty of Versailles offered vehement opposition to a reparations policy that would stifle the German economy in the aftermath of World War I.

20TH-CENTURY CLASSICS
336 pp.   0-14-018805-3 $12.95

SØREN KIERKEGAARD
1813 – 1855, DANISH

Either/Or
A Fragment of Life
Translated and Abridged with an Introduction and Notes by Alastair Hannay

The first major work by the precursor of existentialism examines the philosophical choice between aesthetic and romantic life versus ethical and domestic life, and offers profound observations on the meaning of choice itself. Sheltering behind the persona of a ficti-tious editor, Kierkegaard brings together a diverse range of material, including reflections on Mozart and the famous "Seducer's Diary."
640 pp.   0-14-044577-3 $16.95

Fear and Trembling
Translated with an Introduction by Alastair Hannay

Abraham's unreserved submission to God's will provides the focus for this religious and ethical polemic. Originally written under the pseudonym of Johannes de Silentio, this is a key work in the psychology of religious belief.
160 pp.   0-14-044449-1 $12.95

Papers and Journals
A Selection
Translated with an Introduction and Notes by Alastair Hannay

Drawn from Kierkegaard's private papers and journals, this meticulously edited volume of philosophical musings, theoretical arguments, and descriptions of everyday life sheds light on the conflicts that gave birth to his radical observations on the nature of choice, offers insights into his rejection of conventional Christianity and the formation of his belief in the "leap of faith," and reveals the moral intensity with which he lived his life.

688 pp.   0-14-044589-7 $13.95

Sickness unto Death

Translated with an Introduction and Notes by Alastair Hannay

Arguing that true Christianity exists only in accordance with free will, Kierkegaard's stern treatise attacks Hegelianism and the established Church, and breaks ground for existentialism and modern theology.

320 pp.   0-14-044533-1 $13.95

RUDYARD KIPLING
1865 – 1936, BRITISH (B. INDIA)
NOBEL PRIZE WINNER

The Jungle Books

Edited with an Introduction by Daniel Karlin

Kipling's knowledge of and love for the jungle animates these delightful fables, many featuring Mowgli the wolf boy.

Both *The Jungle Book* and *The Second Jungle Book* are included in this volume.

20TH-CENTURY CLASSICS

384 pp.   0-14-018316-7 $7.95

Just So Stories

Edited with an Introduction by Peter Levi

Linked by poems and scattered with Kipling's own illustrations, these imaginative fables were inspired by the author's empathy with the animal world and his delight with the foibles of human nature.

20TH-CENTURY CLASSICS

128 pp.   0-14-018351-5 $5.95

RUDYARD KIPLING

Rudyard Kipling was born in Bombay in 1865. During his time at the United Services College, he began to write poetry, privately publishing *Schoolboy Lyrics* in 1881. The following year he started work as a journalist in India, and while there produced a body of work, stories, sketches, and poems—including "Mandalay" "Gunga Din," and "Danny Deever"—which made him an instant literary celebrity when he returned to England in 1889. While living in Vermont with his wife, an American, Kipling wrote *The Jungle Books, Just So Stories*, and *Kim*—which became widely regarded as his greatest long work, putting him high among the chroniclers of British expansion. Kipling returned to England in 1902, but he continued to travel widely and write, though he never enjoyed the literary esteem of his early years. In 1907, he became the first British writer to be awarded the Nobel Prize. He died in 1936.

Kim

Edited with an Introduction by Edward W. Said

The story of a young boy who moves through two cultures, *Kim* captures India's opulent, exotic landscape, overshadowed by the uneasy presence of British rule.

20TH-CENTURY CLASSICS

320 pp.   0-14-018352-3 $5.95

Plain Tales from the Hills

Edited by H. R. Woudhuysen with an Introduction and Notes by David Trotter

Originally intended for a provincial readership familiar with colonial life, these stories of "heat and bewilderment and wasted effort and broken faith" re-create the sights and smells of India.

20TH-CENTURY CLASSICS

288 pp.   0-14-018312-4 $10.95

See *The Penguin Book of First World War Poetry*.

HEINRICH VON KLEIST
1777 – 1811, GERMAN

The Marquise of O— and Other Stories

Translated with an Introduction by David Luke and Nigel Reeves

Between 1799, when he left the Prussian Army, and his suicide in 1811, Kleist developed into a writer of unprecedented and tragically isolated genius. This collection of works from the last period of his life also includes "The Earthquake in Chile," "Michael Kohlhaas," "The Beggarwoman of Locarno," "St. Cecilia or The Power of Music," "The Betrothal in Santo Domingo," "The Foundling," and "The Duel."

320 pp.   0-14-044359-2 $10.95

CHODERLOS DE LACLOS
1741 – 1803, FRENCH

Les Liaisons Dangereuses

Translated with an Introduction by P. W. K. Stone

One of the most notorious novels of all time, this eighteenth-century work describes the intrigues of a depraved pair of aristocrats plotting the seduction of a young convent girl.

400 pp.   0-14-044116-6 $8.95

MADAME DE LAFAYETTE
1634 – 1693, FRENCH

The Princesse de Clèves

Translated with an Introduction and Notes by Robin Buss

This romance about a woman's dangerous but platonic liaison is one of the first feminist novels and a precursor to the psychological realism of Proust.

192 pp.   0-14-044587-0 $10.95

JULES LAFORGUE
1860 – 1887, FRENCH

Laforgue: Selected Poems
With a Plain Prose Translation,
and an Introduction by
Graham Dunstan Martin

This extensive, bilingual edition of one of the originators of modern free verse illuminates Laforgue's unique voice and vision. Deeply nihilistic yet full of yearning, tender yet savagely self-mocking, his poems are presented here in the original French with running prose translations.

352 pp.   0-14-043626-X $12.95

WILLIAM LANGLAND
c. 1330 – c. 1400, BRITISH

Piers the Ploughman
Translated with an Introduction by
J. F. Goodridge

Written by a fourteenth-century cleric, this spiritual allegory explores man in relation to his ultimate destiny against the background of teeming, colorful medieval life.

320 pp.   0-14-044087-9 $10.95

LAO TZU
c. 6TH CENT. B.C., CHINESE

Tao Te Ching
Translated with an Introduction and
Notes by D. C. Lau

The principal classic in the thought of Taoism is a treatise on both personal conduct and government that advances a philosophy of meekness as the surest path to survival.

192 pp.   0-14-044131-X $7.95

RING LARDNER
1885 – 1933, AMERICAN

Selected Stories
Edited with an Introduction by
Jonathan Yardley

This collection brings together twenty-one of Lardner's best pieces, including the six Jack Keefe stories that comprise *You Know Me, Al,* as well as such familiar favorites as "Alibi Ike," "Some Like Them Cold," and "Guillible's Travels."
20TH-CENTURY CLASSICS
400 pp.   0-14-118018-8 $10.95

FRANÇOIS DE LA ROCHEFOUCAULD
1613 – 1680, FRENCH

Maxims
Translated with an Introduction by
Leonard W. Tancock

The philosophy of La Rochefoucauld, which influenced French intellectuals as diverse as Voltaire and the Jansenists, is captured here in more than 600 penetrating and pithy aphorisms.

128 pp.   0-14-044095-X $10.95

NELLA LARSEN
1891 – 1964, AMERICAN

Passing

Edited with an Introduction and Notes by Thadious M. Davis

First published in 1929, this landmark novel by the Harlem Renaissance's premier woman writer candidly explores the destabilization of racial and sexual boundaries.

20TH-CENTURY CLASSICS

160 pp.   0-14-118025-0 $8.95

BARTOLOMÉ DE LAS CASAS
1484 – 1576, SPANISH

A Short Account of the Destruction of the Indies

Translated by Nigel Griffin with an Introduction by Anthony Pagden

No work is a stronger, more exacting, heartbreaking record of the Spanish atrocities in the genocidal enterprise of colonization in the Americas. This account provides an eyewitness's history of the process in the territory of Columbus.

192 pp.   0-14-044562-5 $11.95

LE COMTE DE LAUTRÉAMONT
1846 – 1870, FRENCH

Maldoror and Poems

Translated with an Introduction by Paul Knight

One of the earliest and most astonishing examples of surrealist writing, the hallucinatory tale *Maldoror* was hailed as a work of genius by Gide, Breton, Modigliani, and Verlaine. This edition includes a translation of the epigrammatic *Poésies*.

288 pp.   0-14-044342-8 $11.95

MARY LAVIN
1912 – 1996, IRISH (B. AMERICA)

In a Café
Selected Stories

Edited by Elizabeth Walsh Peavoy, with a Foreword by Tomas Kilroy

Compiled by her daughter, *In a Café* presents some of the masterworks of Mary Lavin, one of the twentieth-century's most gifted and influential practitioners of the short story. Among the sixteen stories here are "In the Middle of the Fields," "A Family Likeness," and the title piece.

20TH-CENTURY CLASSICS

336pp.   0-14-118040-4 $13.95

> **"Mary Lavin's stories have always given me a feeling of wonder and security...she is, after all, so original and astonishing."**
>
> —ALICE MUNROE

D. H. LAWRENCE
1885 – 1930, BRITISH

"The greatest writer of imaginative literature in the twentieth century."

—E. M. FORSTER

Aaron's Rod

Edited by Mara Kalnins with an Introduction and Notes by Steven Vine

Aaron Sisson resolves to renounce his marriage and satisfy his need for individual freedom, friendship, passion, and art.

20TH-CENTURY CLASSICS

368 pp.   0-14-018814-2 $11.95

Apocalypse

Edited with an Introduction and Notes by Mara Kalnins

Apocalypse interweaves Lawrence's thoughts on psychology, science, politics, art, God, and man in a radical critique of the foundations of Western civilization—including a fierce attack on Christianity.

20TH-CENTURY CLASSICS

240 pp.   0-14-018781-2 $11.95

The Boy in the Bush

Edited with an Introduction and Notes by Paul Eggert

In portraying one man's struggles to survive in the desolate land of Australia and the ultimate triumph of his spirit, Lawrence not only celebrates nature in all of its beauty and wildness, but asserts its redemptive power over humankind.

20TH-CENTURY CLASSICS

432 pp.   0-14-018817-7 $12.95

Complete Poems

Collected and Edited with an Introduction and Notes by Vivian de Sola Pinto and F. Warren Roberts

This definitive collection of Lawrence's poems, with appendices containing juvenilia, variants, and early drafts, and Lawrence's own critical introductions to his poems, also includes full textual

---

D. H. LAWRENCE

The son of a miner, the prolific novelist, poet, and travel writer David Herbert Lawrence was born in Eastwood, Nottinghamshire, in 1885. He attended Nottingham University and found employment as a schoolteacher. His first novel, *The White Peacock*, was published in 1911, the same year his beloved mother died and he quit teaching after contracting pneumonia. The next year Lawrence published *Sons and Lovers* and ran off to Germany with Frieda Weekley, his former tutor's wife. His masterpieces *The Rainbow* and *Women in Love* were completed in quick succession, but the first was suppressed as indecent and the second was not published until 1920. Lawrence's lyrical writings challenged convention, promoting a return to an ideal of nature where sex is seen as a sacrament. In 1925 Lawrence's final novel, *Lady Chatterley's Lover*, was banned in England and the United States for indecency. He died of tuberculosis in 1930 in Venice.

and explanatory notes, a glossary, and an index for the work of one of the greatest poets of the twentieth century.

20TH-CENTURY CLASSICS

1,088 pp.   0-14-018657-3 $24.95

D. H. Lawrence and Italy
Twilight in Italy/Sea and Sardinia/ Etruscan Places

Introduction by Anthony Burgess

Taken together, these masterful, often rhapsodic impressions of the Italian countryside constitute "an indispensable guide to the sensibility of one of the most astonishing writers of our century" (Anthony Burgess).

20TH-CENTURY CLASSICS

512 pp.   0-14-118030-7 $15.95

The Fox/The Captain's Doll/ The Ladybird

Edited by Dieter Mehl with an Introduction and Notes by David Ellis

Set during and after the First World War, these three short novels feature struggles between men and women, a theme common to much of Lawrence's work.

20TH-CENTURY CLASSICS

272 pp.   0-14-018779-0 $13.95

Lady Chatterley's Lover

Edited with an Introduction and Notes by Michael Squires

This restored text of Lawrence's most famous work explicitly chronicles the affair between Constance Chatterley and the gamekeeper Mellors and includes the author's "Á Propos of Lady Chatterley's Lover," his final thoughts on the male-female relationship in the modern world.

20TH-CENTURY CLASSICS

400 pp.   0-14-018786-3 $10.95

Mr. Noon

Edited with Notes by Lindeth Vasey and an Introduction by Peter Preston

This edition of *Mr. Noon* brings to paperback readers the first authoritative, annotated version of an autobiographical novel that is, as David Lodge wrote in the *New York Review of Books*, a "vivid illumination on the early days of Lawrence's union with Frieda Weekley."

20TH-CENTURY CLASSICS

368 pp.   0-14-018973-4 $12.95

The Prussian Officer and Other Stories

Edited by John Worthen with an Introduction and Notes by Brian Finney

Written between 1907 and 1914, these

twelve stories illuminate Lawrence's increasing interest in the conflict between immediate human experience and the eternal, impersonal forces that operate at the level of the unconscious.

20TH-CENTURY CLASSICS

304 pp.   0-14-018780-4 $12.95

The Rainbow

Edited by Mark Kinkead-Weekes with an Introduction and Notes by Anne Fernihough

Set in the rural midlands of England, *The Rainbow* revolves around three generations of the Brangwen. When Tom Brangwen marries a Polish widow, Lydia Lensky, and adopts her daughter, Anna, as his own, he is unprepared for the conflict and passion that erupts between them. This edition reproduces the Cambridge text, which is based on Lawrence's original manuscript.

20TH-CENTURY CLASSICS

528 pp.   0-14-018813-4 $8.95

Sea and Sardinia

Edited by Mara Kalnins with an Introduction and Notes by Jill Franks

In January 1921, D. H. Lawrence and his wife, Frieda visited Sardinia. Although the trip lasted only nine days, his intriguing account of Sicilian life not only evokes the place, people, local customs, and wildlife but is also deeply revealing about the writer himself. This edition restores censored passages for the first time and corrects corrupt textual readings.

20TH-CENTURY CLASSICS

256 pp.   0-14-118076-5 $13.95

Sketches of Etruscan Places And Other Italian Essays

Edited with an Introduction by Simonetta de Filippis

For Lawrence, Italy was the place of spiritual rejuvenation to which he frequently visited to escape the bourgeois conventions and grim materialism of his native England. These eight, highly personal short essays include sketches of Tuscany, Florence, and the Etruscan lifestyle.

20TH-CENTURY CLASSICS

384pp.   0-14-118105-2 $14.95

Sons and Lovers

Edited with an Introduction and Notes by Helen Baron and Carl Baron

Presented in paperback for the first time in its complete form, including the restoration of eighty pages missing from previous editions, *Sons and Lovers* examines the tensions in the Morel family as the world around them moves from the agricultural past to the industrial future and their own dreams and illusions change.

20TH-CENTURY CLASSICS

544 pp.   0-14-018832-0 $10.95

Studies in Classic American Literature

Lawrence expounds on Franklin's *Auto-biography*, Cooper's *Leatherstocking* novels, Poe's tales, *The Scarlet Letter*, *Moby-Dick*, *Leaves of Grass*, and other works.

20TH-CENTURY CLASSICS
192 pp.   0-14-018377-9 $12.95

Twilight in Italy and Other Essays

Edited by Paul Eggert with an Introduction and Notes by Stefania Michelucci

In 1912, Lawrence left England for the first time, visiting Germany, the Alps, and Italy. Although *Twilight in Italy*, about his experiences on his voyage, was his first travel book, as Anaïs Nin said "it cannot be read as an ordinary travel book, for his voyage is a philosophic, as well as a symbolic and sensuous one."

20TH-CENTURY CLASSICS
288 pp.   0-14-018994-7 $12.95

The Woman Who Rode Away and Other Stories

Edited by Dieter Mehl and Christa Jansohn with an Introduction and Notes by Neil Reeve

The thirteen stories here, written between 1924 and 1928, draw on Lawrence's experiences in New Mexico, Mexico, Italy, Germany, and England, and feature thinly disguised, often malicious, portraits of friends and acquaintances.

20TH-CENTURY CLASSICS
224 pp.   0-14-018806-1 $12.95

Women in Love

Edited by David Farmer, Lindeth Vasey, and John Worthen with an Introduction and Notes by Mark Kinkhead-Weekes

Considered by many critics to be Lawrence's masterpiece, *Women in Love* is a powerful, sexually explicit depiction of the destructiveness of human relations.

20TH-CENTURY CLASSICS
592 pp.   0-14-018816-9 $10.95

VLADIMIR ILICH LENIN
1870 – 1924, RUSSIAN

The State and Revolution

Translated with an Introduction and Glossary by Robert Service

In this seminal work of Soviet literature and Bolshevism, Lenin calls for the destruction of the bourgeoisie and capitalism and the establishment of a new postrevolutionary order.

20TH-CENTURY CLASSICS
192 pp.   0-14-018435-X $11.95

MIKHAIL LERMONTOV
1814 – 1841, RUSSIAN

A Hero of Our Time

Translated with an Introduction by Paul Foote

Lermontov's portrait of a cynical, flamboyant man influenced Tolstoy,

Dostoyevsky, Chekhov, and other nineteenth-century masters.

192 pp.   0-14-044176-X $10.95

PRIMO LEVI
1919 – 1987, ITALIAN

If Not Now, When?

Translated by William Weaver with an Introduction by Irving Howe

Based on a true story and set in the final days of World War II, this powerful novel chronicles the adventures of a band of Jewish partisans making their way from Russia to Italy and waging a personal war of revenge against the Nazis.

20TH-CENTURY CLASSICS

360 pp.   0-14-018893-2 $13.95

Moments of Reprieve

Translated by Ruth Feldman

Against the terrifying, tragic background of Auschwitz, Levi preserves for future generations the tales of his friends, companions, and even adversaries who shared his hell during the Holocaust.

20TH-CENTURY CLASSICS

176 pp.   0-14-018895-9 $11.95

The Monkey's Wrench

Translated by William Weaver

This exuberant and funny novel, an enchanting collection of tales told between a self-educated construction worker and a writer-chemist, celebrates the joys of work and the art of storytelling.

20TH-CENTURY CLASSICS

176 pp.   0-14-018892-4 $12.95

MATTHEW LEWIS
1775 – 1818, BRITISH

The Monk

Edited with an Introduction by Christopher MacLachlan

Savaged by critics for its blasphemy and obscenity, *The Monk* shows the diabolical decline of Ambrosio, a worthy Capuchin superior who is tempted by Matilda—a young girl who has entered his monastery disguised as a boy—and eventually succumbs to magic, murder, incest, and torture.

416 pp.   0-14-043603-0 $9.95

MERIWETHER LEWIS
1774 – 1809, AMERICAN

WILLIAM CLARK
1770 – 1838, AMERICAN

The Journals of Lewis and Clark

Edited and with an Introduction by Frank Bergon

Meriwether Lewis and William Clark's remarkable chronicle of their Voyage of Discovery across the pristine, uncharted wilderness of the American West occupies a unique place in American history, recording a natural world never seen by white men: Edenic landscapes, mysterious native people, and the first descriptions of hundreds of plants and animals.

NATURE CLASSICS

504 pp.   0-14-025217-7 $13.95

SINCLAIR LEWIS
1885 – 1951, AMERICAN
NOBEL PRIZE WINNER

Babbit

*Introduction and Notes by
James M. Hutchisson*

Babbit captures the flavor of the United States during the economic boom years of the 1920s, and its protagonist has become the symbol of middle-class mediocrity, his name an enduring part of the American lexicon.

20TH-CENTURY CLASSICS

320 pp.   0-14-018902-5 $9.95

Main Street

Introduction and Notes by Martin Bucco

Main Street, Sinclair Lewis's portrait of Gopher Prairie, Minnesota, shattered the myth of the Midwest as God's country and became a symbol of the cultural narrow-mindedness and smug complacency of small towns everywhere.

20TH-CENTURY CLASSICS

448 pp.   0-14-018901-7 $9.95

LI PO
701 – 762, CHINESE

TU FU
712 – 770, CHINESE

Poems

*Selected and Translated with an
Introduction and Notes by Arthur Cooper*

More than forty selections from two eighth-century poets of China cover the whole spectrum of human life and feeling.

256 pp.   0-14-044272-3 $11.95

TITUS LIVY
59 B.C. – A.D. 17, ROMAN

The Early History of Rome

Translated by Aubrey de Sélincourt with an Introduction by R. M. Ogilvie

The first five books of Livy's monumental *History of Rome* trace the foundation of Rome through the Gallic invasion of the fourth century B.C.

424 pp.   0-14-044104-2 $11.95

Rome and Italy

*Translated and Annotated by
Betty Radice with an Introduction by
R. M. Ogilvie*

Books VI to X span a dramatic century —from Rome's apparent collapse after defeat by the Gauls in 386 B.C. to its emergence as the premier power in Italy in 293 B.C.

400 pp.   0-14-044388-6 $12.95

Rome and the Mediterranean

Translated by Henry Bettenson with an Introduction by A. H. McDonald

Books XXXI to XLV cover the years from 201 B.C. to 167 B.C., when Rome emerged as ruler of the Mediterranean.

704 pp.   0-14-044318-5 $14.95

The War with Hannibal

*Edited with an Introduction by
Betty Radice and Translated by
Aubrey de Sélincourt*

Books XXI to XXX cover the declaration of the Second Punic War in 218 B.C. to the battle in 202 B.C. at Zama in Africa, where Hannibal was finally defeated.

712 pp.   0-14-044145-X $14.95

JOHN LOCKE
1632 – 1704, BRITISH

An Essay Concerning Human Understanding

*Edited with an Introduction and Notes
by Roger Woolhouse*

Originally published in 1690, this is a newly edited, unabridged edition of Locke's pioneering investigation into the origins, certainty, and extent of human knowledge, which set the groundwork for modern philosophy and influenced psychology, literature, political theory, and other areas of human thought and expression.

816 pp.   0-14-043482-8 $14.95

See *Divine Right and Democracy.*

JACK LONDON
1876 – 1916, AMERICAN

The Assassination Bureau, Ltd.

Introduction by Donald Pease

London's suspense thriller focuses on the fine distinction between state-justified murder and criminal violence in the Assassination Bureau—an organization whose mandate is to rid the state of all its enemies.

20TH-CENTURY CLASSICS

208 pp.   0-14-018677-8 $10.00

The Call of the Wild, White Fang, and Other Stories

*Edited by Andrew Sinclair with an
Introduction by James Dickey*

This volume contains the best of London's famed adventure stories of the North, including the mythic *Call of the Wild*, a vivid tale of a dog's fight for survival in the Yukon wilderness, and *White Fang*, the story of a wild dog's acclimation to the world of men.

20TH-CENTURY CLASSICS

416 pp.   0-14-018651-4 $7.95

Martin Eden

Introduction by Andrew Sinclair

This semi-autobiographical work depicts a young seaman's struggle for education and literary fame, and his eventual disillusionment with success.

20TH-CENTURY CLASSICS

480 pp.   0-14-018772-3 $12.95

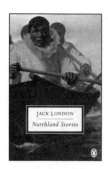

Northland Stories

*Edited with an Introduction and Notes by
Jonathan Auerbach*

Drawing on his own experiences during
the Klondike Gold Rush of 1897, Jack
London's stories, originally published in
three volumes between 1900 and 1902,
bring to life the harrowing hardships of
life in the lawless wilderness.

20TH-CENTURY CLASSICS
400 pp.   0-14-018996-3 $10.95

The Sea-Wolf and Other Stories

*Selected with an Introduction by
Andrew Sinclair*

In the title story, London writes of an
old sea captain who attempts to put the
theories of Spencer and Nietzsche into
practice. Also included here are "The
Sea-Farmer" and "Samuel."

20TH-CENTURY CLASSICS
320 pp.   0-14-018357-4 $9.95

Tales of the Pacific

*Introduction and Afterword by
Andrew Sinclair*

At once rugged and deeply philosophical,
these stories depict man's struggle for
survival, battling not only the elements
and the dangers of the great ocean but
also the stark cruelty that is bondage,

disease, hypocrisy, and secret sin.

20TH-CENTURY CLASSICS
240 pp.   0-14-018358-2 $10.95

HENRY WADSWORTH LONGFELLOW
1807 – 1882, AMERICAN

Selected Poems

*Edited with an Introduction and Notes by
Lawrence Buell*

Longfellow was the most popular poet of
his day. This selection includes generous
samplings from his longer works—*Evangeline, The Courtship of Miles Standish*,
and *Hiawatha*—as well as his shorter
lyrics and less familiar narrative poems.

240 pp.   0-14-039064-2   **$12.95**

See *Nineteenth-Century American Poetry*

LONGUS
C. 2ND OR 3RD CENT. A.D., GREEK

Daphnis and Chloe

*Translated with an Introduction and
Notes by Paul Turner*

At the heart of much romantic literature
of the modern era, this physically
explicit and emotionally charged early
novel holds an important place in the
classical/European canon.

128 pp.   0-14-044059-3 $11.95

ANITA LOOS
1893 – 1981, AMERICAN

Gentlemen Prefer Blondes and But Gentlemen Marry Brunettes

*Introduction by Regina Barreca with
Illustrations by Ralph Barton*

This new combined edition collects two
brilliant satires of the Jazz Age and

American sexual mores, featuring Lorelei Lee—the not-so-dumb blonde flapper from Little Rock. Lorelei's hilarious diaries record her adventures in search of champagne, diamonds, and marriageable millionaires. Intimately illustrated by the inimitable Ralph Barton.

20TH-CENTURY CLASSICS
352 pp.   0-14-118069-2 $12.95

"I think it is beyond doubt that H.P. Lovecraft has yet to be surpassed as the twentieth century's greatest practitioner of the classic horror tale."
—STEPHEN KING

The Call of Cthulhu and Other Weird Stories
Edited with an Introduction and Notes by S. T. Joshi

An original selection of eighteen of Lovecraft's mesmerizing tales, including "Rats in the Walls," "The Colour out of Space," and "The Shadow over Innsmouth."

20TH-CENTURY CLASSICS
304 pp.   0-14-118234-2 $12.95

On the Nature of the Universe
Translated with an Introduction by R. E. Latham and Revised with an Introduction and Notes by John Godwin

This edition of the classic poem and seminal text of Epicurean science and philosophy—which shaped human understanding of the world for centuries—brings new textual research and additional context to Lucretius's explorations of spirit, mind, and soul.

320 pp.   0-14-044610-9 $13.95

Principles of Geology
Edited with an Introduction by James A. Secord

A hugely ambitious attempt to forge links between observable causes—earthquakes, tides, and storms—and the current state of the earth, this work proved crucial in the long-running dispute between science and Scripture. Its clarity, broad sweep, and sheer intellectual passion caught the imagination of Melville, Emerson, and countless readers worldwide.

528 pp.   30 line drawings
0-14-043528-X $15.95

The History of England

*Edited and Abridged with an
Introduction by Hugh Trevor-Roper*

Macaulay's monumental History covers
the period from the accession of James
II through the 1688 revolution and up
to the death of William III in 1702.

576 pp.   0-14-043133-0 $14.95

The Complete Fairy Tales

*Edited with an Introduction and Notes
by U. C. Knoepflmacher*

Admired by his contemporaries including Lewis Carroll and an inspiration for
twentieth-century writers such as C. S.
Lewis and J. R. R. Tolkien, MacDonald's
fairy tales allude to familiar tales but—
employing paradox, play, and non-
sense—are profoundly experimental
and delightfully subversive. This edition brings together all eleven of
MacDonald's fairy stories, including
"The Light Princess" and "The Golden
Keys" as well as his essay "The Fantastic
Imagination."

352 pp.   0-14-043737-1 $13.95

Dom Casmurro

*Translated with an Introduction by
Robert Scott-Buccleuch*

Bentinho, now a taciturn lawyer, looks-
back on his life and tells the Othello-
like story of his adolescent love, their
marriage, and his wife's infidelity—or
so he perceives it through his passionate jealousy.

224 pp.   0-14-044612-5 $10.95

The Discourses

*Edited with an Introduction by
Bernard Crick with Revisions by
Brian Richardson and Translated by
Leslie J. Walker*

Machiavelli examines the glorious
republican past of Rome. In contrast
with *The Prince*, this unfinished work
upholds the Republic as the best and
most enduring style of government.

544 pp.   0-14-044428-9 $10.95

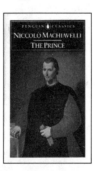

*The Prince
New Edition

*Revised Translation by George Bull with
a New Introduction by Anthony Grafton*

Machiavelli's famous portrait of the
prince still "retains its power to fasci-
nate, frighten and to instruct." Rejecting
the traditional values of political theory,
Machiavelli drew upon his own experiences of office under the turbulent
Florentine republic when he wrote his

celebrated treatise on statecraft. The tough realities of Machiavelli's Italian are well preserved in the clear, unambiguous English of George Bull's revised translation.

144 pp.   0-14-044752-0 $5.95

JAMES MADISON
1751 – 1836, AMERICAN

ALEXANDER HAMILTON
1755 – 1804, AMERICAN

JOHN JAY
1745 – 1829, AMERICAN

The Federalist Papers

Edited with an Introduction by Isaac Kramnick

The definitive exposition of the American Constitution, *The Federalist Papers* were considered by Thomas Jefferson to be the best commentary on the principle of government ever written. This collection of all eighty-five papers contains the complete first-edition text of the collected essays published from 1787 to 1788 in New York by J. and A. McLean. Includes the U.S. Constitution.

528 pp.   0-14-044495-5 $13.95

BERNARD MALAMUD
1914 – 1986, AMERICAN

The Fixer

Based on the actual case of a Jewish Russian worker accused of murder in Kiev, *The Fixer* probes into themes common in Malamud's acclaimed work: the solitude of man ostracized by society and the conflicted legacies of the Jewish people.

20TH-CENTURY CLASSICS

304 pp.   0-14-018515-1 $12.95

God's Grace

A fable at once absurd and profound about a sole survivor—with a tamed chimpanzee—of a nuclear holocaust, *God's Grace* combines "Miltonic ambition and theme with the vernacular crackle of comic dialogue" (*The Washington Post*).

20TH-CENTURY CLASSICS

208 pp.   0-14-018491-0 $11.95

A New Life

Suppressing both fear and self-pity, Sy Levin, a recovering alcoholic, is beginning a new life as an English instructor in the Pacific Northwest, hoping to find peace and renewal. Instead he finds himself the lone liberal fighting a reactionary administration, a crusade made only slightly less onerous by the promise of love—and sex—offered by young students and faculty wives.

20TH-CENTURY CLASSICS

208 pp.   0-14-018681-6 $12.95

Le Morte D'Arthur

Edited with Notes by Janet Cowen and an Introduction by John Lawlor

One of the most readable and moving accounts of the Knights of the Round Table, this version of the Arthurian legend was edited and first published by William Caxton in 1485.

Vol. 1 496 pp. 0-14-043043-1 $10.95
Vol. 2 560 pp. 0-14-043044-X $11.95

An Essay on the Principle of Population

Edited with an Introduction by Antony Flew

In a thesis that explores the disparity between the potential rates of population growth and the means of subsistence, Malthus presents the ultimate demographic choice: starvation or restraint.

304 pp. 0-14-043206-X $10.95

Selected Poems

Selected and Translated by James Greene with an Introduction by Donald Rayfield and Forewords by Nadezhda Mandelstam and Donald Davie

James Greene's acclaimed translations of the poetry of Osip Mandelstam are now in an extensively revised and augmented edition.

20TH-CENTURY CLASSICS
144 pp. 0-14-018474-0 $12.95

The Travels of Sir John Mandeville

Translated with an Introduction by C. W. R. D. Moseley

Though it is still disputed if, and how far, Mandeville actually traveled, his travelogue was consulted for hard geographical information by Leonardo da Vinci and Columbus and stands today as an informative portrait of fourteenth-century Europe.

208 pp. 0-14-044435-1 $12.95

Man of Straw

Written by the older brother of Thomas Mann, this 1918 novel about a self-adoring brutal leader was a prescient and fierce satire of German militarism, which led to the author's imprisonment.

20TH-CENTURY CLASSICS
304 pp. 0-14-018137-7 $13.95

KLAUS MANN
1906 – 1949, German

Mephisto

Translated by Robyn Smyth

Mephisto is the story of an actor who, obsessed with fame and power, renounces his Communist past and deserts his wife and mistress to continue performing in Nazi Germany. The moral consequences of his betrayals eventually haunt him, turning his dream world into a nightmare.

20TH-CENTURY CLASSICS

272 pp.   0-14-018918-1 $13.95

THOMAS MANN
1875 – 1955, German
Nobel Prize winner

Death in Venice and Other Tales

Translated with a Preface by
Joachim Neugroschel

In an acclaimed new translation that restores the controversial passages censored from the original English version, "Death in Venice" recounts a ruinous quest for love and beauty. Also included are eleven other stories, among them "Tonio Kröger" and "The Blood of the Walsungs."

20TH-CENTURY CLASSICS

384 pp.   0-14-118173-7 $9.95

KATHERINE MANSFIELD
1888 – 1923, British
(b. New Zealand)

The Garden Party and Other Stories

In deceptively simple language, Mansfield illuminates complicated relationships and profound, often trou-

THOMAS MANN

Thomas Mann was born in 1875 in the North German town of Lübeck, the younger brother of novelist Heinrich Mann. At the age of nineteen he went to Munich, where he joined an insurance company, while in his free time he studied literature and attended the University of Munich. His earlier major works included *Buddenbrooks*, *Death in Venice*, *Royal Highness*, and *The Magic Mountain*. During the 1920s Mann supported the Weimar Republic on his many lecture tours in Germany and abroad, and in 1929 was awarded the Nobel Prize for literature. With Hitler's rise to power, Mann left Germany for Switzerland and disassociated himself from the National Socialist regime. His German citizenship was taken from him in 1936. He settled in California, where he wrote *Doctor Faustus* and *The Holy Sinner*, eventually becoming an American citizen in 1944. In 1952, he returned to Switzerland, where *The Black Swan* was written. Thomas Mann died there in 1955.

bling, ideas. The fifteen stories in this collection range from "At the Bay," an impressionistic evocation of family life set in her native New Zealand, to the title story, an ironic vignette about a society woman briefly touched by the real world at the funeral of her working-class neighbor.

20TH-CENTURY CLASSICS

192 pp.   0-14-018880-0 $10.95

ALESSANDRO MANZONI
1785 – 1873, ITALIAN

The Betrothed
(I promessi sposi)

Translated with an Introduction by Bruce Penman

Manzoni chronicles the perils of two lovers caught in the turbulence of seventeenth-century Italy.

720 pp.   0-14-044274-X $14.95

MARCUS AURELIUS
121 – 180, ROMAN

Meditations

Translated with an Introduction by Maxwell Staniforth

These musings, maxims, and thoughts on life and death reflect the Roman emperor's profound understanding and expression of Stoic philosophy.

192 pp.   0-14-044140-9 $9.95

MARGUERITE DE NAVARRE
1492 – 1549, BASQUE

The Heptameron

Translated with an Introduction by P. A. Chilton

Inspired by a royal project to produce a French *Decameron*, these seventy stories mirroring Renaissance France's version of the battle of the sexes are attributed to Rabelais's patron, the sister of Francis I.

544 pp.   0-14-044355-X $14.95

MARIE DE FRANCE
C. 12TH CENT., FRENCH

The Lais of Marie de France

Translated with an Introduction by Glyn S. Burgess and Keith Busby

Twelve short story-poems, based on Breton tales of love in crisis, are presented in plain prose translations as close to the twelfth-century original as possible. The volume includes the Old French text of *Laüstic*.

144 pp.   0-14-044476-9 $9.95

CHRISTOPHER MARLOWE
1564 – 1593, BRITISH

The Complete Plays

Edited with an Introduction by J. B. Steane

Reflecting the remarkable range of this Elizabethan dramatist's interests, this volume contains *Dido, Queen of Carthage, Tamburlaine the Great, Doctor*

Faustus, The Jew of Malta, Edward the Second, and *The Massacre at Paris.*

608 pp.   0-14-043037-7 $14.95

ANDREW MARVELL
1621 – 1678, BRITISH

The Complete Poems
Edited by Elizabeth Story Donno

Based on recent studies of existing manuscripts, this collection of works by the seventeenth-century poet much admired by T. S. Eliot includes modern translations of Marvell's Greek and Latin poems, as well as his works in English.

320 pp.   0-14-042213-7 $12.95

See *The Penguin Book of Restoration Verse.*

KARL MARX
1818 – 1883, GERMAN

Capital
Volume 1
Translated by Ben Fowkes

This 1867 study—one of the most influential documents of modern times—looks at the relationship between labor and value, the role of money, and the conflict between the classes.

1,152 pp.   0-14-044568-4 $16.95

Capital
Volume 2
Translated by David Fernbach with an Introduction by Ernest Mandel

The "forgotten" second volume of *Capital,* Marx's world-shaking analysis of economics, politics, and history, contains the vital discussion of commodity, the cornerstone to Marx's theories.

624 pp.   0-14-044569-2 $15.95

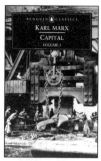

Capital
Volume 3
Translated by David Fernbach with an Introduction by Ernest Mandel

The third volume of the book that changed the course of world history, *Capital*'s final chapters were Marx's most controversial writings on the subject, and were never completed.

1,088 pp.   0-14-044570-6 $15.95

Early Writings
Translated by Gregor Benton and Rodney Livingstone

In this rich body of early work the foundations of Marxism can be seen in essays on alienation, the state, democracy, and human nature.

464 pp.   0-14-044574-9 $15.95

Grundrisse
Foundations of the Critique of Political Economy
Translated with a Foreword by Martin Nickolaus

Written between *The Communist Manifesto* (1848) and the first volume of *Capital* (1867), *Grundrisse*—essential to the understanding of Marx's ideas—provides the only outline of his full political-economic theories.

912 pp.   0-14-044575-7 $18.95

Political Writings: Volume 3
The First International and After

Edited with an Introduction by
David Fernbach

In this third volume of *Political Writings*, Marx applies the pioneering insights of *Capital* to ongoing international events and foresees the possibility of revolution in Russia.

432 pp.   0-14-044573-0 $13.95

KARL MARX
1818 – 1883, GERMAN

FRIEDRICH ENGELS
1820 – 1895, GERMAN

The Communist Manifesto

Introduction and Notes by A. J. P. Taylor

This compelling document is even more relevant today in light of the downfall of Communism. It includes a special Introduction by the noted British historian A. J. P. Taylor.

128 pp.   0-14-044478-5 $6.95

See Friedrich Engels.

PETER MATTHIESSEN
B. 1927, AMERICAN

Blue Meridian
The Search for the Great White Shark

Blue Meridian chronicles the search over thousands of miles of ocean for the most dangerous predator on earth: the legendary Great White Shark. Filled with acute observations of natural history in exotic areas around the world, this harrowing account is one of the

KARL MARX

Karl Marx—who, with Friedrich Engels, formulated the principles of dialectic materialism—was born in the industrial city of Trier, Prussia, in 1818. His family converted to Lutheranism from Judaism to escape persecution when he was six. Marx entered the University of Bonn in 1835 and received his doctorate from the University of Jenna in 1841. The following year he began writing for *Rheinische Zeitung*, a radical newspaper published in Bonn. In contrast to Adam Smith and other mainstream economists, Marx believed that labor creates wealth, hence capitalism is exploitative and antithetical to freedom. He met Engels in Paris in 1844, where they wrote *The Communist Manifesto*. The first volume of his masterpiece *Capital* was published in 1867; Engels compiled the two subsequent volumes after Marx's death in 1883.

great adventures of our time.

NATURE CLASSICS

204 pp.   0-14-026513-9 $12.95

The Cloud Forest

Filled with observations and descriptions of the people and the fading wildlife of the vast world of South America, *The Cloud Forest* is Matthiessen's incisive, wry report of his expedition into some of the last and most exotic wild terrains in the world.

NATURE CLASSICS

280 pp.   0-14-025507-9 $12.95

The Snow Leopard

In 1973 Peter Matthiessen and the field biologist George Schaller went to Nepal to study the Himalayan blue sheep and, possibly, to glimpse the rare and beautiful snow leopard. This National Book Award winner is the account of their five-week trek, unfolding and revealing the narrator and his world.

NATURE CLASSICS

336 pp.   0-14-025508-7 $12.95

"A beautiful, magnificent book... one of the most wonderful accounts I know of journeying in our time."

—W. S. MERWIN

The Tree Where Man Was Born

Skillfully and magically portraying the sights, scenes, and people he observed firsthand in several trips over the course of a dozen years, Peter Matthiessen exquisitely combines nature and travel writing to bring East Africa to vivid life.

NATURE CLASSICS

432 pp.   0-14-023934-0 $12.95

Under the Mountain Wall
A Chronicle of Two Seasons in Stone Age New Guinea

Drawing on his great skills as a naturalist and novelist, Peter Matthiessen offers a remarkable firsthand view of the Kurelu, a Stone Age tribe that survived into the twentieth-century in all its simplicity and violence—on the brink of incalculable change.

NATURE CLASSICS

272 pp.   0-14-025270-3 $12.95

Wildlife in America

Wildlife in America remains one of the most involving and disturbing stories ever told about the character and soul of the American people living among wild creatures, on formerly wild lands, chronicling the destruction of the variety, beauty, and richness of the American wilderness.

NATURE CLASSICS

352 pp.   0-14-004793-X $12.95

CHARLES ROBERT MATURIN
1782 – 1824, IRISH

Melmoth the Wanderer

Edited with an Introduction and Notes by Victor Sage

Melmoth's satanic pact for immortality

condemns him to wander the earth, a tormented outsider. This Gothic masterpiece—first published in 1820—follows in the tradition of both the classics of its genre and the works of Cervantes, Swift, and Sterne.

704 pp.   0-14-044761-X $12.00

(Available in February 2001)

W. SOMERSET MAUGHAM
1874 – 1965, British

Cakes and Ale

In this novel, Maugham creates the unauthorized biography of Edward Driffield, a man lionized by literary society and whose second wife learns more about his less respectable days than she cares to know.

20TH-CENTURY CLASSICS

208 pp.   0-14-018588-7 $12.95

Collected Short Stories
Volume 1

These thirty stories, including the piece "Rain," are set in the Pacific Islands, England, France, and Spain.

20TH-CENTURY CLASSICS

448 pp.   0-14-018589-5 $13.95

Collected Short Stories
Volume 2

The stories collected here, including "The Alien Corn," "Flotsam and Jetsam," and "The Vessel of Wrath," reconfirm Maugham's stature as one of the masters of the short story.

20TH-CENTURY CLASSICS

256 pp.   0-14-018590-9 $13.95

Collected Short Stories
Volume 3

Maugham learned his craft from Maupassant, and these stories, featuring his alter-ego Ashenden, display the unique and remarkable talent that made him an unsurpassed storyteller.

20TH-CENTURY CLASSICS

256 pp.   0-14-018591-7 $13.95

Collected Short Stories
Volume 4

These thirty stories—most set in the colonies at a time when the Empire was still assured, in a world in which men and women were caught between their own essentially European values and the richness and ambiguity of their unfamiliar surroundings—show a master of the genre at the peak of his power.

20TH-CENTURY CLASSICS

464 pp.   0-14-018592-5 $14.95

Liza of Lambeth

Maugham's first novel is about the gloomy, poverty-stricken world of South London in the 1890s and how it affects one young girl who tries to escape from it.

20TH-CENTURY CLASSICS

128 pp.   0-14-018593-3 $10.95

The Magician

The Magician is one of Maugham's most complex and perceptive novels. Running through it is the theme of evil, deftly woven into a story as memorable for its action as for its astonishingly vivid characters.

20TH-CENTURY CLASSICS
208 pp.   0-14-018595-X $12.95

The Moon and Sixpence

Charles Strickland, a dull bourgeois city gent, is driven to abandon his home, wife, and children to devote himself slavishly to painting. In a tiny studio in Paris, he fills canvas after canvas, refusing to sell his works. He drifts to Marseilles and, finally, to Tahiti, where, even after being blinded by leprosy, he produces some of his most passionate and mysterious works of art.

20TH-CENTURY CLASSICS
216 pp.   0-14-018597-6 $9.95

Mrs. Craddock

In this penetrating study of an unequal marriage, Maugham explores the nature of love and happiness and finds that the two rarely coincide.

20TH-CENTURY CLASSICS
256 pp.   0-14-018594-1 $11.95

The Narrow Corner

First published in 1932, this volume recalls many of Maugham's best short stories, featuring a story of love, money, and mutiny.

20TH-CENTURY CLASSICS
224 pp.   0-14-018598-4 $13.95

Of Human Bondage

Introduction by Robert Calder

An obsessive love affair provides the pivot of this powerful evocation of a young man's progress to maturity in the years before the First World War.

20TH-CENTURY CLASSICS
608 pp.   0-14-018522-4 $11.95

The Painted Veil

Set in Hong Kong during the heart of a cholera epidemic, this novel portrays a young woman as she learns the true meaning of love—but her discovery comes too late.

20TH-CENTURY CLASSICS
256 pp.   0-14-018599-2 $11.95

The Razor's Edge

Introduction by Anthony Curtis

Intimate acquaintances, who are less than friends, meet and part in postwar London and Paris, in this story that encompasses the pain, passion, and poignancy of life itself.

20TH-CENTURY CLASSICS
320 pp.   0-14-018523-2 $12.95

The Summing Up

Written to give some account of how Maugham learned his craft and why he became such an acute observer of human beings, *The Summing Up* is like an intimate conversation with one of the great cultured minds of the century.

20TH-CENTURY CLASSICS
208 pp.   0-14-018600-X $12.95

GUY DE MAUPASSANT
1850 – 1893, FRENCH

Bel-Ami

Translated with an Introduction by Douglas Parmée

In this analysis of power and its corrupting influence, Maupassant captures the sleaziness, manipulation, and mediocrity prevalent in the elegant salons of Paris during the belle epoque.

416 pp.   0-14-044315-0 $11.95

Pierre and Jean

Translated with an Introduction by Leonard Tancock

An intensely personal story of suspicion, jealousy, and family love, this novel shows the influence of such masters as Zola and Flaubert on Maupassant's writings.

176 pp.   0-14-044358-4 $10.95

Selected Short Stories

Translated by Roger Colet with an Introduction by Ernest Mandelby

These thirty stories, including "Boule de Suif," "Madame Tellier's Establishment," "The Jewels," "The Mask," "A Duel," and "Mother Savage," range in subject from murder, adultery, and war, to the simple pleasures of eating and drinking.

368 pp.   0-14-044243-X $11.95

A Woman's Life

Translated by H. N. P. Sloman with an Introduction by Ernest Mandelby

In one of his most popular full-length novels, Maupassant exposes with his characteristic detachment and precision the evil around a woman misused by both her husband and her son.

208 pp.   0-14-044161-1 $10.95

FRANÇOIS MAURIAC
1885 – 1970, FRENCH
NOBEL PRIZE WINNER

Thérèse

Translated by Gerard Hopkins

In four stories set in Bordeaux and Paris and in a world bound by conventional morality, Mauriac charts the tortured life of Thérèse Desqueyroux, who dares to act on longings buried deep in her heart and whose refusal to bow to convention condemns her to solitude.

20TH-CENTURY CLASSICS
400 pp.   0-14-018153-9 $12.95

GAVIN MAXWELL
1914 – 1962, SCOTTISH

Ring of Bright Water

Gavin Maxwell's account of his life in the Western Highlands of Scotland is a deeply moving portrait of a land and its inhabitants, including his two remarkable pet otters, Mijbil and Edal.

NATURE CLASSICS
224 pp.   0-14-024972-9 $11.95

HENRY MAYHEW
1812 – 1887, British

London Labour and the London Poor

Selected with an Introduction by Victor Neuburg

This work, representing the height of Mayhew's work as a journalist, originally appeared as newspaper articles in 1849–50. These true scenes of life among Victorian London's lowest classes—detailed, unsentimental, and remarkably free of sociopolitical cant—are among the most shocking ever depicted.

544 pp. 0-14-043241-8 $12.95

HERMAN MELVILLE
1819 – 1891, American

Billy Budd and Other Stories

Selected with an Introduction by Frederick Busch

"Billy Budd, Sailor," a classic confrontation between good and evil, is the story of an innocent young man unable to defend himself from wrongful accusations. Other selections include "Bartleby," "The Piazza," "The Encantadas," "The Bell-Tower," "Benito Cereno," "The Paradise of Bachelors," and "The Tartarus of Maids."

416 pp. 0-14-039053-7 $7.95

The Confidence-Man

Edited with an Introduction and Notes by Stephen Matterson

Part satire, part allegory, part hoax, *The Confidence-Man* is a slippery metaphysical comedy set on April Fool's Day aboard the Mississippi steamer *Fidèle*.

400 pp. 0-14-044547-1 $10.95

Moby-Dick
Or, The Whale

Edited with an Introduction by Andrew Delbanco and Explanatory Commentary by Tom Quirk

The story of an eerily compelling madman pursuing an unholy war against a creature as vast and dangerous and unknowable as the sea itself, Melville's masterpiece is also a profound inquiry into character, faith, and the nature of perception.

624 pp. 0-14-039084-7 $11.95

Penguin Readers Guide Available

Pierre
Or, The Ambiguities

Introduction and Notes by William C. Spengemann

A domestic tragedy and a land-based story, both subject and setting represent striking departures for Melville. But this spiritual autobiography in the guise of a Gothic novel, which describes the literary career of its idealistic hero, is now recognized as Melville's advance into the arena of the modern novel.

400 pp. 0-14-043484-4 $13.95

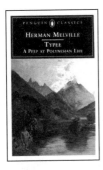

author's Polynesian stay, an examination of the nature of good and evil, and a frank exploration of sensuality and exotic ritual.

320 pp.   0-14-043488-7 $12.95

See *Nineteeth-Century American Poetry*.

Redburn

Edited with an Introduction and Notes by Harold Beaver

Based on his own experiences on a ship sailing between New York and Liverpool, Melville tells a powerful story of pastoral innocence transformed to disenchantment and disillusionment.

448 pp.   0-14-043105-5 $14.95

Typee

Introduction and Explanatory Commentary by John Bryant

Typee is a fast-moving adventure tale, an autobiographical account of the

Plays and Fragments

Translated with an Introduction by Norma Miller

The most innovative dramatist of the Greek New Comedy period, Menander concentrated on his characters' daily lives and colloquial speech in these comedies of manners. This selection contains all but two of Menander's surviving plays, passages attributed to him, and textual notes.

272 pp.   0-14-044501-3 $12.95

HERMAN MELVILLE

Herman Melville was born in New York, the son of a merchant, and largely self-educated. He started writing after having first sailed to Liverpool in 1839, where he joined the whaler *Acushnet* bound for the Pacific. Deserting ship the following year in the Marquesas, he made his way to Tahiti and Honolulu, returning as an ordinary seaman to Boston, where he was discharged in October 1844. Books based on these adventures, which include his masterpiece *Moby-Dick*, won him immediate success. However, this literary renown soon faded; his complexity increasingly alienated readers. Melville died virtually forgotten, and it was not until the 1920s that his reputation underwent the revision that has made him a key figure in American literature.

MENCIUS
c. 4TH CENT. B.C., CHINESE

Mencius

*Translated with an Introduction by
D.C. Lau*

The fullest of the four great Confucian texts, Mencius draws out the implications of the master's moral principles stressing the importance of individual conscience and the necessity for morality in personal and public life.

288 pp.   0-14-044228-6 $10.95

GEORGE MEREDITH
1828 – 1909, BRITISH

The Ordeal of Richard Feverel

*Edited with an Introduction by
Edward Mendelson*

Meredith's 1859 first novel concerns Sir Austin Feverel's misconceived attempts to educate his son, Richard, according to a system based on theories of sexual restraint. This wonderfully ironic and impassioned novel of war between the sexes and the generations shocked Victorian readers but gained a cult following.

560 pp.   0-14-043483-6 $11.95

MICHAEL PSELLUS
1018 – c. 1096, BYZANTINE

Fourteen Byzantine Rulers

*Translated with an Introduction by
E. R. A. Sewter*

This chronicle of the Byzantine Empire, beginning in 1025, shows a profound understanding of the power politics that characterized the empire and led to its decline.

400 pp.   0-14-044169-7 $14.95

THOMAS MIDDLETON
c. 1580 – 1627, BRITISH

Five Plays

*Edited with an Introduction by
Bryan Loughrey and Neil Taylor*

Ranging from ingenious comedy to powerful tragedy, five plays—*A Trick to Catch the Old One, The Revenger's Tragedy, A Chaste Maid in Cheapside, Women Beware Women*, and *The Changeling*—portray the corruptive effects of politics and love in Elizabethan London.

464 pp.   0-14-043219-1 $11.95

See *Three Jacobean Tragedies.*

JOHN STUART MILL
1806 – 1873, BRITISH

Autobiography

*Edited with an Introduction by
John M. Robson*

This 1873 work by the founder of Britain's Utilitarian Society and the author of *System of Logic* and *Principles of Political Economy* describes Mill's intellectual and moral development from his earliest years to maturity.

240 pp.   0-14-043316-3 $11.95

On Liberty

*Edited with an Introduction by
Gertrude Himmelfarb*

Dedicated to the principle of the personal sovereignty of the individual, Mill's most famous work still stands as an essential treatise on the subject of human liberty.

192 pp.   0-14-043207-8 $9.95

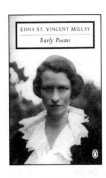

EDNA ST. VINCENT MILLAY
Early Poems

EDNA ST. VINCENT MILLAY
1892 – 1950, AMERICAN

Early Poems

Edited and with an Introduction and Notes by Holly Peppe

Millay's first three books of lyrics and sonnets are collected here: *Renascence, Second April,* and *A Few Figs from This-tles.* With a balanced and appreciative introduction and useful annotations, this volume presents some of the Pulitzer Prize–winning poet's best work in which she weaves intellect, emotion, and irony.

20TH-CENTURY CLASSICS

320 pp.   0-14-118054-4 $12.95

JOHN STUART MILL
1806 – 1873, BRITISH

JEREMY BENTHAM
1748 – 1832, BRITISH

Utilitarianism and Other Essays

Edited with an Introduction by Alan Ryan

Bentham's and Mill's influential socio-political ideas are set forth in essays and selections from larger works, enhanced by Alan Ryan's extensive Introduction analyzing the origins, development, and historical context of these ideas.

352 pp.   0-14-043272-8 $11.95

ARTHUR MILLER
B. 1915, AMERICAN

All My Sons

Introduction by Christopher Bigsby

Winner of the Drama Critics Circle Award for Best New Play in 1947,

ARTHUR MILLER

Arthur Miller was born in New York City in 1915. After attending the University of Michigan, he returned to New York where he began his remarkable career in playwriting after publishing the novel *Focus* in 1945. His first successful play, *All My Sons,* was soon followed by *Death of a Salesman,* which received a Pulitzer Prize in 1949 and established Miller as a preeminent American playwright. Written in 1953, *The Crucible,* a play about the Salem witch trials, is considered by many to be an allegory for the McCarthy hearings, which Miller attended. He wrote the screenplay for the 1961 film *The Misfits* for his second wife, Marilyn Monroe. *A View from the Bridge* garnered Miller his second Pulitzer Prize and the New York Drama Critics Circle Award in 1955. Miller broke ground in contemporary playwriting by portraying the dreams and despair of American working people.

Miller's first major play established him as a leading voice in American theater. In it he introduced themes that would thread their way through his oeuvre: the relationships between fathers and sons and the conflict between business and personal ethics.

20TH-CENTURY CLASSICS
96 pp.   0-14-118546-5 $9.00

The Crucible

Introduction by Christopher Bigsby

Based on historical people and real events, Miller's play about the witch-hunts and trials in Salem, Massachusetts, is a searing portrait of a community engulfed by hysteria. Readers concerned with the increasing polarization of American society today will discover in *The Crucible* not only a play of extraordinary dramatic intensity, but a provocative reminder of the dangers of imposed moralities and "correct thinking."

20TH-CENTURY CLASSICS
176 pp.   0-14-018964-5 $8.95

Death of a Salesman
Certain Private Conversations in Two Acts and a Requiem

Introduction by Christopher Bigsby

Hailed as the first great play to lay bare the emptiness of America's relentless drive for material success, *Death of a Salesman* is Miller's classic portrait of an ordinary man's struggle to leave his mark on the world.

20TH-CENTURY CLASSICS
144 pp.   0-14-118097-8 $10.00

JOHN MILTON
1608 – 1674, ENGLISH

The Complete Poems

Edited with a Preface and Notes by John Leonard

John Milton was a master of almost

JOHN MILTON

John Milton was educated at Cambridge, before being expelled from the university in 1632 for starting a fistfight with his tutor. Upon leaving the school, he abandoned his plan to become a priest. Instead, he took up writing, producing *A Masque* and "Lycidas." A Puritan supporter during the English Civil War, he wrote many political pamphlets and the famous prose piece in defense of freedom of the press, *Areopagitica*. He lost his sight in 1651, but it only proved to stimulate his desire to compose poetry. His great poems were published later in his life, including a ten-book version of *Paradise Lost*, *Paradise Regained*, *Samson Agonistes*, and, later, a twelve-book version of Paradise Lost. In 1674, Milton was struck with gout and died, and was buried next to his father in St. Giles, Cripplegate.

every verse style—from the pastoral, devotional, and tenderly lyrical to the supreme grandeur of his epic, *Paradise Lost*. This comprehensive, fully annotated edition of his poetry includes *Paradise Lost* along with his complete English, Latin, and Greek poems.

1,024pp.   0-14-043363-5 $15.95

Paradise Lost

Edited with an Introduction and Notes by John Leonard

Long regarded as one of the most powerful and influential poems in the English language, Milton's epic work continues to inspire intense debate. Leonard's Introduction reflects on its controversies and contains full notes on language and the many allusions to other works.

512 pp.   0-14-042426-1 $10.00

See *The Penguin Book Restoration Verse.*

MOLIÈRE
1622 – 1673, French

*The Misanthrope and Other Plays
A New Selection
Translated by John Wood and David Coward with an Introduction and Notes by David Coward

The Misanthrope, Molière's richly sophisticated comic drama with its dangerously deluded and obsessive hero is accompanied in this volume by *The Would-be Gentleman, Tartuffe, Such Foolish Affected Ladies, Those Learned Ladies,* and *The Doctor Despite Himself.*

352pp.   0-14-044730-X $8.95

*The Miser and Other Plays
A New Selection
Translated by John Wood and David Coward with an Introduction and Notes by John Wood

This selection of Molière's scandalous, shrewd, and witty commentaries includes *The Miser, The School for Wives, The School for Wives Criticized, Don Juan,* and *The Hypochondriac.*

336 pp.   0-14-044728-8 $8.95

LADY MARY WORTLEY MONTAGU
1689 – 1762, British

Selected Letters

Edited with an Introduction by Isobel Grundy

Lady Mary Wortley Montagu recorded almost every aspect of her intriguing existence in letters about love, politics, science, gossip, and literature.

560 pp.   0-14-043490-9 $14.95

MICHEL DE MONTAIGNE
1533 – 1592, French

An Apology for Raymond Sebond

Translated and Edited with an Introduction and Notes by M. A. Screech

A masterpiece of Counter-Reformation and Renaissance argument, Montaigne's *Apology* is a witty defense of natural theology and an eloquent expression of Christian skepticism.

240 pp.   0-14-044493-9 $10.95

The Complete Essays

Translated and Edited with an Introduction and Notes by M. A. Screech

Montaigne, a great sage of Western

thought, set out to discover himself in his eclectic collection of essays. What he discovered instead was the nature of the human race, poised at the beginning of the Renaissance. This celebrated translation, in plain contemporary English, is true to his frank style.

1,344 pp.   0-14-044604-4 $23.95

The Essays: A Selection

Translated with an Introduction and Notes by M. A. Screech

Reflections by the creator of the essay form display the humane, skeptical, humorous, and honest views of Montaigne, revealing his thoughts on sexuality, religion, cannibals, intellectuals, and other unexpected themes.

480 pp.   0-14-044602-8 $12.95

"Screech is the master of Montaigne."

—ROY PORTER

CHARLES DE MONTESQUIEU
1689 – 1755, FRENCH

Persian Letters

Translated with an Introduction by C. J. Betts

In the form of letters between two Persian travelers in eighteenth-century Europe, this novel was written to show that France was moving from benevolent monarchy to royal tyranny.

352 pp.   0-14-044281-2 $11.95

MARIANNE MOORE
1887 – 1972, AMERICAN

Complete Poems

This definitive edition contains sixty years of Marianne Moore's poems, incorporating her text revisions and her own entertaining notes that reveal the inspiration for complete poems and individual lines.

20TH-CENTURY CLASSICS

320 pp.   0-14-018851-7 $14.95

Selected Letters

Edited with an Introduction by Bonnie Costello

Including correspondence with Eliot, Pound, and Elizabeth Bishop, this collection shows the gradual development of an authoritative woman of letters while documenting the first two-thirds of our century.

20TH-CENTURY CLASSICS

624 pp.   0-14-118120-6 $15.95

SIR THOMAS MORE
1478 – 1535, BRITISH

Utopia

Translated with an Introduction by Paul Turner

Utopia revolutionized Plato's classic blueprint for the perfect republic—later seen as a source of Anabaptism, Mormonism, and even Communism.

160 pp.   0-14-044165-4 $7.95

WILLIAM MORRIS
1834 – 1896, British

News from Nowhere and Other Writings

Edited with an Introduction and Notes by Clive Wilmer

Contained within one volume are the brilliant utopian novel *News from Nowhere* (1891) and essays by the socialist, pioneering environmentalist, designer-craftsman William Morris, whose antipathy toward the dehumanization of the Industrial Revolution was well known.

480 pp.   0-14-043330-9 $12.95

JOHN MUIR
1838 – 1914, American (b. Scotland)

The Mountains of California

With an Introduction by Edward Hoagland

This rhapsodic record of John Muir's time in the Sierras has become an American classic—appreciated both as an account of his life in the mountains and as a call for the preservation of America's forests and the establishment of national parks and reservations.

NATURE CLASSICS

264 pp.   0-14-026661-5 $9.95

My First Summer in the Sierra

With an Introduction by Gretel Ehrlich

In a rapturous tribute to the place he loved most, John Muir tells the story of his first contact with the awe-inspiring mountains he dubbed "The Range of Light." This edition includes more than twenty of Muir's original sketches.

NATURE CLASSICS

264 pp.   0-14-025570-2 $9.95

Travels in Alaska

With an Introduction by Richard Nelson

The three rigorous, exhilarating trips John Muir took through Alaska between 1879 and 1890 are recorded here in all their incomprehensible beauty. All admirers of nature are indebted to Muir for these powerful and informative journals.

NATURE CLASSICS

248 pp.   0-14-026832-4 $10.95

MULTATULI
1820 – 1887, Dutch

Max Havelaar
Or, The Coffee Auctions of the Dutch Trading Company

Translated with Notes by Roy Edwards and an Introduction by R. P. Meijer

Based on the author's actual experiences, *Max Havelaar* is one of the most forceful indictments of colonialism ever written. Its portrayal of colonial cruelty in Indonesia is rendered in prose that ranges from colloquial informality to cadences of biblical resonance, and the sophistication of its satire led D. H. Lawrence to compare it to the works of Swift, Gogol, and Twain.

352 pp.   0-14-044516-1 $13.95

MURASAKI SHIKIBU
c. 978 – 1026, JAPANESE

The Diary of Lady Murasaki
Translated with an Introduction and Notes by Richard Bowring

Witty portraits of quarrelsome ladies-in-waiting and cowardly courtiers, delightful anecdotes about intrigues both political and romantic, and intimate musings are brilliantly interwoven with detailed accounts of official court events and ceremonies in Lady Murasaki's magnificent record of her life as a member of Empress Akiko's entourage during the years 1005 to 1010.

160 pp.   0-14-043576-X $9.95

IRIS MURDOCH
1919 – 1999, BRITISH

A Fairly Honourable Defeat
Introduction by Peter Reed

A dark comedy of errors, this novel portrays the mischief wrought by Julius, a cynical intellectual who decides to demonstrate through a Machiavellian experiment how easily loving couples, caring friends, and devoted siblings can be induced to betray their loyalties.

20TH-CENTURY CLASSICS

464 pp.   0-14-118617-8 $15.00

(Available in March 2001)

The Sea, the Sea
Introduction by Mary Kinzie

A celebrated actor, director, and playwright retires from the theater to write his memoir but it becomes, instead, a chronicle of strange events and unexpected visitors—some real, some spectral—that disrupt his world and shake his oversized ego to its very core.

20TH-CENTURY CLASSICS

528 pp.   0-14-118616-X $15.00

Penguin Readers Guide Available
(Available in March 2001)

SHIVA NAIPAUL
1945 – 1985, TRINIDADIAN

North of South
An African Journey

Based on Naipaul's travels through Kenya, Tanzania, and Zambia in search of answers, this is a travel narrative in the classic tradition—and a scathing, comic, and poignant portrait of the reality behind the rhetoric of liberation.

20TH-CENTURY CLASSICS

352 pp.   0-14-018826-6 $12.95

R. K. NARAYAN
B. 1906, INDIAN

The Guide

Raju was India's most corrupt tourist guide until a peasant mistakes him for a holy man. Gradually he begins to play the part—so well, in fact, that God himself intervenes to put Raju's new holiness to the test.

20TH-CENTURY CLASSICS
224 pp.   0-14-018547-X $12.95

Malgudi Days

In this marvelous collection of stories, all kinds of people—simple and not so simple—are drawn in full color and endearing domestic detail as the author creates the imaginary city of Malgudi.

20TH-CENTURY CLASSICS
256 pp.   0-14-018543-7 $10.95

The Man-Eater of Malgudi

Narayan slyly and sometimes wickedly weaves a story of comedic and vastly human conflict in the enchanted city of Malgudi when an entangling dispute errupts between the local owner of a small printing press and his tenant, Vasu, a pugnacious taxidermist in search of an elephant for his stuffed collection.

20TH-CENTURY CLASSICS
176 pp.   0-14-018548-8 $10.95

The Rāmayāna

This shortened modern prose version of the Indian epic—parts of which date from 500 B.C.—was composed by one of today's supreme storytellers.

20TH-CENTURY CLASSICS
192 pp.   0-14-018700-6 $9.95

A Tiger for Malgudi

A comic view of human absurdities told from the point of view of a tiger named Raja, and one of Narayan's beloved Malgudi novels, this work is infused with Hindu mysticism and delightful humor.

20TH-CENTURY CLASSICS
160 pp.   0-14-018545-3 $10.95

R. K. NARAYAN

R. K. Narayan was born in Madras, South India, in 1906, and educated there and at Maharaja's College in Mysore. His first novel, *Swami and Friends* and its successor, *The Bachelor of Arts* are both set in the enchanting fictional territory of Malgudi and are only two out of the twelve novels he based there. In 1958 Narayan's work *The Guide* won him the National Prize of the Indian Literary Academy, his country's highest literary honor. In addition to his novels, Narayan has authored five collections of short stories, including *A Horse and Two Goats, Malgudi Days*, and *Under the Banyan Tree*, two travel books, two volumes of essays, a volume of memoirs, and the re-told legends *Gods, Demons and Others, The Rāmāyana*, and *The Mahabharata*. In 1980 he was awarded the A. C. Benson Medal by the Royal Society of Literature and in 1982 he was made an Honorary Member of the American Academy and Institute of Arts and Letters.

The Vendor of Sweets

A widower of firm Ghandian principles, Jagan nonetheless harbors a warm and embarrassed affection for his wastrel son Mali. When Mali shows up with a half-American wife and a grand plan for selling novel-writing machines, Jagan's patience begins to fray. Father and son are forced to confront each other and are taken by surprise.

20TH-CENTURY CLASSICS
144 pp.   0-14-018550-X $11.95

THOMAS NASHE
1567 – C. 1601, BRITISH

The Unfortunate Traveller and Other Works

Edited with an Introduction by J. B. Steane

Elizabethan manners, morality, and mirth are captured in this selection from the works of Thomas Nashe—pamphleteer, poet, satirist, scholar, moralist, and jester.

512 pp.   0-14-043067-9 $13.95

PABLO NERUDA
1904 – 1973, CHILEAN
NOBEL PRIZE WINNER

Memoirs

Neruda's *Memoirs* is as full of the passionate, volatile, and profoundly generous personality as lovers of his poetry would expect. García Lorca, Vallejo, Picasso, Gandhi, Mao Tse-Tung, Castro, and Allende appear here too, making Neruda's life story of truly universal reach and significance, as well as one of the richest accounts

we have of Latin American history, politics, art, and literature.

20TH-CENTURY CLASSICS
388 pp.   0-14-018628-X $13.95

Twenty Love Poems and a Song of Despair

Translated by W. S. Merwin

This edition of Neruda's most enduring and popular work—love poems of daring symbolism and sensuality—contains the original Spanish text with the English translation on facing pages.

20TH-CENTURY CLASSICS
88 pp.   0-14-018648-4 $9.95

GÉRARD DE NERVAL
1808 – 1855, FRENCH

Selected Writings

Translated with Introductions by Richard Sieburth

This selection provides the most inclusive and comprehensive overview in English of the brilliant and eccentric poet, belletrist, short-story writer, and autobiographer admired by Baudelaire, Proust, Breton, and Artaud. Including "Aurélia," "Sylvie," the sonnets of "The Chimeras," the *Doppelgänger* tales, correspondence, and more, this volume won the PEN/Book-of-the-Month Club Translation Prize.

448 pp.   0-14-044601-X $13.95

"The most gorgeous lines in the French language."

—MARCEL PROUST

JOHN HENRY NEWMAN
1801 – 1890, BRITISH

Apologia pro Vita Sua

Edited with an Introduction by Ian Ker

This spiritual autobiography of great power was written in response to personal attacks and conceived as a justification of his own actions when Newman's conversion to Roman Catholicism rocked the Church of England and escalated the spread of anti-Catholicism in Victorian England.

608 pp.   0-14-043374-0 $15.95

THOMAS NICKERSON
1805 – 1883, AMERICAN

OWEN CHASE
1796 – 1869, AMERICAN

The Loss of the Ship *Essex*, Sunk by a Whale
First Person Accounts

Edited by Thomas Philbrick with an Introduction by Nathaniel Philbrick

In 1820, the Nantucket whaleship *Essex* was rammed and sunk by an angry sperm whale. The incident was the *Titanic* story of its day and provided the inspiration for Melville's *Moby-Dick*. This edition combines the only extant

first-person narratives of the doomed voyage with every relevant contemporary account.

256 pp.   0-14-043796-7 $12.95

Penguin Classics Readers Guide for *Moby-Dick* features material from *The Loss of the Ship Essex, Sunk by a Whale.*

FRIEDRICH NIETZSCHE
1844 – 1900, GERMAN

Beyond Good and Evil

Translated by R. J. Hollingdale with a New Introduction by Michael Tanner

Nietzsche discusses how cultures lose their creative drives and become decadent, offering a wealth of fresh insights into such themes as the self-destructive urge of Christianity, the prevalence of "slave moralities," and the dangers of the pursuit of philosophical or scientific truth.

240 pp.   0-14-044513-7 $11.95

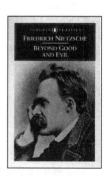

The Birth of Tragedy

Edited with an Introduction by Michael Tanner and Translated by Shaun Whiteside

Nietzsche's first book, published in 1871 and now a seminal work of Western culture, is filled with passionate energy and argument probing the relationship between our experiences of suffering in life and in art, myths, and legends.

160 pp.   0-14-043339-2 $9.95

Ecce Homo

Translated by R. J. Hollingdale with an Introduction by Michael Tanner

This strange and moving autobiography of Nietzsche was begun in late 1888, weeks before his final psychological breakdown.

144 pp.   0-14-044515-3 $10.95

A Nietzsche Reader

Selected and Translated with an Introduction by R. J. Hollingdale

Designed to give an overview of Nietzsche's thought, of his approach to the conventional problems of Western philosophy, and of his own philosophy of "the will to power," this anthology includes 240 thematically arranged passages from his major philosophical works.

288 pp.   0-14-044329-0 $12.95

Thus Spake Zarathustra

Translated with an Introduction by R. J. Hollingdale

Nietzsche's most accessible work, this spiritual odyssey through the modern world influenced such writers as Shaw, Lawrence, Mann, and Sartre.

352 pp.   0-14-044118-2 $12.95

Twilight of the Idols and The Anti-Christ

Translated by R. J. Hollingdale with a New Introduction by Michael Tanner

Written in 1888, before he succumbed to insanity, *Twilight of the Idols* is a fascinating summation of Nietzsche's rejection of the prevalent ideas of his

FRIEDRICH NIETZSCHE

The philosopher Friedrich Nietzsche was born in Prussia in 1844. After the death of his father, a Lutheran minister, Nietzsche was raised from the age of five by his mother in a household of women. In 1869 he was appointed Professor of Classical Philology at the University of Basel, where he taught until 1879 when poor health forced him to retire. He never recovered from a nervous breakdown in 1889 and died eleven years later. Known for saying that "god is dead," Nietzsche propounded his metaphysical construct of the superiority of the disciplined individual (superman) living in the present over traditional values derived from Christianity and its emphasis on heavenly rewards. His ideas were appropriated by the Fascists, who turned his theories into social realities that he had never intended.

time; *The Anti-Christ* is his passionate challenge to institutional Christianity.

208 pp.   0-14-044514-5 $10.95

FRANK NORRIS
1870 – 1902, AMERICAN

McTeague
A Story of San Francisco

Introduction by Kevin Starr

Set against the harsh California landscape, this novel by one of America's foremost literary realists preserves, in almost obsessive detail, the darker side of a still-young San Francisco.

496 pp.   0-14-018769-3 $10.95

The Octopus
A Story of California

Introduction by Kevin Starr

Based on an actual violent dispute in California's Great Central Valley, *The Octopus* (1901) depicts the clash between classic opposing interests of the Progressive Era—the farmers and the land-hungry railroads that distributed their wheat.

496 pp.   0-14-018770-7 $14.95

The Pit
A Story of Chicago

Introduction and Notes by Joseph A. McElrath, Jr. and Gwendolyn Jones

This classic literary critique of turn-of-the-century capitalism in the United States reveals Norris's powerful story of an obsessed trader intent on cornering the wheat market and the consequences of his unchecked greed.

496 pp.   0-14-018758-8 $13.95

NOTKER THE STAMMERER

See Einhard.

SEAN O'CASEY

See J. M. Synge.

MARGARET OLIPHANT
1828 – 1897, SCOTTISH

Miss Marjoribanks

Edited with an Introduction and Notes by Elizabeth Jay

The esteemed English critic Q. D. Leavis declared Oliphant's heroine, Lucilla, to be the "missing link" in nineteenth-century literature between Jane Austen's Emma and George Eliot's Dorothea Brooke, and "more entertaining, more impressive, and more likeable than either."

512 pp.   0-14-043630-8 $12.95

SIGURD OLSON
1900 – 1982, AMERICAN

Songs of the North

Edited with an Introduction by Howard Frank Mosher

In these simple, eloquent essays, Sigurd Olson brings briskly to life the primitive and lovely land of deep icy lakes, unmapped streams, and the thick forests of the Quetico-Superior country of northern Minnesota and Ontario.

NATURE CLASSICS

268 pp.   0-14-025218-5 $11.99

The Rubaiyat of Omar Khayyám

Selected and Translated with an Introduction by Peter Avery and John Heath-Stubbs

This contemporary edition of Khayyám has been selected and translated by Persian scholar Peter Avery and poet John Heath-Stubbs.

120 pp.   0-14-044384-3 $9.95

The Erotic Poems

Translated with an Introduction and Notes by Peter Green

These works by the foremost erotic poet of the Augustan period—*The Art of Love*, the *Amores, Cures for Love*, and *On Facial Treatment for Ladies*—give

testament to the whole spectrum of sexual behavior.

464 pp.   0-14-044360-6 $12.95

Fasti

Translated and Edited with an Introduction, Notes, and Glossary by A. J. Boyle and R. D. Woodward

The Fasti is both a poem on the Roman religious calendar and a witty sequence of stories—comic, tragic, elegiac, epic, and erotic—that also contain uncomfortable political echoes. Ovid's final poem playfully subverts the values of the emperor who sent him into exile.

432 pp.   0-14-044690-7 $14.00

Heroides

Translated with an Introduction and Notes by Harold Isbell

Dramatic monologues in the form of love letters written between mythological lovers—such as Paris and Helen, and Hero and Leander—demonstrate Ovid's gift for psychological insight.

288 pp.   0-14-042355-9 $13.95

Metamorphoses

Translated with an Introduction by Mary M. Innes

Culled from Greek poems and myths, Latin folklore, and tales from Babylon and the East, Ovid's *Metamorphoses* is examined in historical and literary context in Mary Innes's Introduction.

368 pp.   0-14-044058-5 $9.95

Ovid in English

Edited with an Introduction by Christopher Martin

Witty, erotic, skeptical, and subversive, Ovid remains the most influential of Roman poets. Drawing from English translations of his work throughout the centuries, this collection reveals the range of Ovid's genius and his unrivalled impact on the English imagination.

464 pp.   0-14-044669-9 $14.95

The Poems of Exile
Translated with an Introduction, Notes, and Glossary by Peter Green

These poems, written during his exile from Rome on charges of literary obscenity, reveal Ovid's political opinions and his laments for his homeland.

568 pp.   0-14-044407-6 $10.95

THOMAS PAINE
1737 – 1809, AMERICAN

Common Sense
Edited with an Introduction by Isaac Kramnick

Published anonymously in 1776, *Common Sense* was instrumental in initiating the movement that established the independence of the United States. Drawn from Paine's experience of revolutionary politics, this treatise formulates the principles of fundamental human rights later expounded in his *Rights of Man*.

128 pp.   0-14-039016-2 $7.95

Rights of Man
Edited with an Introduction by Eric Foner and Notes by Henry Collins

Written in reply to Burke's *Reflections on the Revolution in France*, Paine's *Rights of Man* enshrines the radical democratic attitude in its purest form.

288 pp.   0-14-039015-4 $9.95

The Thomas Paine Reader
Edited with an Introduction by Michael Foot and Isaac Kramnick

This collection focuses on Paine as the political theorist who was an inspiration to Americans in their struggle for independence, a great defender of individual rights, and the most incendiary of radical writers.

544 pp.   0-14-044496-3 $13.95

DOROTHY PARKER
1893 – 1967, AMERICAN

Complete Poems
Introduction by Colleen Breese

The first complete edition of Parker's poetry brings together all of the poems published in *Enough Rope, Sunset Gun,* and *Death and Taxes* along with a hundred other previously uncollected works.

20TH-CENTURY CLASSICS

320 pp.   0-14-118022-6 $13.95

Complete Stories
Edited by Colleen Breese with an Introduction by Regina Barreca

Parker's talents extended far beyond brash one-liners and clever rhymes.

Her stories lay bare the uncertainties and disappointments of ordinary people living ordinary lives. Included are her best-known stories, thirteen stories never previously collected, and a selection of sardonic sketches.

20TH-CENTURY CLASSICS
352 pp.   0-14-018939-4 $13.95

FRANCIS PARKMAN, JR.
1823 – 1893, AMERICAN

The Oregon Trail
Edited with an Introduction by David Levin

On April 28, 1846, Francis Parkman left Saint Louis on his first expedition west. *The Oregon Trail* documents his adventures in the wilderness, sheds light on America's westward expansion, and celebrates the American spirit.

504 pp.   0-14-039042-1 $11.95

BLAISE PASCAL
1623 – 1662, FRENCH

Pensées
Translated with a Revised Introduction by A. J. Krailsheimer

This collection of short writings ponders the contrast between man in his fallen state and in a state of grace. It is a work of extraordinary power; a lucid, eloquent, and often satirical look at human illusions, self-deceptions, and follies.

368 pp.   0-14-044645-1 $9.95

PAUSANIAS
C. 143 – C. 176, GREEK

Guide to Greece
Translated with an Introduction by Peter Levi

Pausanias's classic account of every Greek city and sanctuary includes historical introductions and a record of local customs and beliefs. Volume 1 covers central Greece, the country around Athens, Delphi, and Mycenae; Volume 2 describes southern Greece, including Olympia, Sparta, Arcadia, and Bassae.

Vol. 1 592 pp. 0-14-044225-1 $14.95
Vol. 2 544 pp. 0-14-044226-X $13.95

THOMAS LOVE PEACOCK
1785 – 1866, BRITISH

Nightmare Abbey/Crotchet Castle
Edited with an Introduction by Raymond Wright

Two of Peacock's wittiest works, parodies of the Gothic novel's excesses, are included here in one volume.

288 pp.   0-14-043045-8 $13.95

GEORGES PEREC
1936 – 1982, FRENCH

Species of Spaces and Other Pieces
Edited and Translated with an Introduction by John Sturrock

This volume features ingenious contemplations on the ways in which we occupy urban and domestic space; engrossing accounts of Perec's experience with psychoanalysis; depictions of the Paris of his childhood; and thought-provoking examinations of the "infra ordinary" and of how the commonplace items of our lives elude our attention.

20TH-CENTURY CLASSICS

304 pp.   0-14-018986-6 $14.95

PERSIUS

See Horace.

PETRONIUS
D. A.D. 66, ROMAN

SENECA
C. 4 B.C. – A.D. 65, ROMAN

The Satyricon/The Apocolocyntosis
Translated with an Introduction and Notes by J. P. Sullivan

In *The Satyricon*, the racy adventures of the impotent Encolpius and his friends and lovers provide the definitive portrait of the age of Nero. *The Apocolocyntosis* is a malicious skit on the "deification of Claudius the Clod," designed by Seneca to ingratiate himself with Claudius's successor, Nero.

256 pp.   0-14-044489-0 $11.95

See Lucius Annaeus Seneca.

PINDAR
C. 518 – C. 438 B.C., GREEK

The Odes
Translated with an Introduction by C. M. Bowra

The entire spectrum of Greek moral order, from earthly competition to fate and mythology, is covered in Pindar's *Epinicia*—choral songs extolling victories in the games at Olympia, Delphi, Nemea, and Corinth.

256 pp.   0-14-044209-X $11.95

LUIGI PIRANDELLO
1867 – 1936, ITALIAN
NOBEL PRIZE WINNER

Six Characters in Search of an Author and Other Plays
Translated by Mark Musa

Inverting the conventions of theater and "real" life, Pirandello suggested that people are simply characters acting out the drama of their lives, for which theater provides an absurd, yet strangely logical, mirror. Besides *Six Characters in Search of an Author*, his best-known work, this volume also includes *Henry IV* and *So It Is (If You Think So)*.

20TH-CENTURY CLASSICS

224 pp.   0-14-018922-X $11.95

CHRISTINE DE PISAN
1364 – C. 1430, FRENCH

The Book of the City of Ladies

*Translated with an Introduction by
Rosalind Brown-Grant*

In this sequel to *The Treasure of the City
of Ladies*, de Pisan, with the help of Reason, Rectitude, and Justice, constructs an allegorical city in which to defend womankind and confront the misogyny of fourteenth-century Europe.

336 pp.   0-14-044689-3 $12.95

The Treasure of the City of the Ladies
Or, The Book of Three Virtues

*Translated with an Introduction by
Sarah Lawson*

A valuable counterbalance to chronicles of medieval life written by men, this 1405 "survival manual" addresses all women, from those at the royal court to prostitutes, and portrays their lives in fine and often wry detail.

192 pp.   0-14-044453-X $11.95

PLATO
C. 427 – C. 347 B.C., GREEK

Early Socratic Dialogues

*Edited with a General Introduction by
Trevor J. Saunders and Translated with
Introductions by Trevor J. Saunders,
Iain Lane, Donald Watt, and
Robin Waterfield*

Rich in drama and humor, seven dialogues provide a definitive portrait of Socrates's thought and times. The selection includes *Ion, Laches, Lysis, Charmides, Hippias Major, Hippias Minor,* and *Euthydemus.*

400 pp.   0-14-044447-5 $12.95

Gorgias

*Translated with an Introduction by
Walter Hamilton*

Though Gorgias was a teacher of oratory, this dialogue is more concerned with ethics than with the art of public speaking.

160 pp.   0-14-044094-1 $8.95

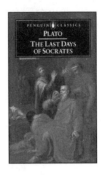

The Last Days of Socrates
Euthyphro/The Apology/Crito/Phaedo

*Translated by Hugh Tredennick and
Harold Tarrant with a New Introduction
and Notes by Harold Tarrant*

The four superb Platonic dialogues that form the classic account of the trial and death of Socrates—presented in this volume in a revised translation with extensive notes—have almost as central a place in Western consciousness as the trial and death of Jesus.

256 pp.   0-14-044582-X $11.95

The Laws

*Translated with an Introduction by
Trevor J. Saunders*

In his last and longest work, Plato sets forth a detailed code of immutable laws for the ideal state that contrasts sharply with the notion of the philosopher-king developed in *The Republic.* This edition

includes a list of crimes and punishments and an appendix of Plato's letters.
560 pp.   0-14-044222-7 $11.95

Phaedrus and Letters VII and VIII

Translated with an Introduction by Walter Hamilton

Phaedrus, chiefly valued for its idyllic setting and magnificent myth, is concerned with establishing the principles of rhetoric based on the knowledge of truth inspired by love. The seventh and eighth letters reflect Plato's involvement in Sicilian politics and reveal fascinating glimpses into the contemporary power struggle.
160 pp.   0-14-044275-8 $9.95

Philebus

Translated with an Introduction by Robin Waterfield

This is Plato's most deliberate and thorough attempt to describe the good life and the way people ought to achieve it, presented with an extensive critical Introduction covering the main stages

of the dialogue.
160 pp.   0-14-044395-9 $9.95

Protagoras and Meno

Translated with an Introduction by W. K. C. Guthrie

These two dialogues explore the question of virtue, the first concluding that all virtues are united by knowledge, the second arguing that virtue is teachable.
160 pp.   0-14-044068-2 $9.95

PLATO

Plato was born into a noble Athenian family that was engaged in politics. Disturbed by the endemic political violence and corruption in Athens, and by the execution of his mentor, Socrates, on charges of impiety and corruption of youth in 399 B.C., Plato turned from the life of politics to philosophy. Plato wrote his famous dialogues, including *The Republic*, to interpret Socratic philosophy, using the character of Socrates to espouse his own views. Plato held that abstract concepts such as "good" are absolute and must be understood in order to be experienced. He returned to Athens around 387 B.C. and founded the Academy in Athens—the prototypical Western university, featuring philosophy, mathematics, astronomy, and natural history—in order to train "philosopher-kings." Aristotle was one of his students. Lasting for almost one thousand years, the Academy was suppressed by the Emperor Justinian in A.D. 529.

The Republic

Translated with an Introduction by Desmond Lee

The first great piece of utopian writing, Plato's treatise on an ideal state applies philosophical principles to political affairs.

472 pp.   0-14-044048-8 $8.95

*The Symposium

Translated with an Introduction and Notes by Christopher Gill

This magnificent modern translation of Plato's dialogue on the power of love conveys all of the drama, humor, and sharply drawn characters of the original. Perhaps no other single work from antiquity retains such direct and immediate relevance for readers today.

144 pp.   0-14-044616-8 $8.95

Theaetetus

Translated with a Critical Essay by Robin Waterfield

Plato examines the idea of knowledge, putting forth and criticizing opposing definitions in this pioneering work in epistemology.

256 pp.   0-14-044450-5 $10.95

Timaeus and Critias

Translated with an Introduction by Desmond Lee

The earliest Greek account of a divine creation, *Timaeus* is concerned with cosmology and anthropology. The unfinished *Critias*, Plato's only work on the natural sciences, tells the story of the lost civilization of Atlantis.

176 pp.   0-14-044261-8 $9.95

PLAUTUS
C. 254 – 184 B.C., ROMAN

The Pot of Gold and Other Plays

Translated by E. F. Watling

Plautus's broad humor, reflecting Roman manners and contemporary life, is revealed in these five plays: *The Pot of Gold (Aulularia)*, *The Prisoners (Captivi)*, *The Brothers Menaechmus (Menaechmi)*, *The Swaggering Soldier (Miles Gloriosus)*, and *Pseudolus*.

272 pp.   0-14-044149-2 $10.95

The Rope and Other Plays

Translated with an Introduction by E. F. Watling

This modern translation presents, in a form suitable for the modern stage, *The Ghost (Mostellaria)*, *The Rope (Rudens)*, *A Three-Dollar Day (Trinummus)*, and *Amphitruo*.

288 pp.   0-14-044136-0 $10.95

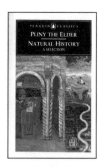

famous account of the destruction of Pompeii and his celebrated correspondence with the Emperor Trajan about the early Christians.

320 pp.   0-14-044127-1 $11.95

The Enneads

Translated by Stephen MacKenna and Abridged with an Introduction and Notes by John Dillon

Here is a highly original synthesis of Platonism, mystic passion, ideas from Greek philosophy, and variants of the Trinity and other central tenets of Christian doctrine by the brilliant thinker who has had an immense influence on mystics and religious writers.

688 pp.   0-14-044520-X $14.95

Natural History
A Selection

Translated with an Introduction and Notes by John F. Healey

This encyclopedic account of the state of science, art, and technology in the first century A.D. also provides a substantial volume of evidence about Pliny's character, temperament, and attitude toward life. Including more than 20,000 facts—from agriculture, astronomy, botany, and chemistry to geography, pharmacy, and zoology—this work is the major source of ancient beliefs about every form of useful knowledge.

448 pp.   0-14-044413-0 $13.95

The Age of Alexander

Translated and Annotated by Ian Scott-Kilvert with an Introduction by G. T. Griffith

Taken from *The Parallel Lives*, this history of nine great Greek statesmen—Agesilaus, Pelopidas, Dion, Timoleon, Demosthenes, Phocion, Alexander, Demetrius, and Pyrrhus—traces a crucial phase of ancient history, from the fall of Athens to the rise of Macedonia.

448 pp.   0-14-044286-3 $13.95

The Letters of the Younger Pliny

Translated with an Introduction by Betty Radice

This modern translation of the ten books of Pliny's *Letters* provides a wealth of information on the social and political history of Rome at the turn of the first century, including Pliny's

Essays

Edited with an Introduction and Notes by Ian Kidd and Translated by Robin Waterfield

Whether he is offering abstract speculations or practical ethics, reflections on the benefits of military versus intellectual glory, or the reasoning powers of animals, Plutarch's encyclopedic writings form a treasure trove of ancient wisdom.

448 p.   0-14-044564-1 $13.95

The Fall of the Roman Republic

Translated by Rex Warner with an Introduction and Notes by Robin Seager

Selections on Gaius, Marius, Sulla, Crassus, Pompey, Caesar, and Cicero are taken from *The Parallel Lives*. Plutarch records, simply and dramatically, the long and bloody period of foreign and civil war that marked the collapse of the Roman Republic and ushered in the Empire.

368 pp.   0-14-044084-4 $13.95

Makers of Rome

Translated with an Introduction by Ian Scott-Kilvert

Nine of Plutarch's *Roman Lives*—Coriolanus, Fabius Maximus, Marcellus, Cato the Elder, Tiberius Gracchus, Gaius Gracchus, Sertorius, Brutus, and Mark Antony—illustrate the courage and tenacity of the Romans in war and their genius for political compromise, from the earliest years of the Republic to the establishment of the Empire.

368 pp.   0-14-044158-1 $12.95

Plutarch on Sparta

Translated with an Introduction and Notes by Richard J. A. Talbert

Rich in anecdote and personal idiosyncrasy, Plutarch's writings are a literary, philosophical, and social exploration of this extraordinary Greek city.

224 pp.   0-14-044463-7 $11.95

The Rise and Fall of Athens
Nine Greek Lives

Translated with an Introduction by Ian Scott-Kilvert

Nine Greek biographies illustrate the rise and fall of Athens, from the legendary days of Theseus, the city's founder, through Solon, Themistocles, Aristides, Cimon, Pericles, Nicias, and Alcibiades, to the razing of its walls by Lysander.

320 pp.   0-14-044102-6 $12.95

EDGAR ALLAN POE
1809 – 1849, AMERICAN

The Fall of the House of Usher and Other Writings

Edited with an Introduction and Notes by David Galloway

This selection includes seventeen poems, among them "The Raven," "Annabel Lee," and "The Bells"; nineteen tales, including "The Fall of the House of Usher," "The Murders in the Rue Morgue," "The Tell-Tale Heart," "The Masque of the Red Death," and "The Pit and the Pendulum"; and sixteen essays and reviews.

544 pp.   0-14-043291-4 $9.95

*The Narrative of Arthur Gordon Pym of Nantucket

Edited with an Introduction and Notes by Richard Kopley

A stowaway aboard the whaling ship *Grampus*, Pym finds himself bound for the high southern latitudes on an extraordinary voyage.

320 pp.   0-14-043748-7 $8.95

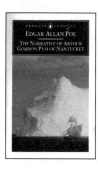

The Science Fiction of Edgar Allan Poe

Edited with an Introduction and Commentary by Harold Beaver

The sixteen stories in this collection, including the celebrated "Eureka," reveal Poe as both an apocalyptic prophet and a pioneer of science fiction.

432 pp.   0-14-043106-3 $12.95

See *Nineteenth-Century American Poetry*.

MARCO POLO
1254 – 1324, VENETIAN

The Travels

Translated with an Introduction by Ronald Latham

Despite piracy, shipwreck, brigandage, and wild beasts, Polo moved in a world of highly organized commerce. This chronicle of his travels through Asia, whether read as fact or fiction, is alive with adventures, geographical information, and descriptions of natural phenomena.

384 pp.   0-14-044057-7 $13.95

POLYBIUS
C. 200 – C. 118 B.C., GREEK

The Rise of the Roman Empire

Translated by Ian Scott-Kilvert with an Introduction by F. W. Walbank

The forty books of Polybius's *Universal History*, covering events in the third and second centuries B.C. that led to the supremacy of Rome, present the first panoramic view of history.

576 pp.   0-14-044362-2 $14.95

JAN POTOCKI
1761 – 1815, POLISH

The Manuscript Found in Saragossa

Translated with an Introduction by Ian Maclean

A rich and wondrous mélange of literary styles and narrative voices, full of philosophical insights, highly charged erotica, and side-splitting humor. "One of the great masterpieces of European literature…this new translation offers us the work as a whole in English for the first time, in the dizzyingly elaborate form envisioned by the author's extraordinary imagination."—*The New York Times Book Review*

656 pp.   0-14-044580-3 $14.95

> **"A Polish classic….It reads like the most brilliant modern novel."**
>
> —SALMAN RUSHDIE

JOHN WESLEY POWELL
1834 – 1902, AMERICAN

The Exploration of the Colorado River and Its Canyons

With an Introduction by Wallace Stegner

In May 1869, a Civil War veteran and nine men descended with four boats in a branch of the Colorado River for an excursion through the last uncharted territory of the United States. Three months and one thousand miles later, six emaciated men in two boats emerged from the open water. Their story, recounted by John Wesley Powell in his journals, remains as fresh and exciting today as it did when it first appeared in 1874.

NATURE CLASSICS

400 pp.   0-14-025569-9 $10.95

ABBÉ PRÉVOST
1697 – 1753, FRENCH

Manon Lescaut

Translated by Leonard Tancock with a New Introduction and Notes by Jean Sgard

Young Chevalier des Grieux's account discloses his love affair with Manon, a femme fatale who makes his life a torment—and without whom it is meaningless.

192 pp.   0-14-044559-5 $10.95

MARY PRINCE
1788 – AFTER 1833 BRITISH
(B. BERMUDA)

The History of Mary Prince

Edited with an Introduction and Notes by Sara Salih

The first account of the life of a black woman ever published in Britain, this moving, painstakingly detailed record of slavery was an instant bestseller that set off immense public controversy and became an instrumental document in the anti-slavery movement's campaign. This edition includes supplementary primary material on enslavement and the case of Mary Prince.

160 pp.   0-14-043749-5 $12.00

(Available in February 2001)

PROCOPIUS
C. 6TH CENT., BYZANTINE

The Secret History

Translated with an Introduction by G. A. Williamson

The other side of sixth-century Byzantium is revealed as Procopius exposes the vicious, scheming nature of the splendid empire and its rulers.

208 pp.   0-14-044182-4 $11.95

MARCEL PROUST
1871 – 1922, FRENCH

Swann's Way

Translated by C. K. Scott-Moncrieff

The themes introduced in *Swann's Way*—the destructive force of obsessive love, the allure and the consequences of transgressive sex, and the selective eye that shapes memories—form the threads that unite all the volumes of *Remembrance of Things Past*.

20TH-CENTURY CLASSICS

224 pp.   0-14-118058-7 $12.95

ALEXANDER PUSHKIN
1799 – 1837, RUSSIAN

Eugene Onegin

Translated by Charles Johnston with an Introduction by John Bayley

Hailed by critics as the finest English-language rendering ever achieved, Charles Johnston's verse translation of *Eugene Onegin* captures the lyric intensity and gusto of Pushkin's incomparable poem.

240 pp.   0-14-044394-0 $9.95

The Queen of Spades and Other Stories

Translated with an Introduction by Rosemary Edmonds

Known as Russia's greatest poet, Pushkin was equally at ease working in other literary forms. The prose collected here includes "The Captain's Daughter," which chronicles the Pugachev Rebellion of 1770, "The Negro of Peter the Great," and "Dubrovsky."

320 pp.   0-14-044119-0 $14.00

Tales of Belkin and Other Prose Writings

Translated by Ronald Wilks with an Introduction by John Bayley

These stories are wonderful in their purity of form, humor, and understatement. This collection also contains a selection of other Pushkin writings, including the fragment *Roslavlev*, *Egyptian Nights*, and the autobiographical *Journey to Arzrum*.

224 pp.   0-14-044675-3 $10.95

MARCEL PROUST

Marcel Proust was born in Auteil in 1871. His father was an eminent Catholic physician; his mother came from a wealthy Jewish family. Despite developing asthma at the age of nine, Proust served in the military from 1889 to 1890 and received degrees in law and literature from the Écoles des Science Politiques in 1893 and 1895. In 1913, he published the first volume of his epic masterpiece, *À la recherche du temps perdu*, known in English as *Remembrance of Things Past*. In 1919, his story *À l'ombre des jeunes filles en fleurs* won the Prix Goncourt. Describing his technique, Proust said, "My instrument is not a microscope, but a telescope directed upon time." He died in 1922; the last three parts of *Remembrance of Things Past* were published posthumously.

THOMAS PYNCHON
B. 1937, AMERICAN

Gravity's Rainbow

A few months after the Germans' secret V-2 rocket bombs begin falling on London, British Intelligence discovers that a map of the city pinpointing the sexual conquests of one Lieutenant Tyrone Slothrop, U.S. Army, corresponds identically to a map showing V-2 impact sites. The implications of this discovery launch Slothrop on a wildly comic extravaganza.

20TH-CENTURY CLASSICS
528 pp.   0-14-018859-2 $16.95

"The most profound and accomplished American novel since the end of World War II."

—EDWARD MENDELSON

Vineland

Pynchon freely combines disparate elements from American pop culture— spy thrillers, Ninja potboilers, TV soap operas, sci-fi fantasies—in this story of sixties survivors.

20TH-CENTURY CLASSICS
400 pp.   0-14-118063-3 $13.95

EÇA DE QUEIRÓS
1845 – 1900, PORTUGUESE

The Maias

Translated by Patricia McGowan Pinheiro and Ann Stevens with an Introduction by Nigel Griffin

A masterpiece of Portuguese literature, this portrait of a decadent landowning family and their declining fortunes over three generations is at once a damning critique of Portugal and a supreme work of humor and irony.

656 pp.   0-14-044694-X $15.95

FRANCISCO DE QUEVEDO
1580 – 1645, SPANISH

Two Spanish Picaresque Novels

Translated by Michael Alpert

A vigorous and earthy humor animates these sixteenth- and seventeenth-century novels, de Quevedo's *El Buscón (The Swindler)* and *Lazarillo de Tormes*, author unknown, in which a slightly disreputable hero who lives by his wits replaces the romantic hero of earlier writings.

216 pp.   0-14-044211-1 $12.95

FRANÇOIS RABELAIS
C. 1483 – 1553, FRENCH

Gargantua and Pantagruel

Translated with an Introduction by J. M. Cohen

Written by a Franciscan monk who was at the center of the sixteenth-century humanist movement, this robust epic parodies everyone from classic authors to Rabelais's own contemporaries.

720 pp.   0-14-044047-X $13.95

Iphigenia/Phaedra/Athaliah

Translated by John Cairncross

Themes of ruthless and unrelenting tragedy are at the heart of these plays. The first two are based on Greek legend, while *Athaliah* depicts the vengeance and the power of the Old Testament Jehovah.

320 pp.   0-14-044122-0 $10.95

Phèdre

Translated with a Foreword by Margaret Rawlings

A favorite among modern readers, students, amateur companies, and repertory theaters alike, Racine's *Phèdre* is the supreme achievement of French neoclassic tragedy. This edition provides both the English and French texts.

192 pp.   0-14-044591-9 $11.95

The Italian

Edited by Robert Miles

Set in the mid-eighteenth-century against a dramatic, lush backdrop of the Bay of Naples, *The Italian* is a tale of passion, deceit, abduction, and the horrors of the Inquisition and one of the most powerful Gothic tales ever written. Its villain, the scheming monk, Schedoni, has become an archetype of Romantic literature.

544 pp.   0-14-043754-1 $10.00

(Available in February 2001)

Ten Days That Shook the World

Introductions by A. J. P. Taylor and V. I. Lenin

Reed's classic eyewitness account of the events in Petrograd in November of 1917 "rises above every other contemporary record" (George F. Kennan).

20TH-CENTURY CLASSICS

368 pp.   0-14-018293-4 $11.95

Clarissa

Edited with an Introduction by Angus Ross

This tale of attracted lovers—one a virtuous young woman, the other a charming and wicked young man—is, like *Pamela*, a novel told in psychologically revealing letters.

1,536 pp.   0-14-043215-9 $24.95

Pamela

*Edited by Peter Sabor with an
Introduction by Margaret A. Doody*

Told in a series of letters, this story of a
maid pursued by her dead mistress's son
features the first British heroine to work
for a living and deals with such matters
as the perversion of sex into power, a
radical theme in 1740.

544 pp.   0-14-043140-3 $7.95

JACOB A. RIIS
1849 – 1914, AMERICAN

How the Other Half Lives

Introduction and Notes by Luc Sante

Published in 1890, Jacob Riis's remarkable study of the horrendous living
conditions of the poor in New York
City had an immediate and extraordinary impact on society, inspiring
reforms that affected the lives of mil-
lions of people. Riis brings life to the
various ethnic groups who lived in the
slums of the Lower East Side, relying on
such specific hard facts as the weapons
of social criticism. His photographs
(included in this edition) made this
book a landmark in photojournalism.

224 pp.   photos throughout
0-14-043679-0 $9.95

ARTHUR RIMBAUD
1854 – 1891, FRENCH

Collected Poems

*Translated with an Introduction by
Oliver Bernard*

All the symbolist poet's well-known
poems are included in this volume,
along with a selection of Rimbaud's letters. Both letters and poems are presented in English prose translations as
well as the original French.

384 pp.   0-14-042064-9 $13.95

EDWIN ARLINGTON
ROBINSON
1869 – 1935, AMERICAN

Selected Poems

*Edited with an Introduction by
Robert Faggen*

Edwin Arlington Robinson's finely
crafted, formal rhythms mirror the
tension the poet sees between life's
immutable circumstances and
humanity's often tragic attempts to
exert control. At once dramatic and
witty, his poems lay bare the loneliness
and despair of life in small genteel
towns, the tyranny of love, and
unspoken, unnoticed suffering.

20TH-CENTURY CLASSICS

288 pp.   0-14-018988-2 $12.95

JEAN-JACQUES
ROUSSEAU
1712 – 1778, SWISS-FRENCH

The Confessions

*Translated with an Introduction by
J. M. Cohen*

The posthumously published *Confessions*,
which describes the first fifty-three years

of the author's life with a refreshing frankness, has left an indelible imprint on the thought of successive generations, influencing, among others, Proust, Goethe, and Tolstoy.

608 pp.   0-14-044033-X $13.00

A Discourse on Inequality

Translated and Annotated with an Introduction and Notes by Maurice Cranston

The most influential of Rousseau's writings, the "Second Discourse" set forth a theory of human evolution that prefigured the discoveries of Darwin, revolutionized the study of anthropology and linguistics, and made a seminal contribution to political and social thought—leading to both the French Revolution and the birth of social science.

208 pp.   0-14-044439-4 $9.95

Reveries of the Solitary Walker

Translated with an Introduction and a Brief Chronology by Peter France

Ten meditations written in the two years before Rousseau's death in 1778 provide an excellent introduction to the thinker's complex world, expressing in its full force the agony of isolation and alienation.

160 pp.   0-14-044363-0 $9.95

The Social Contract

Translated with an Introduction by Maurice Cranston

The Social Contract describes the basic principles of democratic government, stressing that law is derived from the will of the people.

192 pp.   0-14-044201-4 $7.95

SUSANNA ROWSON
1762 – 1828, AMERICAN
(B. ENGLAND)

Charlotte Temple and Lucy Temple

Edited with an Introduction by Ann Douglas

Rowson's tale of a young girl who elopes to the United States only to be abandoned by her fiancé was once the bestselling novel in American literary history. This edition also includes *Lucy Temple*, the fascinating story of Charlotte's orphaned daughter.

320 pp.   0-14-039080-4 $12.95

JOHN RUSKIN
1819 – 1900, BRITISH

Unto This Last and Other Writings

Edited with an Introduction, Commentary, and Notes by Clive Wilmer

The complete text of *Unto This Last*, Ruskin's influential critique of the science of political economy and the doctrine of unhindered industrialization, is presented with selections from *Modern Painters*, *The Stones of Venice*, and *Fors Clavigera*.

368 pp.   0-14-043211-6 $12.95

NICOLA SACCO
1891 – 1927, AMERICAN
(B. ITALY)

BARTOLOMEO VANZETTI
1888 – 1927, AMERICAN
(B. ITALY)

The Letters of Sacco and Vanzetti

Edited by Gardner Jackson and Marion D. Frankfurter with an Introduction by Richard Polenberg

First published in 1928, *The Letters of Sacco and Vanzetti* represents one of the great personal documents of the twentieth century: a volume of primary source material as famous for the splendor of its impassioned prose as for the brilliant light it sheds on the characters of the two dedicated anarchists— executed for the holdup murder of two guards—who became the focus of worldwide attention.

20TH-CENTURY CLASSICS

320 pp.   0-14-118026-9 $13.95

LEOPOLD VON SACHER-MASOCH
1836 – 1895, GALICIAN

Venus in Furs

Translated with Notes by Joachim Neugroschel with an Introduction by Larry Wolff

First published in 1870, *Venus in Furs* earned its author a degree of immortality when the word "masochism"— derived from his name—entered the psychiatric lexicon. The term remains a classic literary statement on sexual submission and control.

144 pp.   0-14-044781-4 $8.95

SALLUST
C. 86 – 35 B.C., ROMAN

The Jugurthine War and The Conspiracy of Catiline

Translated with an Introduction by S. A. Hanford

These are the only surviving works by a man who held various public offices in Rome and was a friend of Caesar and an opponent of Cicero.

240 pp.   0-14-044132-8 $11.95

IGNATIUS SANCHO
1729 – 1780, AFRO-BRITON

Letters of the Late Ignatius Sancho, an African

Edited with an Introduction and Notes by Vincent Carretta

Born in 1729 on a slave ship bound for the West Indies, Ignatius Sancho became the most celebrated Afro-Briton of his time. His letters reveal a man of sensitivity, intellect, and charm, and present his thoughts on race and politics.

352 pp.   0-14-043637-5 $11.95

As I Crossed a Bridge of Dreams
Recollections of a Woman in Eleventh-Century Japan

Translated with an Introduction by Ivan Morris

Born at the height of the Heian period, the pseudonymous Lady Sarashina reveals much about the Japanese literary tradition in this haunting self-portrait.

176 pp.   0-14-044282-0 $11.95

Facundo
Or, Civilization and Barbarism

Translated by Mary Peabody Mann with an Introduction by Ilan Stavans

Written in political exile by one of Argentina's greatest statesmen, *Facundo* is ostensibly a biography of the gaucho barbarian Juan Facundo Quiroga. But it is also a complex, passionate work of history, sociology, and political commentary, and Latin America's most important essay of the nineteenth century.

320 pp.   0-14-043677-4 $12.95

"The single most influential literary work of modern Spanish American culture."
—EDWIN WILLIAMSON

Mary Stuart

Translated with an Introduction and Notes by F. J. Lamport

This masterful and vivid drama of the legendary conflict—and fictitious confrontation—between England's Queen Elizabeth I and Mary, Queen of Scots demonstrates a perfect balance between the classical, the Shakespearean, and the romantic elements of Schiller's genius.

144 pp.   0-14-044711-3 $10.95

The Robbers and Wallenstein

Translated with an Introduction by F. J. Lamport

The foremost dramatist of German classicism wrote *The Robbers*, his first play, in 1781; in the trilogy *Wallenstein*, written nineteen years later, Schiller attempted to combine the strengths of Sophocles, Shakespeare, and French classical drama.

480 pp.   0-14-044368-1 $13.95

Essays and Aphorisms

Selected and Translated with an Introduction by R. J. Hollingdale

This selection of thoughts on religion, ethics, politics, women, suicide, books, and much more is taken from Schopenhauer's last work, *Parerga and Paralipomena*, published in 1851.

240 pp.   0-14-044227-8 $12.95

OLIVE SCHREINER
1855 – 1920, SOUTH AFRICAN

The Story of an African Farm
Introduction by Dan Jacobson

Written by an avid feminist and political activist and first published in 1883, this masterful novel reveals much about colonial history as it tells the story of two orphaned sisters growing up on a lonely farm in a Bible-dominated area of South Africa during the 1860s.

304 pp.   0-14-043184-5 $11.95

BRUNO SCHULZ
1892 – 1942, POLISH

The Street of Crocodiles
Translated by Celina Wieniewski with an Introduction by Jerzy Ficowski

In the Polish city of Drogobych is a street of memories and dreams where recollections of Schulz's boyhood are evoked in a startling blend of the real and the fantastic.

20TH-CENTURY CLASSICS
160 pp.   0-14-018625-5 $11.95

SIR WALTER SCOTT
1771 – 1832, SCOTTISH

The Penguin Classics texts are based on the acclaimed Edinburgh Editions of the Waverley novels

The Antiquary
Edited by David Hewitt with an Introduction by David Punter

The third novel in Scott's Waverley series and his personal favorite, *The Antiquary* centers on a young man who, without wealth or title, wins the daughter of a titled landowner through an extraordinary act of courage.

512 pp.   0-14-043652-9 $13.95

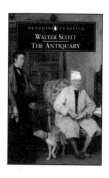

SIR WALTER SCOTT

Sir Walter Scott was born and educated in Edinburgh, but his family roots were in the Borders and he began to collect ballads and tales of that region. His many Romantic narrative poems set in the Border country were a financial success, and though Scott began the Waverley novels in 1805, he abandoned them twice for more marketable work. These novels were published anonymously and followed by many others including, *Ivanhoe*, *The Tale of Old Mortality*, and *Rob Roy*. Scott also issued, under his own editorship at a publishing business he financed with the Ballantyne brothers, a great deal of dramatic work and wrote numerous historical, literary, and antiquarian books. He was created a baronet in 1820.

The Heart of Midlothian

Edited with an Introduction and Notes by Tony Inglis

The inventor and master of the historical novel tells the story of a determined heroine's dramatic confrontation with the justice system in a trial for infanticide, mixing historical fact with folklore from the uneasy, changing world of 1730s Scotland.

848 pp.   0-14-043129-2 $12.95

*Ivanhoe

Edited with an Introduction and Notes by Graham Tulloch

A stirring and exciting recreation of the age of chivalry, alive with such legends as Richard-the-Lion-Hearted and Robin Hood, this is Scott's most popular novel.

544 pp.   0-14-043658-8 $9.00

Kenilworth

Edited with an Introduction by J. H. Alexander

Scott magnificently recreates the drama and the strange mixture of assurance and unease of the Elizabethan Age through the story of Amy Robsart, whose husband, one of the queen's favorites, must keep his marriage secret or incur royal displeasure.

528 pp.   1 line drawing   2 maps
0-14-043654-5 $13.95

Rob Roy

An adventure tale filled with brave deeds and cowardly conspiracies, noble heroes and despicable traitors, *Rob Roy* sweeps readers into the turmoil that erupted in England and Scotland after the death of Queen Anne. Based on the real-life Rob Roy MacGregor, it explores a common theme in Scott's work: the disappearance of the heroic values of chivalry as society became more ordered and prosperous.

512 pp.   0-14-043554-9 $8.95

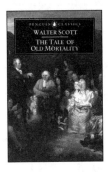

*The Tale of Old Mortality

Edited with an Introduction by Douglas S. Mack

The story of two sets of "cruel and bloody bigots" at war in the late seventeenth-century, this is a fast-paced chronicle of a rebellious religious movement and its impact on peasant and nobleman alike.

496 pp.   0-14-043653-7 $13.95

Waverley

Edited with an Introduction by Andrew Hook

This highly readable story of a young man involved in the Jacobite Rebellion of 1754 blends realism and romance in a classic example of Scott's "invention" —the historical novel.

608 pp.   0-14-043071-7 $10.95

CATHARINE MARIA SEDGWICK
1789 – 1869, AMERICAN

Hope Leslie
Or, Early Times in the Massachusetts

Edited with an Introduction and Notes by Carolyn L. Karcher

Set in seventeenth-century New England in the aftermath of the Pequot War, *Hope Leslie* not only chronicles the role of women in building the republic but also refocuses the emergent national literature on the lives, domestic mores, and values of American women.

464 pp.   0-14-043676-6 $ 13.95

JORGE SEMPRUN
B. 1923, SPANISH

The Long Voyage

Translated by Richard Seaver

The Long Voyage represents both an internal and external voyage for Semprun. It is a profound literary account, fierce and moving, of the time when he was captured fighting with the French Resistance.

20TH-CENTURY CLASSICS

248 pp.   0-14-118029-3 $11.95

LUCIUS ANNAEUS SENECA
C. 4 B.C. – A.D. 65, ROMAN

Dialogues and Letters

Translated with an Introduction by C. D. N. Costa

Included in this volume are the dialogues *On the Shortness of Life* and *On Tranquility of Mind*, which are eloquent classic statements of Stoic ideals of fortitude and self-reliance. This selection also features extracts from *Natural Questions* and the *Consolation of Helvia*.

160 pp.   0-14-044679-6 $12.95

Four Tragedies and Octavia

Translated with an Introduction by E. F. Watling

Although their themes are borrowed from Greek drama, these exuberant and often macabre plays focus on action rather than moral concerns and are strikingly different in style from Seneca's prose writing. This collection includes *Phaedra*, *Oedipus*, *Thyestes*, and *The Trojan Women*.

320 pp.   0-14-044174-3 $12.95

Letters from a Stoic

Selected and Translated with an Introduction by Robin Campbell

Ranging from lively epistles to serious essays, these 124 letters selected from *Epistulae Morales* and *Lucilium* espouse the philosophy of Stoicism. This volume includes Tacitus's account of Seneca's death.

256 pp.   0-14-044210-3 $11.95

MADAME DE SÉVIGNÉ
1626 – 1696, FRENCH

Selected Letters

Edited and Translated with an Introduction by Leonard Tancock

An extraordinarily vivid picture of social, literary, and political life in Louis XIV's France is captured in this selection of letters.

320 pp.   0-14-044405-X $13.95

WILLIAM SHAKESPEARE
1564 – 1616, BRITISH

See page 236-238 for titles available in the Pelican Shakespeare Series.

Four Comedies

Edited with Introductions and Notes by G. R. Hibbard, Stanley Wells, H. J. Oliver, and M. M. Mahood

This collection—including *The Taming of the Shrew*, *A Midsummer Night's Dream*, *As You Like It*, and *Twelfth Night* in the New Penguin Shakespeare text—is engagingly introduced and skillfully annotated, bringing together four of Shakespeare's most spirited comedies.

688 pp.   0-14-043454-2 $12.95

Four Histories

Edited with Introductions and Notes by Stanley Wells, P. H. Davison, and A. R. Humphreys

Shakespeare explores matters of honor, history, tradition, and change in this cycle of plays chronicling the turbulent transition of the British monarchy. Included are *Richard II*; *Henry IV, Parts 1* and *2*; and *Henry V*.

576 pp.   0-14-043450-X $12.95

Four Tragedies

Edited with Introductions and Notes by T. J. B. Spencer, Anne Barton, Kenneth Muir, and G. K. Hunter

These four tragedies—*Hamlet*, *Othello*, *King Lear*, and *Macbeth* in the New Penguin Shakespeare text—contain some of Shakespeare's most celebrated protagonists and finest dramatic poetry.

960 pp.   0-14-043458-5 $12.95

The Sonnets and A Lover's Complaint

Edited with an Introduction by John Kerrigan

This volume of poetry was originally entitled *Shake-speares Sonnets. Neuer before Imprinted* and appeared in 1609 but his inspiration for these masterpieces of wit and erotic word-play remain shrouded in mystery.

464 pp.   0-14-043684-7 $7.95

Three Roman Plays

Edited with Introductions and Notes by Norman Sanders, Emrys Jones, and G. R. Hibbard

Each of these plays, previously published separately in the New Penguin Shakespeare series, investigates political action and the relationship between the personal and the political. In this volume are *Coriolanus*, *Julius Caesar*, and *Antony and Cleopatra*.

672 pp.   0-14-043461-5 $11.95

VARLAM SHALAMOV
1907 – 1982, RUSSIAN

Kolyma Tales

Translated with a Foreword by John Glad

Out of his seventeen years in the Siberian labor camps of Kolyma, Shalamov fashioned a fictional recreation of that world and created this powerful collection of stories from the raw cruelty of Soviet history.

20TH-CENTURY CLASSICS

544 pp.   0-14-018695-6 $13.95

GEORGE BERNARD SHAW
1856 – 1950, IRISH
NOBEL PRIZE WINNER

THE BERNARD SHAW LIBRARY

Edited by Dan H. Laurence

*Heartbreak House

Introduction by David Hare

Shaw's favorite play, *Heartbreak House* is a comedy of manners that takes a probing look at the conflict between "old-fashioned" idealism and the realities of the modern age.

176 pp.   0-14-043787-8 $9.00

*Man and Superman

Introduction by Stanley Weintraub

A wonderfully original twist on the Don Juan myth, this finely tuned combination of intellectual seriousness and popular comedy is a classic exposé of the eternal struggle between the sexes.

288 pp.   0-14-043788-6 $10.00

*Plays Unpleasant

Introduction by David Edgar

This 1898 collection includes *Widowers'*

BERNARD SHAW

George Bernard Shaw was born in Dublin in 1856. Essentially shy, he created the persona of G.B.S., the showman, satirist, critic, wit, and dramatist. Commentators brought a new adjective into English: Shavian, a term used to embody all his brilliant qualities. After his arrival in London in 1876 he became an active Socialist and platform speaker. He undertook his own education at the British museum and consequently became keenly interested in cultural subjects. He invented the comedy of ideas, expounding on social and political problems with a razor-sharp tongue, yet never sacrificing the comic vitality that ensures regular revivals of his plays. Shaw won the Nobel Prize for literature in 1925 and lived long enough to see a few of his plays made into films. He died in 1950.

Houses, *The Philanderer*, and *Mrs. Warren's Profession*, and challenges audiences' moral complacency in the face of serious social problems.

304 pp.   0-14-043793-2 $12.00

*Three Plays for Puritans

Introduction by Michael Billington

Comprising *The Devil's Disciple*, *Caesar and Cleopatra*, and *Captain Brassbound's Conversion*, this volume reveals Shaw's constant delight in turning received wisdom upside down.

368 pp.   0-14-043792-4 $12.00

MARY SHELLEY
1797 – 1851, BRITISH

Frankenstein

Edited with an Introduction by Maurice Hindle

Shelley's Gothic horror tale, written when she was nineteen for her husband and their friend Lord Byron, was an immediate bestseller in 1818. This definitive new edition contains the revised, original text.

320 pp.   0-14-043362-7 $7.95

See *Three Gothic Novels* and Mary Wollstonecraft.

SHEN FU
c. 18TH CENT., CHINESE

Six Records of a Floating Life

Translated with an Introduction and Notes by Leonard Pratt and Chiang Su-Hui

This autobiographical novel, published in 1809, contains lively depictions of the powerful role of the courtesan, the arrogance of untrained officials, and the formal and often strained arranged marriages in turn-of-the-century China.

176 pp.   0-14-044429-7 $10.95

RICHARD BRINSLEY SHERIDAN
1751 – 1816, IRISH

The School for Scandal and Other Plays

Edited with an Introduction by Eric S. Rump

Although Sheridan tried his hand at statesmanship, his reputation as a dramatist was enhanced by these three masterpieces of ingenious plotting, eloquent wit, and biting satire. This edition also includes *The Rivals*, his first play, and *The Critic*.

288 pp.   0-14-043240-X $10.95

WILLIAM TECUMSEH SHERMAN
1820 – 1891, AMERICAN

Memoirs

Introduction and Notes by Michael Fellman

Before his spectacular career as General of the Union forces, Sherman drifted between the Old South and New West.

His *Memoirs* evoke the uncompromising and deeply complex man as well as the turbulent times that transformed America into a world power.

848 pp.   0-14-043798-3 $16.95

SIR PHILIP SIDNEY
1554 – 1586, BRITISH

The Countess of Pembroke's Arcadia

Edited with an Introduction and Notes by Maurice Evans

As much a work of entertainment and wit as of instruction, *Arcadia* affords the best insight we have into the tastes and standards of the Elizabethans and embodies the highest literary aspirations of the age.

880 pp.   0-14-043111-X $12.95

UPTON SINCLAIR
1878 – 1968, AMERICAN

The Jungle

Introduction by Ronald Gottesman

Perhaps the most influential and harrowing of Sinclair's writings, this savage novel of the Chicago stockyards established its author as one of the major modern American propaganda novelists.

20TH-CENTURY CLASSICS

432 pp.   0-14-039031-6 $9.95

ISAAC BASHEVIS SINGER
1904 – 1991, AMERICAN
(B. POLAND)
NOBEL PRIZE WINNER

The Certificate

A penniless writer—and the son of an Orthodox rabbi—enters into a fictitious marriage with a wealthy woman in order to emigrate from Warsaw to Palestine. With characteristic wit and candor, Singer examines the lives of Polish Jews in the context of events sweeping Europe in the 1920s.

20TH-CENTURY CLASSICS

240 pp.   0-14-018785-5 $11.95

The King of the Fields

This magical and resonant fable recreates the birth of the Polish nation and is an "impassioned narrative art which, with roots in Polish-Jewish cultural tradition, brings universal human conditions to life" (Nobel Prize Committee).

20TH-CENTURY CLASSICS

256 pp.   0-14-018668-9 $11.95

I. J. SINGER
1893 – 1944, AMERICAN (B. POLAND)

The Brothers Ashkenazi

Translated by Joseph Singer with an Introduction by Irving Howe

Yiddish novelist Singer's sweeping family saga set against the rise of capitalism and the Jewish bourgeoisie in Lodz, Poland.

20TH-CENTURY CLASSICS

448 pp.   0-14-018777-4 $14.95

CHARLES A. SIRINGO
1855 – 1928, AMERICAN

A Texas Cowboy
Or, Fifteen Years on the Hurricane Deck of a Spanish Pony

Edited with an Introduction and Notes by Richard Etulain

Siringo's 1885 chronicle of his life as a cowboy was one of the first classics about the Old West.

256 pp.   0-14-043751-7 $12.00

JOSHUA SLOCUM
1844 – 1924, AMERICAN

Sailing Alone around the World

Introduction and Notes by Thomas Philbrick

Setting off alone from Boston aboard the thirty-six foot wooden sloop *Spray* in April 1895, Captain Slocum began a three-year solo voyage of more than 46,000 miles that remains unmatched in maritime history for courage, skill, and determination. This autobiographical account endures as one of the greatest adventure narratives ever written.

320 pp.   b/w illustrations throughout
0-14-043736-3 $7.95

"Slocum has become the archetype of the American wanderer: creating himself on the page, he drew a classic hero, as resilient, as full of signification in his own rough-diamond way, as Huckleberry Finn."

—JONATHAN RABAN

ADAM SMITH
1723 – 1790, SCOTTISH

The Wealth of Nations
Books I–III

Edited with an Introduction by Andrew Skinner

In this work, which laid the foundations of economic theory in general and of "classical" economics in particular, Smith pinpointed the division of labor as a major explanation of economic growth.

544 pp.   0-14-043208-6 $11.95

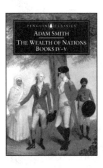

The Wealth of Nations
Books IV-V

Edited with an Introduction and Notes by Andrew Skinner

In these final two books of his land-mark treatise, Smith offers his considered response to the French Physiocrats and famously predicted that America "will be one of the foremost nations of the world."

672 pp.   0-14-043615-4 $13.95

TOBIAS SMOLLETT
1721 – 1771, SCOTTISH

The Expedition of Humphry Clinker

*Edited with an Introduction by
Angus Ross*

Written toward the end of Smollett's
life, this picaresque tour of eighteenth-
century British society abounds with
eccentric characters and comic adventures.

416 pp.   0-14-043021-0 $10.95

SNORRI STURLUSON
1179 – 1241, ICELANDIC

King Harald's Saga

*Translated with an Introduction by
Magnus Magnusson and
Hermann Pálsson*

The biography of one of the most
remarkable and memorable of the
medieval kings of Norway, this saga
culminates in the conflict between
Norway and England in 1066.

192 pp.   0-14-044183-2 $10.95

See *Hrafnkel's Saga.*

SOMADEVA
C. 1070, KASHMIRI

Tales from the Kathāsaritsāgara

*Translated with an Introduction by
Arshia Sattar and a Foreword by
Wendy Doniger*

A compendium of tales passed down
by generations of oral storytellers, the
Kathāsaritsāgara—literally translated as
"ocean of the sea of stories"—is
thought to have been compiled around
1070 for the queen of Kashmir. It brings
together engaging stories of heroic

adventure, love, lust, betrayal, decep-
tion, and revenge in an uninhibited and
bawdy celebration of life.

320 pp.   0-14-044698-2 $12.95

SOPHOCLES
C. 496 – 406 B.C., GREEK

Electra and Other Plays

*Translated with an Introduction by
E. F. Watling*

These verse translations of four plays—
Ajax, Electra, The Women of Trachis, and
Philoctetes—exhibit the structure that
set the standard for most modern dramatic works.

224 pp.   0-14-044028-3 $8.95

The Theban Plays

*Translated with an Introduction by
E. F. Watling*

Based on the legend of the royal house
of Thebes, *King Oedipus, Oedipus at
Colonus,* and *Antigone* are Sophocles's
tragic masterpieces. This verse translation is supplemented by E. F. Watling's
Introduction, which places Sophocles
in historical context, discusses the origins of the art of drama, and interprets
each play in the Theban legend.

168 pp.   0-14-044003-8 $10.95

The Three Theban Plays
Antigone/Oedipus the King/ Oedipus at Colonus
Translated by Robert Fagles with an Introduction and Notes by Bernard Knox

Fagles's lucid modern translation captures the majesty of Sophocles's masterwork and is enhanced by insightful Introductions to each play, an essay on the history of the text, extensive notes, bibliography, and glossary.

432 pp.   0-14-044425-4 $9.95

EDMUND SPENSER
c. 1552 – 1599, British

The Faerie Queene
Edited by Thomas P. Roche, Jr. with C. Patrick O'Connell, Jr.

The first English-language epic, Spenser's masterful extended allegory of knightly virtue and supreme grace brilliantly unites medieval romance to Renaissance epic.

1,248 pp.   0-14-042207-2 $18.95

The Shorter Poems
Edited by Richard A. McCabe

Spenser showed his supreme versatility and skill as a eulogist, satirist, pastoral poet, and prophet in his shorter poetry.

This edition is a sweeping collection of his verse that includes *The Shepheardes Celendar*, *Amoretti*, and *Mother Hubberd's Tale*.

816 pp.   0-14-043445-3 $19.95

SIR RICHARD STEELE
1672 – 1729, British

JOSEPH ADDISON
1672 – 1719, British

Selections from *The Tatler* and *The Spectator*
Edited with an Introduction and Notes by Angus Ross

The essays published in *The Tatler* and *The Spectator* examined everything from conduct and morals to philosophy, political doctrine, science, and literature. This collection sheds light on the ideas at the heart of eighteenth-century thought in both England and Europe and offers an unparalleled glimpse of life among London's intellectual and literary set.

592 pp.   0-14-043298-1 $13.95

EDDIUS STEPHANUS
c. 8th cent., Anglo-Saxon

See Bede.

WALLACE STEGNER
1909 – 1993, American

Angle of Repose
Introduction by Jackson J. Benson

Stegner's Pulitzer Prize–winning novel is at once an enthralling portrait of four generations in the life of an American family and a fascinating illumination of the civilization carved into the surface of America's western frontier.

20TH-CENTURY CLASSICS
592 pp.   0-14-118547-3 $15.00

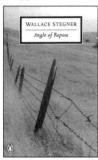

Wolf Willow
A History, a Story, and a Memory of the Last Plains Frontier

Introduction by Page Stegner

A weave of fiction and nonfiction, history and impressions, childhood remembrance and adult reflections form Stegner's unusual portrait of his childhood on the family homestead in southern Saskatchewan.

20TH-CENTURY CLASSICS
320 pp.   0-14-118501-5 $14.00

GERTRUDE STEIN
1874 – 1946, AMERICAN

Three Lives

Introduction by Ann Charters

Redefining the writer's art, *The Good Anna, The Gentle Lena,* and *Melanctha* capture the sensibilities of an author and an age in a way that continues to influence writers of this century.

20TH-CENTURY CLASSICS
320 pp.   0-14-018184-9 $9.95

JOHN STEINBECK
1902 – 1968, AMERICAN
NOBEL PRIZE WINNER

Burning Bright

Written as a play in story form, this novel traces the story of a man ignorant of his own sterility, a wife who commits adultery to give her husband a child, the father of that child, and the outsider whose actions affect them all.

20TH-CENTURY CLASSICS
128 pp.   0-14-018742-1 $10.95

WALLACE STEGNER

Wallace Stegner was born on February 18, 1909 in Lake Mills, Iowa. Among his novels are *The Big Rock Candy Mountain,* 1943; *Joe Hill,* 1950; *All the Little Live Things,* 1967 (Commonwealth Club Gold Medal); *Angle of Repose,* 1972 (Pulitzer Prize); *The Spectator Bird,* 1976 (National Book Award); *Recapitulation,* 1979; and *Crossing to Safety,* 1987. The nonfiction includes *Beyond the Hundredth Meridian,* 1954; *Wolf Willow,* 1962; *The Sound of Mountain Water,* 1969; and *Where the Bluebird Sings to the Lemonade Springs: Living and Writing in the West,* 1992. Three of his short stories have won O. Henry prizes, and in 1980 he received the Robert Kirsch Award from the *Los Angeles Times* for his lifetime achievements. His *Collected Stories* was published in 1990.

Cannery Row

Introduction by Susan Shillinglaw

Steinbeck's tough but loving portrait evokes the lives of Monterey's vital laboring class and their emotional triumph over the bleak existence of life in Cannery Row.

20TH-CENTURY CLASSICS

224 pp.   0-14-018737-5 $9.95

Cup of Gold

Steinbeck's first novel, and the only historical novel he ever wrote, brings to life the exciting, violent adventures of the infamous pirate Henry Morgan.

20TH-CENTURY CLASSICS

272 pp.   0-14-018743-X $11.95

East of Eden

Introduction by David Wyatt

The masterpiece of Steinbeck's later years, *East of Eden* is the powerful and vastly ambitious novel that is both family saga and a modern retelling of the book of Genesis.

20TH-CENTURY CLASSICS

624 pp.   0-14-018639-5 $12.95

The Grapes of Wrath

Introduction by Robert DeMott

This Pulitzer Prize–winning epic of the Great Depression follows the western movement of one family and a nation in search of work and human dignity.

20TH-CENTURY CLASSICS

640 pp.   0-14-018640-9 $13.00

In Dubious Battle

Introduction and Notes by Warren French

This powerful social novel, set in the California apple country, is a story of labor unrest in the migrant community and the search for identity of its protagonist, young Jim Nolan.

20TH-CENTURY CLASSICS

360 pp.   0-14-018641-7 $14.00

The Log from the *Sea of Cortez*

Introduction by Richard Astro

This exciting day-by-day account of Steinbeck's trip to the Gulf of California with biologist Ed Ricketts, drawn from the longer *Sea of Cortez*, is a wonderful combination of science, philosophy, and high-spirited adventure.

20TH-CENTURY CLASSICS

288 pp.   0-14-018744-8 $13.95

The Long Valley

Introduction by John H. Timmerman

First published in 1938, this collection of stories set in the rich farmland of the Salinas Valley includes the O. Henry Prize–winning story "The Murder," as well as one of Steinbeck's most famous short works, "The Snake."

20TH-CENTURY CLASSICS

304 pp.   0-14-018745-6 $12.95

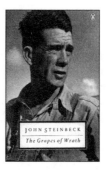

JOHN STEINBECK
The Grapes of Wrath

The Moon Is Down

Introduction by Donald V. Coers

In this masterful tale set in Norway

during World War II, Steinbeck explores the effects of invasion on both the conquered and the conquerors. As he delves into the emotions of the German commander and the Norwegian traitor, and depicts the spirited patriotism of the Norwegian underground, Steinbeck uncovers profound, often unsettling truths about war—and about human nature.

20TH-CENTURY CLASSICS
192 pp.   0-14-018746-4 $10.95

Of Mice and Men

Introduction by Susan Shillinglaw

A parable about commitment, loneliness, hope, and loss, *Of Mice and Men* remains one of America's most widely read and beloved novels.

20TH-CENTURY CLASSICS
160 pp.   0-14-018642-5 $9.95

Once There Was a War

Steinbeck's dispatches filed from the front lines during World War II vividly evoke the human side of the war.

20TH-CENTURY CLASSICS
256 pp.   0-14-018747-2 $12.95

The Pastures of Heaven

Introduction and Notes by James Nagel

Each of these interconnected tales is devoted to a family living in a fertile valley on the outskirts of Monterey, California, and the effects, either intentional or unwitting, that one family has on all of them.

20TH-CENTURY CLASSICS
256 pp.   0-14-018748-0 $11.95

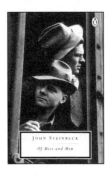

The Pearl

Introduction by Linda Wagner-Martin with Drawings by José Clemente Orozco

The diver Kino believes that his discovery of a beautiful pearl means the

JOHN STEINBECK

Born and raised in Salinas, California, John Steinbeck attended Stanford University from 1919 until 1925 without attaining a degree before working at a series of mostly blue-collar jobs and embarking on his literary career. Profoundly committed to social progress, Steinbeck's novels, such as *The Grapes of Wrath*, *Cannery Row*, and *Tortilla Flat*, raised issues of labor exploitation during the Great Depression. *The Grapes of Wrath* won both the National Book Award and the Pulitzer Prize in 1939. *Travels with Charley*, a travelogue chronicling his tour of the U.S. with his dog, was published in 1962, the same year he received the Nobel Prize in Literature. In 1964, Steinbeck was presented with the United States Medal of Freedom by President Lyndon B. Johnson. Steinbeck died in New York in 1968.

promise of a better life for his impoverished family. His fall from innocence is one of Steinbeck's most moving stories about the American dream.

20TH-CENTURY CLASSICS

128 pp.   0-14-018738-3 $9.95

The Red Pony

Introduction by John Seelye

This cycle of coming-of-age stories tells of a spirited adolescent boy whose encounters with birth and death teach him about loss and profound emptiness, instead of giving him the more conventional hero's pragmatic "maturity."

20TH-CENTURY CLASSICS

128 pp.   0-14-018739-1 $8.95

A Russian Journal

With Photographs by Robert Capa
Introduction by Susan Shillinglaw

First published in 1948, *A Russian Journal* is a remarkable memoir and unique historical document that records the writer and acclaimed war photographer's journey through Cold War Russia.

20TH-CENTURY CLASSICS

224 pp.   70 pp. b/w photographs
0-14-118019-6 $13.95

The Short Reign of Pippin IV

Steinbeck's only work of political satire turns the French Revolution upside down, creating the hilarious characters of the motley royal court of King Pippin.

20TH-CENTURY CLASSICS

176 pp.   0-14-018749-9 $10.95

Sweet Thursday

Returning to the scene of *Cannery Row*—the weedy lot and junk heaps and flophouses of Monterey, California —Steinbeck once more brings to life the denizens of a netherworld of laughter and tears, from Fauna, new headmistress of the local brothel, to Hazel, a bum whose mother must have wanted a daughter.

20TH-CENTURY CLASSICS

288 pp.   0-14-018750-2 $11.95

To a God Unknown

*Introduction and Notes by
Robert DeMott*

Set in familiar Steinbeck territory, *To a God Unknown* is a mystical tale, exploring one man's attempt to control the forces of nature and, ultimately, to understand the ways of God.

20TH-CENTURY CLASSICS

288 pp.   0-14-018751-0 $12.95

Tortilla Flat

Introduction by Thomas Fensch

Adopting the structure and themes of the Arthurian legend, Steinbeck created a "Camelot" on a shabby hillside above Monterey on the California coast and peopled it with a colorful band of knights. As Steinbeck chronicles their thoughts and emotions, temptations and lusts, he spins a tale as compelling, and ultimately as touched by sorrow, as the famous legends of the Round Table.

20TH-CENTURY CLASSICS

192 pp.   0-14-018740-5 $8.95

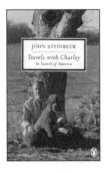

Travels with Charley in Search of America

Introduction by Jay Parini

In September 1960, Steinbeck and his poodle, Charley, embarked on a journey across America. A picaresque tale, this chronicle of their trip meanders along scenic backroads and speeds along anonymous superhighways, moving from small towns to growing cities to glorious wilderness oases.

20TH-CENTURY CLASSICS

288 pp.   0-14-018741-3 $10.95

The Wayward Bus

In this imaginative and unsentimental chronicle of a bus traveling California's back roads, Steinbeck creates a vivid assortment of characters, all running away from their shattered dreams but hoping that they are running toward the promise of a future.

20TH-CENTURY CLASSICS

304 pp.   0-14-018752-9 $13.00

The Winter of Our Discontent

Ethan Hawley works as a clerk in the grocery store owned by an Italian immigrant. His wife is restless, and his teenaged children are hungry for the tantalizing material comforts he cannot provide. Then one day, in a moment of moral crisis, Ethan decides to take a holiday from his own scrupulous standards.

20TH-CENTURY CLASSICS

288 pp.   0-14-018753-7 $11.95

STENDHAL
1783 – 1842, FRENCH

The Charterhouse of Parma

Translated with an Introduction by Margaret R. B. Shaw

This fictionalized account explores the intrigues within a small Italian court during the time of Napoleon's final exile.

504 pp.   0-14-044061-5 $11.95

Love

Translated by Gilbert Sale and Suzanne Sale with an Introduction by Jean Stewart and B. C. J. G. Knight

Stendhal draws on history, literature, and his own experiences in this intensely personal yet universal story of unrequited love.

336 pp.   0-14-044307-X $11.95

Scarlet and Black

Translated with an Introduction by Margaret R. B. Shaw

In the atmosphere of the fearful and greedy drawing-room conformity that followed Waterloo, Julian Sorel rebels against his circumstances and wills himself to make something of his life by adopting a code of hypocrisy and a life of crime.

512 pp.   0-14-044030-5 $8.95

LAURENCE STERNE
1713 – 1768, IRISH

The Life and Opinions of Tristram Shandy

Edited by Melvyn New and Joan New with an Introductory Essay by Christopher Ricks and an Introduction and Notes by Melvyn New

This comic novel about writing a novel is bawdy, profane, irreverent, brazenly illogical, and exceedingly shrewd in its understanding of human behavior and of the infinite possibilities and insurmountable limitations of the art of fiction.

720 pp.   0-14-043505-0 $9.95

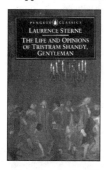

A Sentimental Journey

Edited by Graham Petrie with an Introduction by A. Alvarez

Begun as an account of a trip through France and Italy, this novel is a treasury of dramatic sketches, ironic incidents, philosophical musings, reminiscences, and anecdotes, all recorded in Sterne's delightful, meandering style.

160 pp.   0-14-043026-1 $5.95

ROBERT LOUIS STEVENSON
1850 – 1894, SCOTTISH

"He lighted up one whole side of the globe, and was in himself a whole province of one's imagination."

—HENRY JAMES

Dr. Jekyll and Mr. Hyde and Other Stories

Edited with an Introduction by Jenni Calder

This volume also includes two later stories set in the South Seas, "The Beach of Falesá" (in its unexpurgated form) and "The Ebb-Tide," both of which explore the same moral terrain as *Dr. Jekyll and Mr. Hyde*.

304 pp.   0-14-043117-9 $6.95

In the South Seas

Edited with an Introduction by Neil Rennie

Combining personal anecdote and historical account, autobiography and anthropology, Stevenson and the South

Sea Island, the English novelist's posthumously published work is a classic of travel writing.

336 pp.   1 map   0-14-043436-4 $13.95

Kidnapped

Edited with an Introduction and Notes by Donald McFarlan

Set in the aftermath of the Jacobite Rebellion of 1745, *Kidnapped* is a swashbuckling adventure tale of family treachery, abduction, and murder.

272 pp.   0-14-043401-1 $7.95

The Master of Ballantrae

Edited with an Introduction and Notes by Adrian Poole

In the ancestral home of the Duries, a family divided by the Jacobite risings of 1745, two brothers, James and Henry, carry out a fatal rivalry over a wealthy and beautiful kinswoman who loves one brother but marries the other.

288 pp.   0-14-043446-1 $9.95

Selected Poems

Edited by Angus Calder

This definitive anthology brings together the complete *A Child's Garden of Verses* (1885), substantial extracts from the published collections, and many uncollected poems.

256 pp.   0-14-043548-4 $9.95

Treasure Island

With an Introduction by John Seelye

The quintessential British adventure story, Stevenson's novel is narrated by the teenage Jim Hawkins, who outwits a gang of murderous pirates. This edition includes Stevenson's own essay about the composition of *Treasure Island*, written just before his death.

224 pp.   0-14-043768-1 $5.95

ROBERT LOUIS STEVENSON

Robert Louis Stevenson was born in Edinburgh in 1850. The son of a prosperous civil engineer, he was expected to follow the family profession but, instead, studied law at Edinburgh University. Stevenson reacted violently against the Presbyterian respectability of the city's professional classes and this led to painful clashes with his parents. In his early twenties he became a professional writer. Sickly for most of his life, he traveled to California in 1879 to marry an American ten years his junior and together they spent long periods of time abroad searching for a climate that would be kind to his fragile health. Eventually they settled in Samoa, where he died on December 3, 1894.

Weir of Hermiston

Edited with an Introduction and Notes by Karl Miller

Set in Edinburgh at the end of the eighteenth century, *Weir of Hermiston* is the story of the conflict between Lord Hermiston, a grimly sardonic "hanging judge," and his idealistic son, Archie, who is banished by his father to a country estate. This edition includes an account of Stevenson's projected conclusion to the novel, left unfinished at the time of his death, as well as passages of draft material.

176 pp.   0-14-043560-3 $9.95

ADALBERT STIFTER
1805 – 1868, AUSTRIAN

Brigitta and Other Tales

Translated with an Introduction by Helen Watanabe-O'Kelly

In four tales—*Brigitta*, *Abdias*, *Limestone*, and *The Forest Path*—written in the middle of the nineteenth century, Stifter created fiction with a measured prose that exhibits a highly modern sensibility to the diseased subconscious and reveals the subterranean connections between our earliest experiences and our future selves.

256 pp.   0-14-044630-3 $10.95

ELIZABETH STODDARD
1823 – 1902, AMERICAN

The Morgesons

Edited with an Introduction and Notes by Lawrence Buell and Sandra A. Zagarell

This 1862 female bildungsroman—which explores the conflict between a woman's instinct, passion, and will, and the social taboos, family allegiances, and traditional New England restraint that inhibit her—evoked comparisons during Stoddard's lifetime with Balzac, Tolstoy, Eliot, the Brontës, and Hawthorne.

304 pp.   0-14-043651-0 $11.95

BRAM STOKER
1847 – 1912, IRISH

Dracula

Edited with an Introduction and Notes by Maurice Hindle

The first—and most chilling—portrait of the unbridled lusts and desires of a vampire is still the ultimate terror myth.

560 pp.   0-14-043406-2 $10.95

HARRIET BEECHER STOWE
1811 – 1896, AMERICAN

Dred
A Tale of the Great Dismal Swamp

Edited with an Introduction by Robert S. Levine

Written partly in response to critics of *Uncle Tom's Cabin*, Stowe's compelling second novel brings to life conflicting beliefs about race through the stories of Nina Gorden, the mistress of a slave plantation and Dred, a black revolutionary. Exploring the political and spiritual goals that fuel Dred's rebellion, Stowe creates a figure far different from the acquiescent Christian martyr, Uncle Tom.

656 pp.   0-14-043904-8 $16.00

The Minister's Wooing

Edited with an Introduction by Susan K. Harris and Notes by Susan K. Harris and Danielle Conger

In this novel set in eighteenth-century Newport, Rhode Island, Stowe satirizes Calvinism, celebrating its intellectual and moral integrity while critiquing its rigid theology. With colorful characters and an element of romance, *The Minister's Wooing* combines domestic comedy with regional history to show the convergence of daily life, slavery, and religion in post-Revolutionary New England.

480 pp.   0-14-043702-9 $13.95

Uncle Tom's Cabin
Or, Life Among the Lowly

Edited with an Introduction by Ann Douglas

Perhaps the most powerful document in the history of American abolitionism, this controversial novel goaded thousands of readers to take a stand on the issue of slavery and played a major political and social role in the Civil War period.

640 pp.   0-14-039003-0 $8.95

LYTTON STRACHEY
1880 – 1932, BRITISH

Eminent Victorians

Introduction by Michael Holroyd

Marking an epoch in the art of biography, this volume has been hailed as the "work of a great anarch, a revolutionary textbook on bourgeois society" (Cyril Connolly).

20TH-CENTURY CLASSICS
272 pp.   0-14-018350-7 $12.95

Queen Victoria

In richly detailed, sympathetic descriptions of Victoria's childhood, her relations with other heads of state and with Prime Ministers Melbourne, Peel, Palmerston, and Disraeli, and her obsessive devotion to Prince Albert, Strachey looks beyond the facts of the queen's life to reveal the psychological influences and motivations behind her actions.

20TH-CENTURY CLASSICS
256 pp.   0-14-018393-0 $12.95

Inferno/From an Occult Diary

Selected by Torsten Eklund and
Translated with an Introduction by
Mary Sandbach

Inferno is an intensely powerful record
of Strindberg's mental collapse; *From
an Occult Diary* recounts his obsessive,
unrequited love for his third wife.

448 pp.   0-14-044364-9 $11.95

Three Plays

Translated with an Introduction by
Peter Watts

Combining acute psychological insight
and masterful language, Strindberg
depicts the war between the sexes in
The Father and class struggle in *Miss
Julie; Easter* is a mystical play, written
after Strindberg underwent a religious
conversion.

176 pp.   0-14-044082-8 $9.95

Black List, Section H

Introduction by Colm Tóibín

An underground masterpiece first published in the United States in 1971 after
several rejections by British and Irish
publishers, *Black List, Section H* is a
stark portrait of a wounded and alienated man searching for wholeness and
redemption.

20TH-CENTURY CLASSICS

416 pp.   0-14-018926-2 $13.95

The Twelve Caesars

Translated by Robert Graves and
Revised with an Introduction by
Michael Grant

This fascinating and colorful Latin his-
tory vividly records incidents in the
lives of the first twelve Caesars: Julius,
Augustus, Tiberius, Gaius (Caligula),
Claudius, Nero, Galba, Otho, Vitellius,
Vespasian, Titus, and Domitian.

320 pp.   0-14-044072-0 $12.95

See *Lives of the Later Caesars.*

Sunjata

Translated and Annotated by Gordon Innes
Edited with an Introduction and
Additional Notes by Lucy Durán and
Graham Furniss

The stories brought together here are
central to the culture of the Mande-
speaking peoples. Wars, magic, and the
founding of an empire are related
through vivid translations of one of the
major epic oral traditions in Africa.

160 pp. 1 map 0-14-044736-9 $11.95

JONATHAN SWIFT
1667 – 1745, IRISH

Complete Poems

*Edited with an Introduction by
Pat Rogers*

This complete edition encompasses the poetic works of one of the greatest English-language moralists and satirists.

960 pp.   0-14-042261-7 $19.95

Gulliver's Travels

*Edited by Peter Dixon and John Chalker
with an Introduction by Michael Foot*

Swift's satirical account of Gulliver's visits to Lilliput and Brobdingnag has amused and provoked readers since it was first published in 1726. A profound comment on the Age of Reason, it is perhaps the finest satire in the English language.

368 pp.   0-14-043022-9 $6.95

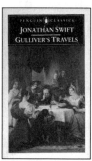

ALGERNON CHARLES SWINBURNE
18377 – 1909, BRITISH

Poems and Ballads and Atalanta in Calydon

Edited by Kenneth Haynes

Collecting Swinburne's passionate, musical verse, this volume brings together *Atalanta in Calydon*, a drama

in classical Greek form, and poems that are opulent hymns to sensual love, to the loss of love, and to death.

448 pp. 1 map   0-14-042250-1 $15.00
(Available in April 2001)

J. M. SYNGE
1871 – 1909, IRISH

The Aran Islands

*Edited with an Introduction by
Tim Robinson*

The dramatic record of Synge's visit to the savagely beautiful Aran Islands at the turn of the century, this work is drenched in the Gaelic soul of Ireland.

208 pp.   0-14-018432-5 $11.95

J. M. SYNGE
1871 – 1909, IRISH

W. B. YEATS
1865 – 1939, IRISH
NOBEL PRIZE WINNER

SEAN O'CASEY
1880 – 1964, IRISH

The Playboy of the Western World and Two Other Irish Plays

Introduction by W. A. Armstrong

This volume brings together three of the greatest and most controversial plays ever presented at the famed Abbey Theatre: *The Playboy of the Western World*, *The Countess Cathleen*, and *Cock-a-doodle Dandy*. These plays mark important stages in the rich explosion of Irish drama that began at the turn of the century.

20TH-CENTURY CLASSICS
224 pp.   0-14-018878-9 $9.95

See W. B. Yeats.

The Agricola and The Germania

Translated with an Introduction by
H. Mattingly and Revised by
S. A. Hanford

The Agricola, Tacitus's eulogistic description of his father-in-law, the governor of Roman Britain, contains the first detailed account of the British Isles. *The Germania*, an ethnographical account of the Germanic tribes, contrasts the primitive virtues of the Germans with the degeneracy of contemporary Rome.

176 pp.   0-14-044241-3 $12.95

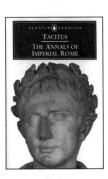

The Annals of Imperial Rome

Translated with an Introduction by
Michael Grant

Surviving passages from Tacitus's last and best-known work cover the reigns of Tiberius, Gaius (Caligula), Claudius, and Nero, and detail the Roman Empire at its zenith.

464 pp.   0-14-044060-7 $14.95

The Histories

Translated with an Introduction by
Kenneth Wellesley

The surviving books of *The Histories* reconstruct the terrible events of the year of the Four Emperors (A.D. 69), which shook the whole edifice of the Empire.

336 pp.   0-14-044150-6 $12.95

The Home and the World

Translated with an Introduction by
Anita Desai

Sir Rabindranath Tagore's powerful novel, set on a Bengali noble's estate in 1908, is both a love story and a novel of political awakening. Today, ninety years after the time it describes, the novel remains astonishingly relevant.

20TH-CENTURY CLASSICS
208 pp.   0-14-018187-3 $11.95

Selected Poems

Translated with an Introduction by
William Radice

Forty-eight selections cover the period 1882 to 1941 and provide a long-overdue reappraisal of the Bengali Nobel laureate's poetry.

20TH-CENTURY CLASSICS
224 pp.   0-14-018366-3 $11.95

Selected Short Stories

Translated with an Introduction by
William Radice

Tagore was the first romantic poet and the first Bengali to write short stories, a form he adopted from his reading of European short stories. This collection is a representative selection from the span of his career.

20TH-CENTURY CLASSICS

336 pp.   0-14-018854-1 $12.95

JOHN TANNER
1780 – UNKNOWN, AMERICAN

The Falcon

With an Introduction by Louise Erdrich

This is the fascinating autobiography of John Tanner (the Falcon), who is captured by the Shawnee tribe in 1789 at the age of nine and sold to an Ojibwa family with whom he spends the first half of his adult life. His effort to return to white society proves unsuccessful and he returns to his tribe, only to be forced to flee after he is wrongfully accused of murder.

NATURE CLASSICS

280 pp.   0-14-028871-6 $13.95

ALFRED, LORD TENNYSON
1809 – 1892, BRITISH

Idylls of the King

Edited with an Introduction and Notes by J. M. Gray

For Tennyson, the *Idylls* embodied the universal and unending war between sense and soul, and Arthur the highest ideals of manhood and kingship, an attitude in keeping with the moral outlook of his day.

376 pp.   0-14-042253-6 $11.00

Selected Poems

Edited by Aidan Day

From a genius at painting human emotions in rich and sensuous imagery, this volume focuses on *In Memoriam* (1850), a record of spiritual conflict considered to be Tennyson's greatest work.

400 pp.   0-14-044545-5 $12.95

TERENCE
C. 186 – 159 B.C., ROMAN

The Comedies

Translated with an Introduction by Betty Radice

All six of the Roman dramatist's comedies—from *The Girl from Andros*, the first romantic comedy ever written, to the socially sophisticated *The Brothers* —show why Terence became a model for playwrights from the Renaissance onward. Also included are *The Self-Tormentor*, *The Eunuch*, *Phormio*, and *The Mother-in-Law*.

400 pp.   0-14-044324-X $12.95

TERESA OF ÁVILA
1515 – 1582, SPANISH

The Life of St. Teresa of Ávila by Herself

Translated with an Introduction by J. M. Cohen

This story of how a willful and unbalanced woman was transformed by profound religious experiences delves into the nature of exalted states. After *Don Quixote*, it is the most widely read prose classic of Spain.

320 pp.   0-14-044073-9 $10.95

WILLIAM MAKEPEACE THACKERAY
1811 – 1863, BRITISH

The History of Henry Esmond

Edited by John Sutherland and Michael Greenfield with an Introduction and Notes by John Sutherland

This blend of psychological drama, romance, and history is set during the reign of Queen Anne and examines the conflicts between England's Tory-Catholic past and its Whiggish-Protestant future.

544 pp.   0-14-043049-0 $7.95

The History of Pendennis

Edited by Donald Hawes with an Introduction by J. I. M. Stewart

This novel of a young man's passage from miserable schoolboy to striving journalist, from carefree Oxbridge to the high (and low) life of London, mirrors Thackeray's life.

816 pp.   0-14-043076-8 $7.95

The Newcomes

Edited with an Introduction and Notes by David Pascoe

In this autobiographical novel, Thackeray depicts the "respectable" social world of London in the 1820s and '30s, a milieu where material wealth determined acceptability, and alliances, including marriage, were pursued with the goal of enhancing a family's position.

896 pp.   0-14-043481-X $13.95

Vanity Fair

Edited with an Introduction and Notes by J. I. M. Stewart

Becky Sharp, one of the most resourceful, engaging, and amoral women in literature, is the heroine of this sparkling satirical panorama of British society during the Napoleonic Wars.

816 pp.   0-14-043035-0 $9.95

THEOCRITUS
c. 300 – 250 B.C., GREEK

The Idylls

Translated with an Introduction and Notes by Robert Wells

From Sicilian legend to the sexual gossip of herdsmen, these second-century B.C. pastorals are presented in modern-verse translations that reveal Theocritus as a varied and compelling poet.

160 pp.   0-14-044523-4 $10.95

See Hesiod.

THOMAS À KEMPIS
c. 1379 – 1471, GERMAN

The Imitation of Christ

Translated with an Introduction by Leo Sherley-Price

One of the most read and influential of Christian classics, this is a seminal work of the Devotio Moderna, the late-medieval reform movement that returned to the original Apostolic zeal and simplicity of Christianity.

232 pp.   0-14-044027-5 $10.95

FLORA THOMPSON
1876 – 1947, BRITISH

Lark Rise to Candleford
A Trilogy

Introduction by H. J. Massingham

In her three enduring books—*Lark Rise, Over to Candleford,* and *Candleford Green*—Flora Thompson created "one of the most sensitive memorials of Victorian rural England" (John Fowles). Her chronicle of the ebb and flow of life in a hamlet, a village, and a market town is based on her own life.

20TH-CENTURY CLASSICS

544 pp.   0-14-018850-9 $12.95

HENRY DAVID THOREAU
1817 – 1862, AMERICAN

Cape Cod

With an Introduction by Paul Theroux

With his unique perceptions and precise descriptions, *Cape Cod* chronicles Thoreau's journey of discovery along this evocative stretch of Massachusetts coastline.

NATURE CLASSICS

320 pp.   0-14-017002-2 $10.95

HENRY DAVID THOREAU

Henry David Thoreau was born in Concord, Massachusetts, in 1817. He graduated from Harvard in 1837, the same year he began his lifelong journal. Inspired by Ralph Waldo Emerson, Thoreau became a key member of the Transcendentalist movement. He tested the Transcendentalists' faith in nature between 1845 and 1847, when he lived for twenty-six months in a homemade hut at Walden Pond. There he worked on the only two books published during his lifetime, *Walden* and *A Week on the Concord and Merrimack Rivers.* Several of his other works were published posthumously. Thoreau died in Concord in 1862.

The Maine Woods

With an Introduction by
Edward Hoagland

Over a period of three years, Thoreau made three trips to the largely unexplored woods of Maine. Using the careful notes made during these journeys, Thoreau managed to capture a wilder side of America and revealed his own adventurous spirit.

NATURE CLASSICS

440 pp.   0-14-017013-8 $12.95

Walden and Civil Disobedience

Introduction by Michael Meyer

Two classic examinations of individuality in relation to nature, society, and government, *Walden* conveys at once a naturalist's wonder at the commonplace and a Transcendentalist's yearning for spiritual truth and self-reliance. "Civil Disobedience" is perhaps the most famous essay in American literature—and the inspiration for social activists around the world, from Gandhi to Martin Luther King, Jr.

440 pp.   0-14-039044-8 $10.95

A Week on the Concord and Merrimack Rivers

Edited with an Introduction by
H. Daniel Peck

Thoreau's account of his 1839 boat trip is a finely crafted tapestry of travel writing, essays, and lyrical poetry. An invaluable companion to *Walden*, it also stands alone as one of the most remarkable literary achievements of the nineteenth century.

384 pp.   0-14-043442-9 $10.95

A Year in Thoreau's Journal: 1851

Introduction and Notes by H. Daniel Peck

Thoreau's journal of 1851 reveals profound ideas and observations in the making, including wonderful writing on the natural history of Concord.

464 pp.   0-14-039085-5 $13.95

See *Nineteenth-Century American Poetry.*

THUCYDIDES
C. 460 – C. 400 B.C., GREEK

The History of the Peloponnesian War
Revised Edition

Translated by Rex Warner with an
Introduction and Notes by M. I. Finley

The eight books of Thucydides's account of the clash between two great powers, Athens and Sparta, are contained in Rex Warner's acclaimed modern translation.

656 pp.   0-14-044039-9 $12.95

Anna Karenin

Translated with an Introduction by
Rosemary Edmonds

Tolstoy's intense, imaginative insight is brilliantly apparent in this psychological novel and its portraits of the passionate Anna, Count Vronsky, and Levin, who may be seen as a reflection of Tolstoy himself.

872 pp.   0-14-044041-0 $9.95

Penguin Readers Guide Available

Childhood/Boyhood/Youth

Translated with an Introduction by
Rosemary Edmonds

These sketches, a mixture of fact and fiction, provide an expressive self-portrait of the young Tolstoy and hints of the man and writer he would become.

320 pp.   0-14-044139-5 $12.95

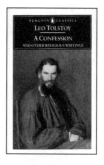

A Confession and Other Religious Writings

Translated with an Introduction by
Jane Kentish

Tolstoy's passionate and iconoclastic writings—on issues of faith, immortality, freedom, violence, and morality—reflect his intellectual search for truth and a religion firmly grounded in reality. The selection includes "A Confession," "Religion and Morality,"

LEO TOLSTOY

Count Leo Nikolayevich Tolstoy was born in 1828 at Yasnaya Polyana in the Tula province of Russia. As a young man, he studied Oriental languages and law at the University of Kazan. After he completed his schooling, Tolstoy fought in the Crimean war while writing *The Sebastopol Stories*, which established his reputation. In 1862, he married Sophie Andreyevna Behrs and the next fifteen years proved to be a period of great happiness; they had thirteen children and Tolstoy managed his vast estates in the Volga Steppes and, in 1868, completed *War and Peace*, following that work with *Anna Karenin* in 1876. *A Confession*, finished in 1882, marked an outward change in his life and works; he became an extreme rationalist and moralist, and in a series of pamphlets he expressed his doctrines such as inner self-perfection, rejection of institutions, indictment of the demands of the flesh, and denunciation of private property. His teaching earned him numerous followers in Russia and abroad, but also much opposition. In 1901, Tolstoy was excommunicated by the Russian holy synod. He died in 1910, in the course of a dramatic flight from home, at the small railway station of Astapovo.

"What Is Religion, and of What Does Its Essence Consist?," and "The Law of Love and the Law of Violence."

240 pp.   0-14-044473-4 $11.95

The Death of Ivan Ilyich and Other Stories

Translated with an Introduction by Rosemary Edmonds

"The Death of Ivan Ilyich" is a magnificent story of a spiritual awakening; "The Cossacks" tells of a disenchanted nobleman who finds happiness amid the simple people of the Caucasus; and "Happily Ever After" traces the maturing of romantic love into "family attachment."

336 pp.   0-14-044508-0 $9.95

How Much Land Does a Man Need? and Other Stories

Edited with an Introduction by A. N. Wilson and Translated by Ronald Wilks

These short works, ranging from Tolstoy's earliest tales to the brilliant title story, are rich in the insights and passion that characterize all of his explorations in love, war, courage, and civilization.

240 pp.   0-14-044506-4 $11.95

The Kreutzer Sonata and Other Stories

Translated with an Introduction by David McDuff

These four tales—the title story plus "The Devil," "The Forged Coupon," and "After the Ball"—embody the moral, religious, and existential themes of Tolstoy's final creative period.

288 pp.   0-14-044469-6 $9.95

Master and Man and Other Stories

Translated with an Introduction by Paul Foote

Written in the 1890s, both "Master and Man" and "Father Sergius" are preoccupied with material desires—for the flesh in one instance and for money in the other. In *Hadji Murat*, Tolstoy offers a precisely written and memorable portrait of a treacherous soldier.

272 pp.   0-14-044331-2 $11.95

"One hesitates to value *Hadji Murat* over all of Tolstoy's other achievements in the short novel...[but] it is my personal touchstone for the sublime of prose fiction, to me the best story in the world, or at least the best that I have ever read."

—HAROLD BLOOM

Resurrection

Translated with an Introduction by Rosemary Edmonds

In this story of a fallen man and an emphatically non-Christian "resurrection," Tolstoy writes a compelling tale of the underworld and turns a highly critical eye on the law, the penal system, and the Church.

576 pp.   0-14-044184-0

$11.95

The Sebastopol Sketches

Translated with an Introduction and Notes by David McDuff

These three short stories stem from Tolstoy's military experience during the Crimean War: "Sebastopol in December," "Sebastopol in May," and "Sebastopol in August 1855."

176 pp.   0-14-044468-8 $9.95

War and Peace

Translated with an Introduction by Rosemary Edmonds

This epic presents a complete tableau of Russian society during the great Napoleonic Wars, from 1805 to 1815.

1,456 pp.   0-14-044417-3 $13.95

What Is Art?

Translated by Richard Pevear and Larissa Volokhonsky with a Preface by Richard Pevear

This profound analysis of the nature of art is the culmination of a series of essays and polemics on issues of morality, social justice, and religion. Considering and rejecting the idea that art reveals and reinvents through beauty, Tolstoy perceives the question of the

nature of art to be a religious one. Ultimately, he concludes, art must be a force for good, for the progress and improvement of mankind.

240 pp.   0-14-044642-7 $11.95

THOMAS TRAHERNE
1637 – 1674, BRITISH

Selected Poems and Prose

Edited with a Preface by Alan Bradford

In poems from the Dobell folio and selections from his prose masterpiece, *Centuries of Meditations*, Traherne explores the boundless potential of the human mind and spirit as he celebrates the wonder and simplicity of the child.

416 pp.   0-14-044543-9 $13.95

ANTHONY TROLLOPE
1815 – 1882, BRITISH

An Autobiography

Edited with an Introduction by David Skilton

As he recounts his journey from an impoverished, unhappy childhood to the fame and prosperity he achieved as a writer, Trollope writes not of moments of great inspiration but of hours of toil and dogged dedication to the trade of writing.

320 pp.   0-14-043405-4 $10.95

Barchester Towers

Edited with an Introduction and Notes by Robin Gilmour and a Preface by I. K. Galbraith

In this second novel of the Barsetshire Chronicles series, Trollope continues the story begun in *The Warden* and explores the conflict between the High and Low Church during the mid-

Victorian period.

576 pp.   0-14-043203-5 $8.95

"Anthony Trollope wrote about conscience and conflict, self-deception and love....His people are recognizably real today and if English men and women no longer talk as his people talk, some intuition tells us that their speech was once precisely as Trollope renders it."

—RUTH RENDELL

Can You Forgive Her?

Edited with an Introduction and Notes by Stephen Wail

The first of Trollope's Palliser novels is concerned with a spirited young woman in London who rejects her faultless fiancé to marry an aggressive opportunist, a decision her Victorian society cannot accept.

848 pp.   0-14-043086-5 $11.95

Dr. Wortle's School

Edited with an Introduction by Mick Imlah

Warmhearted schoolmaster Dr. Wortle comes to the rescue when bigamy and blackmail threaten to undo British Mr. Peacocke and his beautiful American wife. *Dr. Wortle's School* is one of the sharpest and most engaging of Trollope's later novels and the only one to have American scenes—in the Wild West.

256 pp.   0-14-043404-6 $8.95

The Eustace Diamonds

Edited by Stephen Gill and John Sutherland

Trollope examines the many guises of "truth" in this taut novel about Lizzie Eustace, a brave, beautiful, and unscrupulous young woman.

760 pp.   0-14-043041-5 $8.95

Framley Parsonage

Edited with an Introduction and Notes by David Skilton and Peter Miles

In the fourth novel of the Barsetshire Chronicles series, a young Victorian clergyman's social ambition leads him to the brink of ruin.

520 pp.   0-14-043213-2 $9.95

He Knew He Was Right

Edited with an Introduction by Frank Kermode

Written at a time of heated controversy about women's emancipation—and published the same year as John Stuart Mill's *The Subjection of Women*—*He Knew He Was Right* examines the conflict between male fantasies of total possession and a married woman's right to a measure of independence.

864 pp.   0-14-043391-0 $11.95

The Prime Minister

Edited with an Introduction and Notes by David Skilton

In this penultimate book in the Palliser series, Trollope chronicles Plantagenet Palliser's ascent to the highest office in the land and explores how the realities of political life challenge his scrupulously moral hero.

736 pp.   0-14-043349-X $11.95

The Small House at Allington

Edited with an Introduction and Notes by Julian Thompson

This story of Lily Dale and her love for the ambitious, self-seeking, faithless Crosbie offers a vivid portrayal of the social and political changes occurring in the mid–nineteenth century.

752 pp.   0-14-043325-2 $7.95

The Warden

Edited with an Introduction and Notes by Robin Gilmour

The first book in the Barsetshire Chronicles tells the story of an elderly clergyman who resigns his church sinecure when it becomes the center of public controversy.

240 pp.   0-14-043214-0 $8.95

The Way We Live Now

Edited with an Introduction and Notes by Frank Kermode

First published in 1874 and widely regarded as the finest of all Trollope's novels, *The Way We Live Now* satirizes to devastating effect the grip of the monetary ethic on politics, the aristocracy, the literary world, the London scene, and the marriage market.

816 pp.   0-14-043392-9 $12.00

FANNY TROLLOPE
1779 – 1863, BRITISH

Domestic Manners of the Americans

Edited with an Introduction and Notes by Pamela Neville-Sington

Part satire, part masterpiece of nineteenth-century travel writing, this perceptive and humorous book grew from Fanny Trollope's ill-fated attempt to escape growing debts and the oppressively black moods of her husband by fleeing to the United States. After two miserable years she retreated to England, where she launched her remarkably successful literary career with this timeless and biting commentary on a society torn between high ideals and human frailties.

416 pp.   0-14-043561-1 $12.95

SOJOURNER TRUTH
C. 1797 – 1883, AMERICAN

Narrative of Sojourner Truth

Edited with an Introduction and Notes by Nell Irvin Painter

Sojourner Truth's landmark slave narrative, dictated to a neighbor, chronicles her experiences as a slave in upstate

New York and her transformation into a well-known abolitionist, feminist, orator, and preacher. This unique volume is based on the most complete text, the 1884 edition of the *Narrative*.

288 pp.   0-14-043678-2 $9.95

Selected Poems

*Translated with an Introduction by
Elaine Feinstein*

An admired contemporary of Rilke, Akhmatova, and Mandelstam, Russian poet Marina Tsvetayeva bore witness to the turmoil and devastation of the Revolution, and chronicled her difficult life in exile, sustained by the inspiration and power of her modern verse.

20TH-CENTURY CLASSICS

160 pp.   0-14-018759-6 $13.95

See Li Po.

Fathers and Sons

Translated by Rosemary Edmonds

This powerful novel resounds with a recognition of the universal clash between generations, in this instance localized in the hostility between the reactionary 1840s and the revolutionary 1860s. Included is the 1970 Romanes Lecture "Fathers and Children" by Isaiah Berlin.

296 pp.   0-14-044147-6 $9.95

First Love

*Translated by Isaiah Berlin with an
Introduction by V. S. Pritchett*

Isaiah Berlin's translation reproduces in finely wrought English the original story's simplicity, lyricism, and sensitivity.

112 pp.   0-14-044335-5 $8.95

Home of the Gentry

Translated by Richard Freeborn

Through the story of one man, Turgenev describes a whole generation of Russians who discover the emptiness of European ideas and long for a reconciliation with their homeland.

208 pp.   0-14-044224-3 $12.95

A Month in the Country

*Translated with an Introduction by
Isaiah Berlin*

Turgenev's most celebrated play, written in 1850, is a tragicomedy exploring that most universal theme, the love triangle.

128 pp.   0-14-044436-X $8.95

Rudin

*Edited and Translated by
Richard Freeborn*

Rudin, the hero of Turgenev's first
novel, is in part an example of the
banality of the Russian intelligentsia of
the 1840s, in part a hero with the
charms and failings of Don Quixote.

192 pp.   0-14-044304-5 $11.95

Sketches from a Hunter's Album

*Translated with an Introduction and
Notes by Richard Freeborn*

First published in 1852, Turgenev's
impressions of Russian peasant life and
the tyranny of serfdom led to his arrest
and confinement.

416 pp.   0-14-044522-6 $10.95

Spring Torrents

*Translated with an Introduction, Notes,
and a Critical Essay by Leonard Shapiro*

This is an exquisitely written, partly
autobiographical treatment of one of
Turgenev's favorite themes—man's
inability to learn about love without
first losing his innocence.

240 pp.   0-14-044369-X $10.95

MARK TWAIN
1835 – 1910, AMERICAN

The Adventures of Huckleberry Finn

Introduction by John Seelye

A novel of immeasurable richness,
filled with adventures, ironies, and
wonderfully drawn characters, all con-
veyed with Twain's mastery of humor
and language, *Huckleberry Finn* is often
regarded as the masterpiece of
American literature.

384 pp.   0-14-039046-4 $5.95

"All modern American literature comes from one book by Mark Twain called *Huckleberry Finn*."
—ERNEST HEMINGWAY

The Adventures of Tom Sawyer

Introduction by John Seelye

Evoking life in a small Mississippi River
town, *Tom Sawyer* is Twain's hymn to
the secure and fantastic world of boyhood and adventure.

256 pp.   0-14-039083-9 $5.95

A Connecticut Yankee in King Arthur's Court

*Edited with an Introduction by
Justin Kaplan*

This imaginary confrontation of a
nineteenth-century American with life
in sixth-century England is both a rich,
extravagant comedy and an apocalyptic
vision of terrifying violence and
destruction.

416 pp.   0-14-043064-4 $7.95

Life on the Mississippi

Introduction by James M. Cox

Twain's firsthand portrait of the steam-
boat age and the science of riverboat
piloting recalls the history of the

Mississippi River, from its discovery by Europeans to the writer's own time.

464 pp.   0-14-039050-2   **$9.95**

The Prince and the Pauper

Introduction by Jerry Griswold

This 1881 novel about a poor boy, Tom Canty, who exchanges identities with Edward Tudor, the prince of England, is at once an adventure story, a fantasy of timeless appeal, and an intriguing example of the author's abiding preoccupation with separating the true from the false, the genuine from the impostor. Included is the story "A Boy's Adventure," written as part of the novel but published separately.

224 pp.   0-14-043669-3   **$8.95**

Pudd'nhead Wilson

Edited with an Introduction by Malcolm Bradbury

While it retains the comic exuberance of *Huckleberry Finn*, this is Twain's darker and more disturbing account of human nature under slavery.

320 pp.   0-14-043040-7   **$8.95**

Roughing It

Edited with an Introduction by Hamlin Hill

A fascinating picture of the American frontier emerges from Twain's fictionalized recollections of his experiences prospecting for gold, speculating in timber, and writing for a succession of small Western newspapers during the 1860s.

592 pp.   0-14-039010-3   **$12.95**

Tales, Speeches, Essays, and Sketches

Edited with an Introduction by Tom Quirk

Masterful short fiction and prose pieces display the variety of Twain's imaginative invention, his diverse talents, and his extraordinary emotional range. The volume includes "Jim Smiley and His Jumping Frog," "The Man That Corrupted Hadleyburg," "Fenimore Cooper's Literary Offenses," and the spectacularly scatalogical "Date, 1601."

448 pp.   0-14-043417-8   **$12.95**

A Tramp Abroad

Introduction by Robert Gray Bruce and Hamlin Hill

Cast in the form of a walking tour through Germany, Switzerland, France, and Italy, *A Tramp Abroad* sparkles with the author's shrewd observations and highly opinionated comments on Old World culture, and showcases his unparalleled ability to integrate humorous sketches, autobiographical tidbit, and historical anecdotes in consistently entertaining narrative.

640 pp.   0-14-043608-1   **$14.95**

The Obedience of a Christian Man

Edited with an Introduction and Notes by David Daniell

In this 1528 treatise, which would become one of the most important publications of the first phase of the English Reformation, Tyndale boldly develops the argument that ordinary believers should take their spiritual sustenance direct from Scripture. He was the first to translate the Bible into English, a heretical undertaking that eventually led to his execution.

272 pp.   0-14-043477-1 $13.00

Gunnar's Daughter

Edited with an Introduction and Notes by Sherrill Harbison and Translated by Arthur G. Chater

Written in 1909, this swift and compelling tale of a female avenger from the Saga Age was Undset's first published novel with a medieval setting. Unlike most of the Viking-inspired art of its period, it is not a historical romance but addresses questions as troublesome in Undset's own time—and in ours—as they were in the Saga Age: rape and revenge, civil and domestic violence.

20TH-CENTURY CLASSICS
240 pp. 3 maps 0-14-118020-X $11.95

Kristin Lavransdatter
I: The Wreath

Translated with an Introduction and Notes by Tiina Nunnally

Originally published in 1920 and set in fourteenth-century Norway, the first volume of *Kristin Lavransdatter* chronicles the courtship of a strong-willed and

SIGRID UNDSET

Sigrid Undset was born in Denmark, the eldest daughter of a Norwegian daughter and a Danish mother, and moved with her family to Oslo two years later. She published her first novel in 1907 and *Gunnar's Daughter*, her first work set in the Middle Ages followed in 1909. In 1920, Undset published the first volume of *Kristin Lavransdatter*, the medieval trilogy that would become her most famous work. In 1928, Sigrid Undset won the Nobel Prize for literature. During the Nazi occupation of Norway, Undset lived as a refugee in New York City. She returned home in 1945 and lived in Lillehammer until her death in 1949.

passionate young woman and a dangerously charming man. This new translation—nominated for the PEN Center
USA West Translation Prize—brings
Undset's magnificent epic to life with
clarity and lyrical beauty.

20TH-CENTURY CLASSICS
288 pp. 1 map 0-14-118041-2 $11.95

Kristin Lavransdatter
II: The Wife

*Translated with Notes by Tiina Nunnally
and an Introduction by Sherrill Harbison*

The Wife chronicles Kristin's marriage
to Erlend Nikulausson, a man whose
single-minded determination to
become a powerful social and political
figure forces Kristin to manage his
estate while raising their seven sons.
Tiina Nunnally's beautiful new translation, which restores passages ommitted
from the original English-language version, was nominated for both the PEN
Center USA West and the PEN/Book-
of-the-Month Club Translation Prizes.

20TH-CENTURY CLASSICS
352 pp. 2 maps 0-14-118128-1 $11.95

Kristin Lavransdatter
III: The Cross

*Translated with Notes by Tiina Nunnally
and an Introduction by Sherrill Harbison*

In the most devastating and emotional
volume of the trilogy, Kristin returns
with her husband and children to her
childhood home. *The Cross* exquisitely
completes the first new English translation of Undset's masterpiece.

20TH-CENTURY CLASSICS
448 pp. 2 maps 0-14-118235-0 $12.95

Penguin Readers Guide Available for
Kristin Lavransdatter I–III.

BARTOLOMEO VANZETTI

See Nicola Sacco.

GIORGIO VASARI
1511 – 1574, ITALIAN

Lives of the Artists
Volume 1

*Translated and Edited with an
Introduction by George Bull*

Vasari offers insights into the lives and
techniques of twenty artists, from
Cimabue, Giotto, and Leonardo to
Michelangelo and Titian.

480 pp.   0-14-044500-5 $11.95

Lives of the Artists
Volume 2

*Translated and Edited with an
Introduction by George Bull and Notes
on the Artists by Peter Murray*

Vasari's knowledge was based on his
own experience as an early Renaissance
painter and architect. Volume 2 explores
the lives of twenty-five artists, from
Perugino to Giovanni Pisano.

376 pp.   0-14-044460-2 $11.95

THORSTEIN VEBLEN
1857 – 1929, AMERICAN

The Theory of the Leisure Class

Introduction by Robert Lekachman

With exquisite irony, Veblen, the "best critic of America that America has produced" (C. Wright Mills), lays bare the hollowness of our canons of taste and culture.

20TH-CENTURY CLASSICS

144 pp.   0-14-018795-2 $10.95

GIOVANNI VERGA
1840 – 1922, ITALIAN

Cavalleria Rusticana and Other Stories

Translated with an Introduction by G. H. McWilliam

Giovanni Verga's brilliant stories of love, adultery, and honor are set against the scorched landscapes of the slopes of Mount Etna and the Plain of Catalan. This edition contains the first major English translations since those of D. H. Lawrence in the 1920s.

272 pp.   0-14-044741-5 $12.95

GIAMBATTISTA VICO
1668 – 1744, ITALIAN

New Science

Translated by David Marsh with an Introduction by Anthony Grafton

This astonishingly ambitious attempt to provide a comprehensive science of all human society by decoding the history, mythology, and law of the ancient world marked a turning-point in humanist thinking as significant as Newton's contemporary revolution in physics.

560 pp.   0-14-043569-7 $14.95

"My imagination grows every time I read Vico."

—JAMES JOYCE

GORE VIDAL
B. 1925, AMERICAN

Duluth

Spoofing everything from social pretenses, motherhood, law enforcement, marriage, and racism, to literature, television, science fiction, and sex, this wild burlesque tells of two women who die in a snowdrift to be reborn on a popular television show, *Duluth*, and in a romance novel.

20TH-CENTURY CLASSICS

224 pp.   0-14-118042-0 $13.95

Kalki

Vidal takes on the unmitigated follies born of the unholy partnership of religion, the media, and a public that longs for a savior.

20TH-CENTURY CLASSICS

272 pp.   0-14-118037-4 $13.95

The Messiah

A deft and daring blend of satire and prophecy first published in 1954, *The Messiah* eerily anticipates the excesses of Jim Jones, David Koresh, and "Do," the guru of Heaven's Gate.

20TH-CENTURY CLASSICS

256 pp.   0-14-118039-0 $13.95

Myra Breckinridge/Myron

When *Myra Breckinridge* first appeared in 1968, critics were delighted, baffled, and somewhat appalled by this comedy of sex change. Thirty years later, Myra has become literature's most famous transsexual. In the sequel, *Myron* (1974), the Breckinridge saga takes an increasingly bizarre turn. Vidal combines time travel with the ultimate Hollywood fantasy, as Myra attempts to alter cinema history.

20TH-CENTURY CLASSICS

432 pp.   0-14-118028-5 $14.95

GEOFFROI DE VILLEHARDOUIN

See Jean de Joinville.

VIRGIL

70 – 19 B.C., ROMAN

Aeneid

Edited by Frederick M. Keener and Translated by John Dryden

Virgil's epic vividly recounts Aeneas's tortuous journey after the Trojan War and the struggles he faced as he lay the foundations for the greatest continental empire. Rendered into a vigorous and refined English by the most important man of letters of the seventeenth century, this translation of the *Aeneid* "set a new, august standard so influential as to be epochal." For his version, John Dryden drew on his personal experiences during periods of political unrest.

480 pp.   0-14-044627-3 $15.95

VIRGIL

Generally regarded as ancient Rome's greatest poet, Publius Vergilius Maro was born of peasant stock near Mantua in 70 B.C. He was later sent to Rome to further his education and there came under the influence of Epicureanism. *The Georgics*, a superb expression of agricultural living, was composed during the final period of the civil wars, and was dedicated to Maecenas, an important Roman official and art patron. Virgil devoted the last years of his life to writing *The Aeneid*, the epic story of the foundation of Rome and Virgil's embodiment of Roman ideals. In the last year of his life, 19 B.C., he journeyed to Greece to do research for a revision of his epic.

The Aeneid

Translated by W. F. Jackson Knight

In this fresh prose translation, W. F. Jackson Knight discusses *The Aeneid*'s impact on Western civilization and provides a list of variations from the Oxford text.

368 pp.   0-14-044051-8 $9.95

The Aeneid
A New Prose Translation

Translated with an Introduction by David West

This new prose translation by David West has been widely acclaimed for its directness and clarity.

288 pp.   0-14-044457-2 $10.95

The Eclogues

Translated with an Introduction and Notes by Guy Lee

Written between 42 and 37 B.C., ten pastoral poems believed to be the first authentic work by Virgil are presented with the original Latin on the left-hand page and the translation on the right.

144 pp.   0-14-044419-X $11.95

The Georgics

Translated with an Introduction and Notes by L. P. Wilkinson

A eulogy to Italy as the temperate land of perpetual spring, and a celebration of the values of rustic piety, *The Georgics* is probably the supreme achievement of Latin poetry.

160 pp.   0-14-044414-9 $11.95

VOLTAIRE
1694 – 1778, FRENCH

Candide

Translated and Cast in the Form of a Walking Tour through Germany, Switzerland, France, and Italy by John Butt

Voltaire takes Candide and Dr. Pangloss through a variety of ludicrous adventures and reversals of fortune in this satirical challenge to the empty optimism prevalent in Voltaire's eighteenth-century society.

144 pp.   0-14-044004-6 $6.95

Penguin Readers Guide Available

Letters on England

Translated with an Introduction by Leonard Tancock

Also known as the *Lettres anglaises ou philosophiques*, Voltaire's response to his exile in England offered the French public of 1734 a panoramic view of British culture. Perceiving them as a veiled attack against the ancien regime, however, the French government ordered the letters burned and Voltaire persecuted.

160 pp.   0-14-044386-X $9.95

Philosophical Dictionary

Translated and Edited with an Introduction by Theodore Besterman

Voltaire's irony, scrutiny, and passionate love of reason and justice are fully evident in this deliberately revolutionary series of essays on religion, metaphysics, society, and government.

400 pp.   0-14-044257-X $13.95

Zadig/L'Ingénu

Translated with an Introduction by John Butt

One of Voltaire's earliest tales, *Zadig* is set in the exotic East and is told in the comic spirit of *Candide*; *L'Ingénu*, written after *Candide*, is a darker tale in which an American Indian records his impressions of France.

192 pp.   0-14-044126-3 $9.95

JACOBUS DE VORAGINE
C.1229 – 1298, FRENCH

The Golden Legend
Selections

Selected and Translated by Christopher Stace with an Introduction and Notes by Richard Hamer

This single-volume sourcebook of all the core Christian stories attracted a huge audience across thirteenth-century Europe, including Geoffrey Chaucer. The more than seventy biographies here are essential reading for anyone who wants to understand medieval imagery, art, and thought.

432 pp.   0-14-044648-6 $13.95

BOOKER T. WASHINGTON
1856 – 1915, AMERICAN

Up from Slavery

Introduction by Louis R. Harlan

Washington's autobiography reveals the conviction he held that the black man's salvation lay in education, industriousness, and self-reliance.

336 pp.   0-14-039051-0 $9.95

REBECCA WEST
1892 – 1983, BRITISH

Black Lamb and Grey Falcon
A Journey through Yugoslavia

A magnificent blend of cultural commentary, travel journal, and historical insight, this volume—written on the eve of World War II—probes the troubled history of the Balkans and their uneasy alliance of ethnic groups.

20TH-CENTURY CLASSICS
1,200 pp.   0-14-018847-9 $21.95

> "Surely one of the great books of our century."
> —DIANA TRILLING

The Return of the Soldier

Introduction by Samuel Hynes

Writing her first novel during World War I, West examines the relationship between three women and a soldier suffering from shell-shock. This novel of an enclosed world invaded by public events also embodies in its characters the shifts in England's class structures at the beginning of the twentieth century.

20TH-CENTURY CLASSICS
128 pp.   0-14-118065-X $10.95

EDITH WHARTON
1862 – 1937, AMERICAN

The Age of Innocence

Edited with an Introduction by Cynthia Griffin Wolff and Notes by Laura Dluzynski Quinn

Edith Wharton's sharp, ironic wit and Jamesian mastery of form create a disturbingly accurate picture of men and women caught in a society that denies humanity while desperately defending its civilization.

20TH-CENTURY CLASSICS
384 pp.   0-14-018970-X $9.95
Penguin Readers Guide Available

The Custom of the Country

Introduction by Anita Brookner

Wharton blends sharp cultural criticism with a biting indictment of American culture. This is a portrait of a woman advancing herself through matrimony in a world where no business transaction is honest, and no marriage is for love.

20TH-CENTURY CLASSICS
352 pp.   0-14-018190-3 $10.95

EDITH WHARTON

Edith Wharton was born into a prosperous social circle that centered in New York, New England, and Europe. In *The House of Mirth* (1905) and *The Age of Innocence* (1920) she brought to life ironic portraits of aristocratic American society and the constraints it placed upon women with its demands and expectations. Her 1911 tale, *Ethan Frome*, the story of the stifled existence of a snowbound, desolate household, is set in the stark New England landscape that she knew well. After her unhappy marriage had dissolved, Wharton sold "The Mount," her lavish home in western Massachusetts, and moved to France, where she lived independently, and traveled and wrote inexhaustibly, forming friendships with such notables as Henry James and Bernard Berenson.

Ethan Frome

Introduction by Doris Grumbach and Notes by Sarah Higginson Begley

This classic novel of despair, forbidden emotion, and sexual undercurrents set against an austere New England background is different in both theme and tone from Wharton's other writings.

20TH-CENTURY CLASSICS

224 pp.   0-14-018736-7 $7.95

The House of Mirth

Introduction and Notes by Cynthia Griffin Wolff

Published in 1905, this daring novel about the shallow, brutal world of Eastern monied society deals with powerful social and feminist themes.

20TH-CENTURY CLASSICS

384 pp.   0-14-018729-4 $9.95

Penguin Readers Guide Available

The Reef

Introduction by Anita Brookner

In this tale that explores the delicate nature of the human condition, young widow Anna Leath hires as a governess a woman whose arrival unleashes suspicions and exposes secrets that threaten to destroy Anna's carefully ordered world.

20TH-CENTURY CLASSICS

368 pp.   0-14-018731-6 $10.95

Summer

Introduction and Notes by Elizabeth Ammons

The novel Wharton called her "hot Ethan" is set in the Massachusetts Berkshires and delves into the thwarted dreams and sexual passions of a repressed rural woman.

20TH-CENTURY CLASSICS

224 pp.   0-14-018679-4 $9.95

See *Four Stories by American Women.*

PHILLIS WHEATLEY
c. 1753 – 1784, AMERICAN
(B. WESTERN AFRICA)

Complete Writings

Edited and with an Introduction and Notes by Vincent Carretta

This volume collects the astonishing writings of the eighteenth-century American slave who published her first poem at the age of 14. It includes her letters, poetry, hymns, elegies, translations, tales, and epyllions.

192 pp.   0-14-042430-X $12.00

(Available in February 2001)

GILBERT WHITE
1720 – 1793, BRITISH

The Natural History of Selborne

With an Introduction by Edward Hoagland

Gilbert White found a world to explore in his own native village of Selborne. His beautiful evocation of that countryside has gone on to become the best-known natural history book in the English language—a work that has shaped our everyday view of a kindly relationship between human beings and nature.

NATURE CLASSICS

288 pp.   0-14-026486-8 $8.95

PATRICK WHITE
1912 – 1990, Australian
(b. England)
Nobel Prize Winner

The Cockatoos

In this collection of six short novels and stories, including "A Woman's Hand," "The Full Belly," "The Night the Prowler," "Five-Twenty," "Sicilian Vespers," and "The Cockatoos," Australia's masterful writer brilliantly displays his ability to see into the profound meaning of ordinary events.

20TH-CENTURY CLASSICS

288 pp.   0-14-018582-8 $10.95

WALT WHITMAN
1819 – 1892, American

The Complete Poems

Edited with an Introduction by Francis Murphy

Of the nine editions Whitman prepared of his *Leaves of Grass*, this final "deathbed" edition (1891–92) is printed in accordance with a note of instruction left by the poet to his future editors.

896 pp.   0-14-042222-6 $15.95

Leaves of Grass

Edited with an Introduction by Malcolm Cowley

This is the original and complete 1855 edition of one of the greatest masterpieces of American literature, including Whitman's own introduction to the work.

192 pp.   0-14-042199-8 $7.95

See *Nineteenth-Century American Poetry*.

OSCAR WILDE
1854 – 1900, Irish

Complete Short Fiction

Edited with an Introduction and Notes by Ian Small

This volume gathers the short masterpieces that brought Wilde his first fame as a writer of fiction and includes the complete texts of *The Happy Prince and Other Tales*, *A House of Pomegranates*, *Lord Arthur Savile's Crime and Other Stories*, "Poems in Prose," and "Portrait of Mr. W. H."

336 pp.   0-14-043423-2 $10.95

De Profundis and Other Writings

Introduction by Hesketh Pearson

This collection contains many examples of Wilde's humorous and epigrammatic genius that captured the London theater and, by suddenly casting light from an unexpected angle, widened the bounds of truth. Included are "The Soul of Man Under Socialism," "The Decay of Lying," and a selection of poems, including *The Ballad of Reading Gaol*, "Sonnet to Liberty," "Requiescat," and "To My Wife."

256 pp.   0-14-043089-X $10.95

hedonist is a sterling example of Wilde's wit and aestheticism.

272 pp.   0-14-043187-X $7.95

JOHN WILMOT, EARL OF ROCHESTER
1647 – 1680, British

The Complete Works
Edited with an Introduction and Notes by Frank H. Ellis

This volume encompasses the works of the Earl of Rochester—the Restoration's infamous literary rake, hedonist, and master of satire—and includes tragic verse, prose comedy, boisterous songs, rich rhymes and language, and frank explorations of sexual matters.

464 pp.   0-14-042362-1 $12.95

OWEN WISTER
1860 – 1938, American

The Virginian
With an Introduction and Notes by John Seelye

Set in the vast Wyoming territory, Wister's powerful story of the silent stranger who rides into the uncivilized

*The Importance of Being Earnest and Other Plays
Edited by Richard Allen Cave

This volume collects the essential plays of the brilliant, witty, and enduring playwright: *Lady Windermere's Fan, Salomé, A Woman of No Importance, An Ideal Husband, A Florentine Tragedy,* and *The Importance of Being Earnest*—including an excised scene.

464 pp.   0-14-043606-5 $10.00

(Available in March 2001)

The Picture of Dorian Gray
Edited with an Introduction by Peter Ackroyd

First published to scandal and protest in 1891, this story of a flamboyant

OSCAR WILDE

Oscar Wilde was born in Dublin in 1854, the son of an eminent surgeon. He attended Trinity College, Dublin, then Magdalen College, Oxford, where, in the last years of the seventies, he started the cult of "Aetheticism"—of an art of life. He wrote several books, including *The Picture of Dorian Gray* (1891), before he became a successful playwright in both England and France. In 1895 Wilde brought a libel action against the Marquis of Queensberry; he lost the case and was himself sentenced to two years' imprisonment with hard labor for acts of gross indecency. He was released from prison, bankrupt, in 1897 and went to Paris, where he lived until his death in 1900.

West and defeats the forces of evil embodies one of the most enduring themes in American mythology.

458 pp.   0-14-039065-0 $10.00

MARY WOLLSTONECRAFT
1759 – 1797, BRITISH

A Vindication of the Rights of Woman

Edited with an Introduction by Miriam Brody

Published in 1792, this classic treatise applied the egalitarian principles of the French and American revolutions to the social, political, and economic conditions of women.

320 pp.   0-14-043382-1 $10.95

"As a thinker on social issues, Wollstonecraft was bold and original, and expressed her views through essays, fiction, and travel writing."

—CLAIRE TOMALIN

MARY WOLLSTONECRAFT
1759 – 1797, BRITISH

WILLIAM GODWIN
1756 – 1836, BRITISH

A Short Residence in Sweden, Norway, and Denmark and Memoirs of the Author of A Vindication of the Rights of Woman

Edited with an Introduction and Notes by Richard Holmes

Feminist writer Wollstonecraft's record of her Scandinavian journey and her philosopher-husband's memoirs (written after her death) offer insight into the minds of two major figures in the transition from reason to romanticism in Europe.

320 pp.   0-14-043269-8 $11.95

See William Godwin.

MARY WOLLSTONECRAFT
1759 – 1797, BRITISH

MARY SHELLEY
1797 – 1851, BRITISH

Mary/Maria/Matilda

Edited with an Introduction by Janet Todd

Three short novels written by mother and daughter offer insight into the personal lives of both authors as they illuminate struggles for identity within the early feminist movement.

256 pp.   0-14-043371-6 $12.95

See Mary Shelley.

Jacob's Room

Introduction and Notes by Sue Roe

Imparted in a poetic prose style reflecting her experiments with reality, memory, and time, Woolf's third novel signals her bold departure from the traditional methods of the English novel.

20TH-CENTURY CLASSICS
192 pp.   0-14-018570-4 $9.95

Night and Day

Edited with an Introduction and Notes by Julia Briggs

A love story and a social comedy in the tradition of Jane Austen, *Night and Day* transcends traditional romance to raise questions about women's intellectual freedom, marriage, social expectations, and social reform.

20TH-CENTURY CLASSICS
496 pp.   0-14-018568-2 $13.95

The Voyage Out

Edited with an Introduction and Notes by Jane Wheare

Woolf's first novel is the story of an impressionable young British woman sailing to South America, whose innocence makes her susceptible to love and ripe for tragedy.

20TH-CENTURY CLASSICS
432 pp.   0-14-018563-1 $11.95

The Poems
Volume 1

Edited with an Introduction by John O. Hayden

The poems, arranged in chronological order, show the coherent whole of Wordsworth's lifework, the parts of which are a single and organic opus of autobiographical confession depicting the growth of a poet's sensibility. The selection includes "*Lines Written as a School Exercise at Hawkshead*," "*We Are Seven*," "*Surprised by Joy—Impatient as the Wind*," and others.

1,072 pp.   0-14-042211-0 $18.95

The Poems
Volume 2

Edited with an Introduction by John O. Hayden

This volume includes "*Tintern Abbey*," "*The Excursion, By the Sea-Side*," "*Ode on the Installation of His Royal Highness Prince Albert*," and others.

1,104 pp.   0-14-042212-9 $17.95

Selected Poems

Edited by John O. Hayden

This generous selection of Wordsworth's best poems, freshly edited and chronologically arranged, concentrates on his greater short works.

624 pp.   0-14-042375-3 $11.95

Selected Prose Writings

Edited with an Introduction and Notes by John O. Hayden

Twenty thematically arranged essays, letters, and prose pieces display the poet's far-reaching interests in politics, social concerns, aesthetics, and literary theory.

528 pp.   0-14-043292-2 $10.95

See *English Romantic Verse*.

WILLIAM WORDSWORTH
1770 – 1850, British

DOROTHY WORDSWORTH
1771 – 1855, British

Home at Grasmere

Edited by Colette Clark

This perceptive arrangement of Dorothy's journal entries alongside William's poems sheds light on the poet's creative process.

304 pp.   0-14-043136-5 $11.95

SIR THOMAS WYATT
1503 – 1542, British

The Complete Poems

Edited with a Preface and Notes by R. A. Rebholz

The rondeaux, sonnets, epigrams, canzoni, ballades, songs, epistolary satires, psalms, and poems of Renaissance diplomat and Tudor courtier Sir Thomas Wyatt express a high degree of intelligence and culture as surely as did his diplomatic work.

560 pp.   0-14-042227-7 $12.95

XENOPHON
C. 430 – C. 350 B.C., Greek

Conversations of Socrates

Edited with an Introduction by Robin Waterfield and Translated by Hugh Tredennick and Robin Waterfield

Xenophon's complete Socratic works—*Socrates' Defence, Memoirs of Socrates, The Dinner Party*, and *The Estate-Manager*—not only portray the character and teachings of the great philosopher but apply Socratic principles to the daily life of Greece, giving insight into the religious, political, and moral views of the Athenians.

384 pp.   0-14-044517-X $12.95

Hiero the Tyrant and Other Treatises

Translated by Robin Waterfield with an Introduction and Notes by Paul Cartledge

This collection of the essays of a man of penetrating practical intelligence and deep moral commitment includes the dialogue between the poet Simonides and his employer—Hiero, tyrant of Syracuse—is a classic study of absolute power, a pioneering biography of King Agesilaus of Sparta, a bold economic program for democratic Athens, and more. Together they present informed, learned insights into the nature and purposes of leadership.

288 pp.   0-14-044682-6 $13.95

A History of My Times

Translated by Rex Warner with an Introduction and Notes by George Cawkwell

Continuing the story of the Peloponnesian War where Thucydides left off, Xenophon records the politics and battles that brought about the ultimate decline of Greece.

432 pp.   0-14-044175-1 $11.95

The Persian Expedition

Translated by Rex Warner with an Introduction and Notes by George Cawkwell

This historical account tells of Xenophon's march with the Ten Thousand against the barbarian Persians.

376 pp.   0-14-044007-0 $13.95

W. B. YEATS
1865 – 1939, IRISH
NOBEL PRIZE WINNER

Short Fiction

Edited with an Introduction and Notes by G. J. Watson

This volume contains Yeats's best short fiction, including the novel *John Sherman*, all the stories in *The Secret Rose*, and the "companion" stories "The Table of the Law" and "The Adoration of the Magi."

20TH-CENTURY CLASSICS
320 pp.   0-14-018002-8 $13.95

See J. M. Synge.

ANZIA YEZIERSKA
1885 – 1970, AMERICAN
(B. POLAND)

Hungry Hearts

Introduction by Blanche H. Gelfant

In stories that draw heavily on her own life, Anzia Yezierska portrays the immigrant's struggle to become a "real" American, in such stories as "Yekl," "Hunger," "The Fat of the Land," and "How I Found America." Set mostly in New York's Lower East Side, the stories brilliantly evoke the oppressive atmosphere of crowded streets and shabby tenements and lay bare the despair of families trapped in unspeakable poverty, working at demeaning jobs, and coping with the barely hidden prejudices of their new land.

20TH-CENTURY CLASSICS
288 pp.   0-14-118005-6 $10.95

YEVGENY ZAMYATIN
1884 – 1937, RUSSIAN

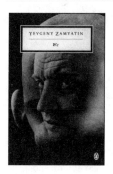

We

Translated with an Introduction and Notes by Clarence Brown

Orwell's inspiration for *1984*, Zamyatin's masterpiece describes life under the regimented totalitarian society of OneState, ruled over by the all-powerful "Benefactor."

20TH-CENTURY CLASSICS

240 pp.   0-14-018585-2 $12.95

"The best single work of science fiction yet written."

—URSULA K. LE GUIN

ÉMILE ZOLA
1840 – 1902, FRENCH

*L'Assommoir (The Dram Shop)

Translated with an Introduction by Robin Buss

Now in a vibrant new translation, this edition of Zola's story of a good-hearted but vulnerable laundress includes Zola's response to critics who denounced the work as immoral. The seventh novel in Les Rougon-Macquart cycle, this dark and gritty exploration of working-class life was a publishing sensation and is widely hailed as Zola's masterpiece.

480 pp.   0-14-044753-9 $11.00

(Available in April 2001)

La Bête Humaine

Translated with an Introduction by Leonard Tancock

In this taut thriller of violent passions, crime, and the law, Zola bitterly attacks the politics and corruption of the French judicial system.

368 pp.   0-14-044327-4 $10.95

The Debacle

Translated with an Introduction by Leonard Tancock

Zola's only purely historical work, this realistic, detailed, and accurate account of France's defeat in the Franco-Prussian War is a grim testament to the human horrors of war.

512 pp.   0-14-044280-4 $13.95

The Earth

Translated with an Introduction by Douglas Parmée

With humor and flashes of tenderness, Zola depicts the human cycle of birth, marriage, and death against the natural changes of the agricultural seasons.

512 pp.   0-14-044387-8 $14.95

Germinal

Translated with an Introduction by Leonard Tancock

Written to draw attention to the misery prevailing among the lower class in France during the Second Empire, *Germinal* depicts the grim struggle between capital and labor in a coal field in northern France.

512 pp.   0-14-044045-3 $8.95

Nana

Translated with an Introduction by George Holden

An evocation of the corrupt world of the Second Empire, this story of a prostitute embodies Zola's theory that behavior is predetermined by one's origin.

472 pp.   0-14-044263-4 $7.95

Thérèse Raquin
Translated with an Introduction by Leonard Tancock

This tale of adultery, murder, and revenge, condemned as pornography when it was published in 1867, is one of Zola's earliest novels.

272 pp.   0-14-044120-4 $10.95

ANONYMOUS

Beowulf
Edited with an Introduction, Notes, and Glossary by Michael Alexander

Rather than a literary translation, this edition presents Anglo-Saxon verse text on the left-hand page, faced by a page on which almost every word is glossed. Succinct footnotes clarify historical and cultural matters.

272 pp.   0-14-043377-5 $12.95

Beowulf
A Verse Translation
Introduction by Michael Alexander

This heroic Old English poem, perhaps the most significant work to survive from the Anglo-Saxon period, is rendered in an eloquent verse translation.

176 pp.   0-14-044268-5 $10.00

Beowulf
A Prose Translation
Introduction by David Wright

Based on a Norse legend, this prose translation of the epic depicts the Scandinavian warrior and his struggles against monsters.

128 pp.   0-14-044070-4 $7.95

The Bhagavad Gita
Translated with an Introduction by Juan Mascaro

One of the most important mystical poems in the Hindu scriptures, *The Bhagavad Gita* ranks among the key religious books of the world.

128 pp.   0-14-044121-2 $8.95

The Classic of Mountains and Seas
Translated with an Introduction and Notes by Anne Birrell

Traditionally ascribed to the mythical figure Yü the Great this treasure trove of colorful fiction and eclectic information is a spectacular guided tour of the known world in antiquity and a major source of Chinese mythology. This is the first complete annotated edition of *The Classic of Mountains and Seas* (third century B.C. to second century A.D.).

336 pp.   9 line drawings
0-14-044719-9 $13.95

The Cloud of Unknowing and Other Works

Translated with an Introduction by Clifton Wolters

This devotional classic springs from the fourteenth century, an age when European mysticism was in full flower, and includes three shorter works attributed to the same writer—*The Epistle of Privy Counsel, Dionysius's Mystical Training (Deonise Hid Divinite)*, and *The Epistle of Prayer*—illuminating the close relationship between medieval spirituality and mysticism.

232 pp.   0-14-044385-1 $11.95

The Death of King Arthur

Translated with an Introduction by James Cable

Set in the twilight of the Arthurian world, this medieval romance tells of Lancelot's adultery with Guinevere, the arrival of the treacherous Mordred, and the deaths of both Arthur and Lancelot.

240 pp.   0-14-044255-3 $12.95

The Dhammapada

Translated with an Introduction by Juan Mascaro

Compiled in the third century B.C., these aphorisms illustrate the Buddhist dhamma, or moral system, pointing out the narrow Path of Perfection that leads toward Nirvana.

96 pp.   0-14-044284-7 $8.95

Egil's Saga

Translated with an Introduction by Hermann Pálsson and Paul Edwards

Thought to have been written in 1230, *Egil's Saga* chronicles the histories of the ruling clans of Iceland and Norway, giving a wide-ranging view of the Viking world in the ninth and tenth centuries.

256 pp.   0-14-044321-5 $12.95

The Epic of Gilgamesh

Translated with an Introduction by N.K. Sandars

Fifteen centuries before Homer, this Mesopotamian cycle of poems tells of Gilgamesh, the great King, Uruk, and his long and arduous journey to the spring of youth in search of immortality.

128 pp.   0-14-044100-X $8.95

The Epic of Gilgamesh
A New Translation

Translated with an Introduction by Andrew George

George's gripping new translation brilliantly brings together all the variant traditions and transforms a "damaged masterpiece" into a fluent, coherent narrative.

288 pp.   28 line drawings   1 map
0-14-044721-0 $9.00

Eyrbyggja Saga

Translated with an Introduction by Hermann Pálsson and Paul Edwards

This saga dramatizes a thirteenth-century view of the past, from the pagan anarchy of the Viking Age to the settlement of Iceland, the coming of Christianity, and the beginnings of organized society.

192 pp.   0-14-044530-7 $12.95

The Greek Alexander Romance

Translated with an Introduction by Richard Stoneman

One of the most influential works of late classical Greek literature, this fast-paced, wonderfully exuberant entertainment portrays the fabulous adventures of Alexander the Great.

208 pp. 0-14-044560-9 $11.95

Hrafnkel's Saga

Translated with an Introduction by Hermann Pálsson

These seven stories, dating from the thirteenth century, combine pagan elements and Christian ethics; some are set in the pastoral society of Iceland, while others are concerned with the royal courts of Norway and Denmark.

144 pp. 0-14-044238-3 $11.95

See Snorri Sturluson.

King Arthur's Death
Morte Arthure/Le Morte Arthur

Translated with Introductions by Brian Stone

Modern verse translations of two Midlands Arthurian epics provide a vivid contrast of medieval poetic tone and narrative style: the alliterative *Morte Arthure* (Northeast Midlands, c. 1400) and the stanzaic *Le Morte Arthur* (Northwest Midlands, c. 1350).

320 pp. 0-14-044445-9 $11.95

The Koran

Translated with an Introduction and Notes by N. J. Dawood

N. J. Dawood's vivid revised translation is presented with opposing-page parallel Arabic text in the traditional calligraphic style. The volume includes a comprehensive index. Oversized format.

1,088 pp. 0-14-044542-0 $23.95

The Koran
Revised Edition

Translated with an Introduction and Notes by N. J. Dawood

This classic, authoritative translation has been revised to fully reflect the characteristic flavor and rhythm of Islam's most sacred work, following the original sequence of the Koranic suras.

456 pp. 0-14-044558-7 $9.95

The Laws of Manu

Translated by Wendy Doniger O'Flaherty with Brian K. Smith

No understanding of modern India is possible without this extraordinary model of jurisprudence, philosophy, and religion, written from 200 B.C. to A.D. 200.

368 pp. 0-14-044540-4 $13.95

Laxdaela Saga

Translated with an Introduction by Magnus Magnusson and Hermann Pálsson

This dynastic chronicle, composed around 1245, sweeps across 150 years of Iceland's early history.

272 pp. 0-14-044218-9 $12.95

Lives of the Later Caesars

Translated with an Introduction by Anthony Birley

Covering the emperors from Hadrian to Heliogabalus (A.D. 117–222),

this edition contains the only true
sequel to Suetonius's *The Twelve
Caesars*.

336 pp.   0-14-044308-8 $11.95

The Mabinogion

*Translated with an Introduction by
Jeffrey Gantz*

These tales from the Welsh oral tradition were first written down in the thirteenth century and remain an alluring
combination of fact and fantasy, myth,
history, and folklore.

376 pp.   0-14-044322-3 $9.95

The Nibelungenlied

*Translated with an Introduction by
A. T. Hatto*

This great German epic poem, written
during the thirteenth century, is the
principal literary source of Richard
Wagner's *The Ring*.

416 pp.   0-14-044137-9 $11.95

Njal's Saga

*Translated with an Introduction by
Magnus Magnusson and
Hermann Pálsson*

Based on historical events in tenth-
century Iceland, this spare, simple narrative describes a fifty-year blood feud

from its violent beginnings to its tragic
end.

384 pp.   0-14-044103-4 $13.95

Orkneyinga Saga
The History of the Earls of Orkney

*Translated with an Introduction by
Hermann Pálsson and Paul Edwards*

Describing the conquest of the Orkney
Islands by the Kings of Norway, this is
the only medieval Norse chronicle concerned with what is now part of the
British Isles.

256 pp.   0-14-044383-5 $13.95

The Poem of the Cid

*Translated by Rita Hamilton and Janet
Perry with an Introduction and Notes by
Ian Michael*

This epic poem, the only one to have
survived from medieval Spain, depicts
the career of the warlord El Cid in a
unique blend of fiction and historical
fact. Both English and Spanish texts are
provided.

256 pp.   0-14-044446-7 $10.95

The Quest of the Holy Grail

*Translated with an Introduction by
P. M. Matarasso*

This classic tale of chivalrous adventures was intended as an allegory of
man's perilous search for the grace of
God.

304 pp.   0-14-044220-0 $12.95

The Rig Veda

*Selected, Translated, and Annotated by
Wendy Doniger O'Flaherty*

This collection of more than 1,000
Sanskrit hymns from the timeless
world of myth and ritual forms a

unique insight into early Indian mythology, philosophy, and religion.
512 pp.   0-14-044402-5 $12.95

The Saga of King Hrolf Kraki

Translated with an Introduction by Jesse L. Byock

Written in fourteenth-century Iceland, this extraordinary saga ranks among the masterworks of the Middle Ages.

144 pp. 1 map   0-14-043593-X $11.95

The Saga of the Volsungs

Translated with an Introduction, Notes, and Glossary by Jesse L. Byock

Based on Viking Age poems and composed in thirteenth-century Iceland, this saga combines mythology, legend, and sheer human drama to relate the heroic deeds of Sigurd the dragon slayer. Yet its setting is a very human world that incorporates oral memories of the fourth and fifth centuries.

160 pp. 2 maps 0-14-044738-5 $11.95

Sir Gawain and the Green Knight

Edited by J. A. Burrow

Written in the latter part of the fourteenth century, this subtle and accomplished poem is roughly contemporary with *The Canterbury Tales*, though written in a more provincial dialect. The aim of this edition has been to remove unnecessary impediments while retaining the integrity of the original.

176 pp.   0-14-042295-1 $9.95

Sir Gawain and the Green Knight

Translated with an Introduction by Brian Stone

This masterpiece of medieval alliterative poetry by an unknown fourteenth-century author is both magical and human, full of drama and descriptive beauty.

176 pp.   0-14-044092-5 $8.95

The Song of Roland

Translated with an Introduction and Notes by Glyn Burgess

Chronicling the massacre in A.D. 778 of Charlemagne's army at Roncesvalles, this age-old French epic transforms a legendary defeat into an allegorical clash between Christianity and paganism.

224 pp.   0-14-044532-3 $8.95

The Song of Roland

Translated by Dorothy Sayers

Nowhere in literature is the medieval code of chivalry more perfectly expressed than in this masterly and exciting poem, translated here by Dorothy Sayers, an expert in medieval literature perhaps best known for her sixteen crime novels.

208 pp.   0-14-044075-5 $11.95

Tales from the Thousand and One Nights

Translated with an Introduction by N. J. Dawood

This volume includes the finest and best known of the *Tales*, representing an expression of the secular imagination in revolt against the religious austerity of other works of medieval Near Eastern literature.

416 pp.   0-14-044289-8 $12.95

The Upanishads

Selected and Translated with an Introduction by Juan Mascaro

First written in Sanskrit between 800 and 400 B.C., these spiritual treatises form the foundation of Hindu beliefs.

144 pp.   0-14-044163-8 $8.95

The Vinland Sagas and The Norse Discovery of America

Translated by Magnus Magnusson and Hermann Pálsson

These two Icelandic sagas tell the arresting stories of the discovery of North America five centuries before the arrival of Christopher Columbus.

128 pp.   0-14-044154-9 $10.95

ANTHOLOGIES AND COLLECTIONS

Against Slavery
An Abolitionist Reader

Edited and with an Introduction by Mason Lowance

An original anthology of primary documents from the eighteenth- and nineteenth-century antislavery and abolitionist movements, including speeches, lectures, and essays by Garrison, Douglass, Emerson, and Lydia Maria Child.

20TH-CENTURY CLASSICS
384 pp.   0-14-043758-4 $13.95

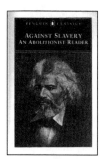

American Local Color Writing, 1880–1920

Edited with an Introduction by Elizabeth Ammons and Valerie Rohy

Organized geographically, *American Local Color Writing* features familiar writers such as Kate Chopin, Hamlin Garland, Joel Chandler Harris, and Sarah Orne Jewett, and introduces lesser-known voices like Abraham Cahan, Sui Sin Far, and Zitkala-Ša. The writing sheds light on varying concepts of the "American identity": the African American experience; shifting notions of gender and sexuality; and racial, class, and ethnic stereotypes.

400 pp.   0-14-043688-X $13.95

See Abraham Cahan, Kate Chopin, Hamlin Garland, Joel Chandler Harris, and Sarah Orne Jewett.

Augustan Critical Writing

Edited with an Introduction and Notes by David Womersley

English literary criticism from 1660 to 1750 is collected in this engaging look back to a time before literary criticism had become codified and professionalized—when literary art, and readers' reactions to it, were considered not a separate sphere but an integral part of political, cultural, and social life.

464 pp.   0-14-043373-2 $14.95

Buddhist Scriptures

Selected and Translated by
Edward Conze

This selection of writings from the golden age of Buddhist literature (A.D. 100–400) focuses on texts intended for the layperson rather than for the monk and exhibits the humanity rather than the profundity of the scriptures. Passages from the *Dhammapada*, the *Buddhacarita*, the *Questions of King Milinda*, and the *Tibetan Book of the Dead* are included.

256 pp.   0-14-044088-7 $12.95

A Celtic Miscellany

Selected and Translated with a Preface and Notes by Kenneth Hurlstone Jackson

More than 240 thematically arranged selections of Celtic poetry and prose, translated from the Welsh, Irish, Scottish Gaelic, Cornish, Breton, and Manx languages, provide insight into the Celtic mind from the earliest times to the nineteenth century.

352 pp.   0-14-044247-2 $12.95

The Cistercian World
Monastic Writings of the Twelfth Century

Edited and Translated with an Introduction by Pauline Matarasso

Collected in this volume are letters, sermons, biographies, satires, and stories by the influential abbot St. Bernard of Clairvaux and other monks of the Cistercian Order—a medieval order devoted to strict asceticism and a life of poverty.

336 pp.   0-14-043356-2 $14.95

Classical Literary Criticism

Translated with an Introduction by
T. S. Dorsch

This collection presents three classical discussions of creative writing: Aristotle's *Poetics*, Horace's *Ars Poetica*, and the treatise *On the Sublime*, falsely attributed to Dionysius Longinus.

160 pp.   0-14-044155-7 $11.95

See Aristotle and Horace.

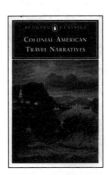

Colonial American Travel Narratives

Edited with an Introduction by
Wendy Martin

Four journeys by early Americans Mary Rowlandson, Sarah Kemble Knight, William Byrd II, and Dr. Alexander Hamilton recount the vivid physical and psychological challenges of colonial life. Essential primary texts in the study of early American cultural life, they are now conveniently collected in a single volume.

336 pp.   0-14-039088-X $13.95

Divine Right and Democracy
An Anthology of Political Writing in Stuart England

Edited with an Introduction by David Wooton

Reflecting the political debate that characterized England's century of revolution, these thirty-three thematically arranged selections prefigure modern conceptions of political rights and social change. The volume includes anonymous writers as well as James VI and James I, John Lilburne, Charles I, Richard Hooker, Roger Williams, Gerrard Winstanley, Francis Bacon, Algernon Sidney, John Locke, Bernard Mandeville, and others.

512 pp.   0-14-043250-7 $14.95

See Francis Bacon and John Locke.

The Earliest English Poems
Third Revised Edition

Translated with an Introduction by Michael Alexander

This select volume includes translations of heroic poems (including the oldest poem in the English language), a passage from *Beowulf*, "riddles" from *The Exeter Book*, and elegies in Anglo-Saxon meter and alliteration.

176 pp.   0-14-044594-3 $11.95

See *Beowolf: A Verse Translation.*

Early American Drama

Edited with an Introduction and Notes by Jeffrey H. Richards

This unique volume includes eight early dramas that mirror American literary, social, and cultural history: Royall Tyler's *The Contrast* (1789); William Dunlap's *André* (1798); James Nelson

Barker's *The Indian Princess* (1808); Robert Montgomery Bird's *The Gladiator* (1831); William Henry Smith's *The Drunkard* (1844); Anna Cora Mowatt's *Fashion* (1845); George Aiken's *Uncle Tom's Cabin* (1852); and Dion Boucicault's *The Octoroon* (1859).

576 pp.   0-14-043588-3 $13.95

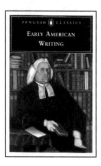

Early American Writing

Edited with an Introduction by Giles Gunn

Drawing materials from journals and diaries, political documents and religious sermons, prose and poetry, Giles Gunn's anthology provides a panoramic survey of early American life and literature—including voices black and white, male and female, Hispanic, French, and Native American.

720 pp.   0-14-039087-1 $14.95

Early Christian Lives

Translated and Edited by Carolinne White

Shedding light on the men who were the founding fathers of monasticism in both the eastern and western areas of the Roman Empire, these accounts—Athanasius's *Life of Antony*; St. Jerome's *Life of Paul of Thebes, Life of Hilarion,* and *Life of Malchus*; Sulpicius Severus's *Life of Martin of Tours*; and Pope Gregory the Great's *Life of Benedict*—also illuminate the beliefs and values of their celebrated authors.

288 pp.   0-14-043526-3 $13.95

Early Christian Writings
The Apostolic Fathers

Translated by Maxwell Staniforth with Revised Translation, Introductions, and New Editorial Material by Andrew Louth

These letters and short theological treatises provide a rich guide to the emerging traditions and organization of the infant Church.

208 pp.   0-14-044475-0 $12.95

Early Greek Philosophy

Translated and Edited with an Introduction by Jonathan Barnes

The earliest Western philosophers, the pre-Socratics, are profiled in this omnibus, which includes a general Introduction and a synopsis of their historical and ideological development, as well as brief introductions to each philosopher's work.

320 pp.   0-14-044461-0 $12.95

Early Irish Myths and Sagas

Translated with an Introduction and Notes by Jeffrey Gantz

These fourteen myths and tales, probably first written down around the eighth century A.D., represent the oral tradition of Iron Age Celts who flourished in Europe during the seven centuries before Christ.

288 pp.   0-14-044397-5 $11.95

English Romantic Verse

Edited with an Introduction by David Wright

Nearly all the famous and beloved masterworks can be found here—"Intimations of Immortality," "Rime of the Ancient Mariner," and "The Tyger"—as well as some less familiar poems from such writers as Christopher Smart, Walter Savage Landor, John Clare, and Thomas Lovell Beddoes.

384 pp.   0-14-042102-5 $8.95

See William Blake, Samuel Coleridge, and William Wordsworth.

Four Stories by American Women

Edited with an Introduction by Cynthia Griffin Wolff

Representing four prominent American women writers who flourished in the period following the Civil War, this collection comprises "Life in the Iron Mills," Rebecca Harding Davis; "The Yellow Wallpaper," Charlotte Perkins Gilman; "The Country of the Pointed Firs," Sarah Orne Jewett; and "Souls Belated," Edith Wharton.

240 pp.   0-14-039076-6 $9.95

See Charlotte Perkins Gilman, Sarah Orne Jewett, and Edith Wharton.

German Idealist Philosophy

*Edited with an Introduction by
Rüdiger Bubner*

In this masterful introduction to German idealism, Rüdiger Bubner brings together key texts and lesser-known extracts from works of four powerful intellects—Immanuel Kant, Johann Fichte, Friederich Schelling, and George Hegel—with insightful overviews of each philosopher and an account of the movement as a whole.

368 pp.   0-14-044660-5 $13.95

See Georg Wilhelm Friedrich Hegel.

Hindu Myths

Translated by Wendy Doniger O'Flaherty

This selection and translation of seventy-five myths spans a wide range of Indian sources, from the serpent-slaying Indra of the Vedas to the medieval pantheon.

272 pp.   0-14-044306-1 $12.95

Hippocratic Writings

*Edited with an Introduction by
G. E. R. Lloyd and Translated by
J. Chadwick, W. N. Mann,
E. T. Withington, and I. M. Lonie*

The origins of Western medicine and the ideal of ethical practice, as well as the origin of the scientific method are revealed in these writings by Hippocrates and other medical pioneers.

384 pp.   0-14-044451-3 $13.95

Japanese Nō Dramas

*Translated with an Introduction and
Notes by Royall Tyler*

These twenty-four plays of mesmerizing beauty fuse the spiritual and the sensual in the esoteric Nō art form, which combines music, dance, costume, and language. The collection includes full notes and stage directions, as well as new interpretations of the plays that influenced writers such as Yeats, Pound, and Brecht.

384 pp.   0-14-044539-0 $14.95

Medieval English Verse

*Edited and Translated with an
Introduction by Brian Stone*

Short narrative poems, religious and secular lyrics, and moral, political, and comic verses are all included in this comprehensive collection of works from the thirteenth and fourteenth centuries.

256 pp.   0-14-044144-1 $13.95

The Metaphysical Poets

*Edited with an Introduction by
Helen Gardner*

These select works feature thirty-eight poets, among them Carew, Crashaw, Donne, Herbert, Jonson, Lovelace, Marvell, Suckling, and Vaughan.

332 pp.   0-14-042038-X $9.95

See John Donne, George Herbert, and Ben Jonson.

Nineteenth-Century American Poetry

Edited with an Introduction and Notes by William C. Spengemann with Jessica F. Roberts

Whitman, Dickinson, and Melville occupy the center of this anthology of nearly three hundred poems, spanning the course of the century, from Joel Barlow to Edwin Arlington Robinson, by way of Bryant, Emerson, Longfellow, Whittier, Poe, Holmes, Jones Very, Thoreau, Lowell, and Lanier.

480 pp.   0-14-043587-5 $14.95

See Ralph Waldo Emerson, Henry Wadsworth Longfellow, Herman Melville, Edgar Allan Poe, Henry David Thoreau, and Walt Whitman.

The Penguin Book of First World War Poetry

Edited with an Introduction by Jon Silkin

More than photographs or eyewitness reports of the First World War, it is the poetry written during this devastating conflict that has embedded the horror of that time in our consciousness. Now supplemented with five new poems, the works of thirty-eight British, European, and American writers collected here include some of the most outstanding and poignant poems of this century.

20TH-CENTURY CLASSICS

320 pp.   0-14-118009-9 $12.95

See Thomas Hardy and Rudyard Kipling.

The Penguin Book of French Poetry 1820–1950

Edited by William Rees

This anthology offers a broad range of French poetry from writers such as Theophile Gautier, Stephane Mallarmé, Charles Baudelaire, and Guillaume Appollinaire. The French text is accompanied by English prose translations.

856 pp.   0-14-042385-0 $19.95

See Charles Baudelaire.

The Penguin Book of Modern African Poetry
Fourth Edition

Edited with an Introduction by Gerald Moore and Ulli Beier

The definitive one-volume survey of modern African poetry, this edition contains the poetry of ninety-nine from twenty-seven countries and displays the wide-ranging forms of African verse: war songs, satires, political protests, and poems about love, nature, and life's surprises.

20TH-CENTURY CLASSICS

480 pp.   0-14-118100-1 $15.95

The Penguin Book of Renaissance Verse
1509–1659
Edited by H. R. Woudhuysen and Selected with an Introduction by David Norbrook

Organized thematically, this superbly edited anthology offers a new view of one of the most fertile periods in the history of English literature. Generous space is devoted to writings of women, works of popular culture, and regional noncourtly poetry.

960 pp.   0-14-042346-X $22.95

The Penguin Book of Restoration Verse
Edited with an Introduction by Harold Love

Organized by themes ranging from libertines to moralists and visionaries, from poems of love to poems honoring the dead, this anthology reflects recent developments in restoration scholarship and features many works by women poets. Writings by such well-known poets as Milton, Dryden, Marvell, and Aphra Behn are included, along with selections by less-familiar authors.

384 pp.   0-14-042407-5 $14.95

See Aphra Behn, Andrew Marvell, and John Milton.

The Penguin Book of Victorian Verse
Selected and Edited with an Introduction by Daniel Karlin

Works by almost 150 poets, from late Romantics to high modernists, are included in this rich, far-ranging survey. Cross-references and complete biographical and textual notes make this the ideal anthology for general readers and students alike.

20TH-CENTURY CLASSICS

928 pp.   0-14-044578-1 $17.95

Poems of Heaven and Hell from Ancient Mesopotamia
Translated with an Introduction by N. K. Sandars

Five poems from the height of Babylonian civilization reflect the cyclical nature of the lives and beliefs of the Mesopotamian culture. Included are *The Babylonian Creation, The Sumerian Underworld, Inanna's Journey to Hell, Adapa: The Man,* and *A Prayer to the Gods of Night.*

192 pp.   0-14-044249-9 $11.95

Romantic Fairy Tales
Translated and Edited with an Introduction by Carol Tully

This enchanting and disturbing collection vividly illustrates the development of German Romanticism through four key "literary fairy tales": Goethe's *The Fairy Tale* (1795), Tieck's *Eckbert the Fair* (1797), Fouqué's *Undine* (1811), and Brentano's *The Tale of Honest Casper and Fair Annie* (1817).

192 pp.   0-14-044732-6 $11.00

See John Wolfgang von Goethe.

Seven Viking Romances
Translated with an Introduction by Hermann Pálsson and Paul Edwards

Incorporating local myths and legends, as well as sources from Homer to French romances, these medieval stories feature famous kings, difficult gods, and great adventures.

304 pp.   0-14-044474-2 $13.95

Six Yüan Plays

Translated with an Introduction by
Liu Jung-En

Six vibrant plays from the thirteenth century represent the first real Chinese theater to develop free from conservative Confucianism: *The Orphan of Chao, The Soul of Ch'ien-Nü Leaves Her Body, The Injustice Done to Tou Ngo, Chang Boils the Sea, Autumn in Han Palace,* and *A Stratagem of Interlocking Rings.*

288 pp.   0-14-044262-6 $11.95

Speaking of Śiva

Translated with an Introduction by
A. K. Ramanujan

This volume contains a collection of *vacanas* (free-verse lyrics) centering on the Hindu god Shiva, written by four saints of the great bhakti protest movement of the tenth century A.D.: Basvanna, Devara Dāsimayya, Mahaādeviyakka, and Allama Prabhu.

208 pp.   0-14-044270-7 $13.00

Three Gothic Novels

Edited by Peter Fairclough with an
Introduction by Mario Praz

Horace Walpole's *The Castle of Otranto,* published in 1765, is the prototype of all Gothic novels; William Beckford's *Vathek* combines Gothic romanticism with Oriental exoticism; and Mary Shelley's *Frankenstein* is a masterpiece of Gothic horror.

512 pp.   0-14-043036-9 $10.95

See Mary Shelley.

Three Jacobean Tragedies

Edited with an Introduction by
Gāmini Salgādo

From the early seventeenth century, three of the finest examples of Jacobean revenge tragedy make up this collection: *The White Devil* by John Webster, *The Revenger's Tragedy* by Cyril Tourneur, and *The Changeling* by Thomas Middleton and William Rowley.

368 pp.   0-14-043006-7 $12.95

See Thomas Middleton.

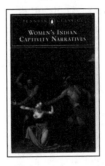

Women's Indian Captivity Narratives

Edited with an Introduction and Notes
by Kathryn Zabelle Derounian-Stodola

Enthralling generations of readers, the narrative of capture by Native Americans is an archtype of American literature. Most such narratives were fact-based, but the stories themselves were often transformed into spiritual autobiographies, spellbinding adventure stories, sentimental tales, or anti-Indian propaganda. The ten narratives here span two hundred years (1682–1892), and depict the experiences of women such as Mary Rowlandson, Hannah Dunstan, Sarah Wakefield, and Mary Jemison.

224 pp.   0-14-043671-5 $13.95

The new Pelican Shakespeare series incorporates the most up-to-date scholarship since the acclaimed series first appeared a generation ago under the editorial aegis of Alfred Harbage. Stephen Orgel and A.R. Braunmuller, the general editors of the revised series, have assembled a team of eminent scholars who have prepared introductions and notes to the forty new volumes.

"I feel that I have spent half my career with one or another Pelican Shakespeare in my back pocket. Convenience, however, is the least important aspect of the new Pelican Shakespeare series. Here is an elegant and clear text for either the study or the rehearsal room, notes where you need them and the distinguished scholarship of the general editors, Stephen Orgel and A. R. Braunmuller who understand that these are plays for performance as well as great texts for contemplation."

—PATRICK STEWART

NOW AVAILABLE

Antony and Cleopatra
Edited by A. R. Braunmuller
160 pp.   0-14-071452-9 $4.95

As You Like It
Edited by Frances E. Dolan
128 pp.   0-14-071471-5 $3.95

The Comedy of Errors
Edited by Frances E. Dolan
224 pp.   0-14-071474-X $4.95

Coriolanus
Edited by Jonathan Crewe
160 pp.   0-14-071473-1 $5.95

Cymbeline
Edited by Peter Holland
176 pp.   0-14-071472-3 $5.95

Henry IV, Part 1
Edited by Claire McEachern
144 pp.   0-14-071456-1 $3.95

Henry IV, Part 2
144 pp.   0-14-071457-x $4.95

Henry V
Edited by Claire McEachern
176 pp.   0-14-071458-8 $4.95

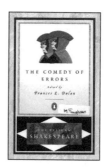

Henry VI, Part 1

Edited by William Montgomery with an Introduction by Janis Lull

256 pp.   0-14-071465-0 $5.95

Henry VI, Part 2

304 pp.   0-14-071466-9 $5.95

Henry VI, Part 3

304 pp.   0-14-071467-7 $5.95

Julius Caesar

Edited by William Montgomery with an Introduction by Douglas Trevor

144 pp.   0-14-071468-5 $3.95

King John

Edited by Claire McEachern

384 pp.   0-14-071459-6 $5.95

King Lear

Edited by Stephen Orgel

176 pp.   0-14-071476-6 $3.95

King Lear
(The Quarto and the Folio Texts)

Edited by Stephen Orgel

176 pp.   0-14-071490-1 $4.95

Love's Labor's Lost

Edited by Peter Holland

144 pp.   0-14-071477-4 $5.95

Macbeth

Edited by Stephen Orgel

128 pp.   0-14-071478-2 $3.95

Measure for Measure

Edited by Jonathan Crewe

144 pp.   0-14-071479-0 $4.95

The Merchant of Venice

Edited by A. R. Braunmuller

144 pp.   0-14-071462-6 $3.95

A Midsummer Night's Dream

Edited by Russ McDonald

128 pp.   0-14-071455-3 $3.95

Much Ado About Nothing

Edited by Peter Holland

128 pp.   0-14-071480-4 $3.95

The Narrative Poems

Edited by Jonathan Crewe

192 pp.   0-14-071481-2 $5.95

Richard II

Edited by Frances E. Dolan

144 pp.   0-14-071482-0 $4.95

Richard III

Edited by Peter Holland

192 pp.   0-14-071483-9 $4.95

Romeo and Juliet

Edited by Peter Holland

160 pp.   0-14-071484-7 $3.95

ROMEO
AND JULIET
edited by Peter Holland

THE PELICAN SHAKESPEARE

The Taming of the Shrew

Edited by Stephen Orgel

144 pp.   0-14-071451-0 $3.95

The Tempest

Edited by Peter Holland

144 pp.   0-14-071485-5 $3.95

Timon of Athens
Edited by Frances E. Dolan
176 pp.   0-14-071487-1 $5.95

Titus Andronicus
Edited by Russ McDonald
176 pp.   0-14-071491-X $5.95

Troilus and Cressida
Edited by Jonathan Crewe
160 pp.   0-14-071486-3 $5.95

Twelfth Night
Edited by Jonathan Crewe
128 pp.   0-14-071489-8 $4.95

The Two Gentlemen of Verona
Edited by Mary Beth Rose
224 pp.   0-14-071461-8 $5.95

The Winter's Tale
Edited by Frances E. Dolan
144 pp.   0-14-071488-X $4.95

COMING IN 2001

All's Well That Ends Well
Edited by Claire McEachern
144 pp.   0-14-071460-X $5.95

Hamlet
Edited by A. R. Braunmuller
192 pp.   0-14-071454-5 $3.95

Henry VIII
Edited by Jonathan Crewe
160 pp.   0-14-071475-8 $5.95

Merry Wives of Windsor
Edited by Russ McDonald
128 pp.   0-14-071464-2 $5.95

Othello
Edited by Russ McDonald
160 pp.   0-14-071463-4 $3.95

Pericles
Edited by Stephen Orgel
208 pp.   0-14-071469-3 $5.95

Sonnets
*Edited by Stephen Orgel with an
Introduction by John Hollander*
192 pp.   0-14-071453-7 $4.95

SUBJECT CATEGORIES

ART/ARCHITECTURE

Henry Adams
Mont-Saint-Michel and Chartres

Leon Battista Alberti
On Painting

Charles Baudelaire
Selected Writings on Art and Literature

Benvenuto Cellini
Autobiography

Vincent van Gogh
The Letters of Vincent van Gogh

Georg Wilhelm Friedrich Hegel
Introductory Lectures on Aesthetics

William Morris
News from Nowhere and Other Writings

Sir Joshua Reynolds
Discourses

Leo Tolstoy
What Is Art?

Giorgio Vasari
Lives of the Artists, Volumes 1 and 2

AUTOBIOGRAPHY/BIOGRAPHY

Abélard and Héloïse
The Letters of Abélard and Héloïse

Henry Adams
The Education of Henry Adams

Jane Addams
Twenty Years at Hull-House

Adomnán of Iona
Life of St. Columba

Mary Antin
The Promised Land

John Aubrey
Brief Lives

Saint Augustine
Confessions

James Boswell
The Life of Samuel Johnson

Vera Brittain
Testament of Youth

John Bunyan
Grace Abounding to the Chief of Sinners

Benvenuto Cellini
Autobiography

Quentin Crisp
The Naked Civil Servant

Frederick Douglass
Narrative of the Life of Frederick
    Douglass, an American Slave

Olaudah Equiano
The Interesting Narrative and Other
    Writings

Geoge Fox
The Journal

Benjamin Franklin
The Autobiography and Other Writings

Hamlin Garland
A Son of the Middle Border

Elizabeth Gaskell
The Life of Charlotte Brontë

Maxim Gorky
My Childhood

Ulysses S. Grant
Personal Memoirs

Lady Isabella Gregory
Selected Writings

Thomas Wentworth Higginson
Army Life in a Black Regiment
    and Other Writings

Elspeth Huxley
The Flame Trees of Thika

Harriet Jacobs
Incidents in the Life of a Slave Girl

Margery Kempe
The Book of Margery Kempe

Primo Levi
Moments of Reprieve

W. Somerset Maugham
The Summing Up

John Stuart Mill
Autobiography

Lady Mary Wortley Montagu
Selected Letters

Marianne Moore
Selected Letters

Murasaki Shikibu
The Diary of Lady Murasaki

Pablo Neruda
Memoirs

Gérard de Nerval
Selected Writings

John Henry Newman
Apologia pro Vita Sua

Friedrich Nietzsche
Ecce Homo

Mary Prince
The History of Mary Prince

Jean-Jacques Rousseau
The Confessions

Lady Sarashina
As I Crossed a Bridge of Dreams:
    Recollections of a Woman in
    Eleventh-Century Japan

Madame de Sévigné
Selected Letters

William Tecumseh Sherman
Memoirs

Charles A. Siringo
A Texas Cowboy

Joshua Slocum
Sailing Alone around the World

Wallace Stegner
Wolf Willow

Lytton Strachey
Eminent Victorians
Queen Victoria

Teresa of Ávila
The Life of St. Teresa of Ávila by Herself

Anthony Trollope
An Autobiography

Sojourner Truth
Narrative of Sojourner Truth

Giorgio Vasari
Lives of the Artists, Volumes 1 and 2

Booker T. Washington
Up from Slavery

Mary Wollstonecraft and William Godwin
A Short Residence in Sweden, Norway,
    and Denmark and Memoirs of the
    Author of A Vindication of the Rights
    of Woman

Women's Indian Captivity Narratives

DRAMA

Aeschylus
The Oresteia: Agamemnon/
    The Libation Bearers/The Eumenides
The Oresteian Trilogy
Prometheus Bound and Other Plays

Aristophanes
The Frogs and Other Plays
The Knights/The Peace/The Birds/
    The Assembly Women/Wealth
Lysistrata and Other Plays

Pierre-Augustin Caron de Beaumarchais
The Barber of Seville and
    The Marriage of Figaro

Georg Büchner
Complete Plays, Lenz, and Other Writings

Anton Chekhov
Plays

Pierre Corneille
The Cid/Cinna/The Theatrical Illusion

Euripides
The Bacchae and Other Plays
Electra and Other Plays
Medea and Other Plays
Orestes and Other Plays

John Ford
Three Plays

John Gay
The Beggar's Opera

Johann Wolfgang von Goethe
Faust, Part 1 and Part 2

Lady Isabella Gregory
Selected Writings

Henrik Ibsen
Brand
A Doll's House and Other Plays
Ghosts and Other Plays
Hedda Gabler and Other Plays
The Master Builder and Other Plays
Peer Gynt

Ben Jonson
Three Comedies

Christopher Marlowe
The Complete Plays

Menander
Plays and Fragments

Thomas Middleton
Five Plays

Arthur Miller
All My Sons
The Crucible
Death of a Salesman: Certain Private
    Conversations in Two Acts and a
    Requiem

Molière
The Misanthrope and Other Plays
The Miser and Other Plays

Luigi Pirandello
Six Characters in Search of an Author
    and Other Plays

Plautus
The Pot of Gold and Other Plays
The Rope and Other Plays

Jean Racine
Iphigenia/Phaedra/Athaliah
Phèdre

Friedrich Schiller
Mary Stuart
The Robbers and Wallenstein

Lucius Annaeus Seneca
Four Tragedies and Octavia

William Shakespeare
Four Comedies
Four Histories
Four Tragedies
Three Roman Plays

George Bernard Shaw
Heartbreak House
Man and Superman
Plays Unpleasant
Three Plays for Puritans

Richard Brinsley Sheridan
The School for Scandal and Other Plays

Sophocles
Electra and Other Plays
The Theban Plays
The Three Theban Plays: Antigone/
    Oedipus the King/Oedipus at Colonus

August Strindberg
Three Plays

**J. M. Synge, W. B. Yeats, and
Sean O'Casey**
The Playboy of the Western World and
    Two Other Irish Plays

Terence
The Comedies

Ivan Turgenev
A Month in the Country

Oscar Wilde
The Importance of Being Earnest and
Other Plays

Early American Drama
Japanese Nō Dramas
Six Yüan Plays
Three Jacobean Tragedies

ECONOMICS

John Maynard Keynes
The Economic Consequences of the Peace

Thomas Robert Malthus
An Essay on the Principle of Population

Bernard Mandeville
The Fable of the Bees

Karl Marx
Capital, Volumes 1, 2, and 3
Grundrisse: Foundations of the Critique
of Political Economy

Adam Smith
The Wealth of Nations, Books I–III
The Wealth of Nations, Books IV-V

Thorstein Veblen
The Theory of the Leisure Class

FOOD/COOKING

Jean-Anthelme Brillat-Savarin
The Physiology of Taste

Elizabeth David
French Provincial Cooking
Italian Food

HISTORY/POLITICS

Henry Adams
The Education of Henry Adams

Alfred the Great and Assar
Alfred the Great

Ammianus Marcellinus
The Later Roman Empire (A.D. 354–378)

Anna Comnena
The Alexiad of Anna Comnena

Appian
The Civil Wars

Hannah Arendt
Eichmann in Jerusalem: A Report on the
Banality of Evil
On Revolution

Arrian
The Campaigns of Alexander

Bede
The Age of Bede
Ecclesiastical History of the English
People

Jacob Burckhardt
The Civilization of the Renaissance
in Italy

Edmund Burke
Reflections on the Revolution in France

Julius Caesar
The Civil War
The Conquest of Gaul

Charles W. Chesnutt
The Marrow of Tradition

Marcus Tullius Cicero
Murder Trials
On Government
Selected Political Speeches
Selected Works

Carl von Clausewitz
On War

Christopher Columbus
The Four Voyages

J. Hector St. John de Crèvecoeur
Letters from an American Farmer and
Sketches of Eighteenth-Century
America

Quintus Curtius Rufus
The History of Alexander

Bernal Díaz del Castillo
The Conquest of New Spain

Cassius Dio
The Roman History: The Reign of
    Augustus

W. E. B. Du Bois
The Souls of Black Folk

Einhard and Notker the Stammerer
Two Lives of Charlemagne

Friedrich Engels
The Condition of the Working Class in
    England

Jean Froissart
Chronicles

Geoffrey of Monmouth
The History of the Kings of Britain

Gerald of Wales
The History and Topography of Ireland
The Journey Through Wales/The
    Description of Wales

Edward Gibbon
The Decline and Fall of the Roman
    Empire, An Abridged Version
The History of the Decline and Fall of the
    Roman Empire, Volumes I, II, and III

Gregory of Tours
A History of the Franks

Richard Hakluyt
Voyages and Discoveries

Herodotus
The Histories

Thomas Wentworth Higginson
Army Life in a Black Regiment
    and Other Writings

Thomas Hobbes
Leviathan

Thomas Jefferson
Notes on the State of Virginia

**Jean de Joinville and Geoffroi de
Villehardouin**
Chronicles of the Crusades

Flavius Josephus
The Jewish War, Revised Edition

Justinian I
The Digest of Roman Law: Theft, Rapine,
    Damage, and Insult

Bartolomé de Las Casas
A Short Account of the Destruction of
    the Indies

Vladimir Ilich Lenin
The State and Revolution

Primo Levi
Moments of Reprieve

Titus Livy
The Early History of Rome
Rome and Italy
Rome and the Mediterranean
The War with Hannibal

Lord Thomas Babington Macaulay
The History of England

Niccolò Machiavelli
The Discourses
The Prince

**James Madison, Alexander
Hamilton, and John Jay**
The Federalist Papers

Karl Marx
Capital, Volumes 1, 2, and 3
Early Writings
Grundrisse: Foundations of the
    Critique of Political Economy
Political Writings: Volume 3,
    The First International and After

Karl Marx and Friedrich Engels
The Communist Manifesto

Michael Psellus
Fourteen Byzantine Rulers

John Stuart Mill
On Liberty

Sir Thomas More
Utopia

Thomas Nickerson and Owen Chase
The Loss of the Ship *Essex*, Sunk by a Whale

Robert Owen
A New View of Society and Other Writings

Thomas Paine
Common Sense
Rights of Man
The Thomas Paine Reader

Francis Parkman, Jr.
The Oregon Trail

Pausanias
Guide to Greece, Volumes 1 and 2

Christine de Pisan
The Treasure of the City of the Ladies: Or, The Book of Three Virtues

Pliny the Elder
Natural History: A Selection

Pliny the Younger
The Letters of the Younger Pliny

Plutarch
The Age of Alexander
The Fall of the Roman Republic
Makers of Rome
Plutarch on Sparta
The Rise and Fall of Athens: Nine Greek Lives

Polybius
The Rise of the Roman Empire

Procopius
The Secret History

John Reed
Ten Days That Shook the World

Jacob A. Riis
How the Other Half Lives

Nicola Sacco and Bartolomeo Vanzetti
The Letters of Sacco and Vanzetti

Sallust
The Jugurthine War and The Conspiracy of Catiline

Domingo F. Sarmiento
Facundo

Jorge Semprun
The Long Voyage

Suetonius
The Twelve Caesars

Cornelius Tacitus
The Agricola and The Germania
The Annals of Imperial Rome
The Histories

Thucydides
The History of the Peloponnesian War, Revised Edition

Alfred de Vigny
Servitude and Grandeur of Arms

Voltaire
Letters on England

Rebecca West
Black Lamb and Grey Falcon: A Journey through Yugoslavia

Xenophon
Hiero the Tyrant and Other Treatises
A History of My Times
The Persian Expedition

Colonial American Travel Narratives
Divine Right and Democracy: An Anthology of Political Writing in Stuart England
Early American Writing
Hippocratic Writings
Lives of the Later Caesars
Women's Indian Captivity Narratives

LITERARY CRITICISM

Aristotle
Poetics

Malcolm Cowley
Exile's Return: A Literary Odyssey of the 1920s

D. H. Lawrence
Studies in Classic American Literature

John Ruskin
Unto This Last and Other Writings

Augustan Critical Writing
Classical Literary Criticism

LITERATURE

Edwin A. Abbott
Flatland

Henry Adams
Esther

Aesop
The Complete Fables

Henri Alain-Fournier
Le Grand Meaulnes

Louisa May Alcott
The Inheritance
Little Women
Work: A Story of Experience

Horatio Alger, Jr.
Ragged Dick and Struggling Upward

Kingsley Amis
Lucky Jim

Mulk Raj Anand
Untouchable

Sherwood Anderson
The Egg and Other Stories
Winesburg, Ohio

Mary Antin
The Promised Land

Apollonius of Rhodes
The Voyage of the Argo: The Argonautica

Apuleius
The Golden Ass

Aristotle
Poetics

Jane Austen
Emma
Lady Susan/The Watsons/Sanditon
Mansfield Park
Northanger Abbey
Persuasion
Pride and Prejudice
Sense and Sensibility

Jane Austen and Charlotte Brontë
The Juvenilia of Jane Austen and
    Charlotte Brontë

Isaac Babel
Collected Stories

Honoré de Balzac
The Black Sheep
Cousin Bette
Cousin Pons
Eugénie Grandet
A Harlot High and Low
History of the Thirteen
Lost Illusion
Old Goriot
Selected Short Stories
The Wild Ass's Skin

Charles Baudelaire
Baudelaire in English

L. Frank Baum
The Wonderful World of Oz:
    The Wizard of Oz/The Emerald City
    of Oz/Glinda of Oz

Aphra Behn
Oroonoko, The Rover, and Other Works

Edward Bellamy
Looking Backward, 2000–1887

Saul Bellow
The Adventures of Augie March
Dangling Man
The Dean's December
Henderson the Rain King
Herzog
Him with His Foot in His Mouth
Humboldt's Gift
Mosby's Memoirs and Other Stories
Mr. Sammler's Planet
Seize the Day

To Jerusalem and Back:
  A Personal Account
The Victim

Andrei Bely
Petersburg

Stephen Vincent Benét
The Devil and Daniel Webster

Arnold Bennett
The Old Wives' Tale

Béroul
The Romance of Tristan

Ambrose Bierce
Tales of Soldiers and Civilians

Giovanni Boccaccio
The Decameron

Heinrich T. Böll
Billiards at Half-Past Nine
The Clown
The Lost Honor of Katherina Blum

Tadeusz Borowski
This Way for the Gas, Ladies and
  Gentlemen

Mary Elizabeth Braddon
Lady Audley's Secret

Anne Brontë
Agnes Grey
The Tenant of Wildfell Hall

Charlotte Brontë
Jane Eyre
The Professor
Shirley
Villette

Emily Brontë
Wuthering Heights

Charles Brockden Brown
Edgar Huntly: Or, Memoirs of a
  Sleep-Walker
Wieland and Memoirs of Carwin the
  Biloquist

**William Hill Brown and
Hannah Webster Foster**
The Power of Sympathy and
  The Coquette

Mikhail Bulgakov
The Master and Margarita

Ivan A. Bunin
The Gentleman from San Francisco
  and Other Stories

John Bunyan
The Pilgrim's Progress

Frances Hodgson Burnett
The Secret Garden

Frances Burney
Evelina

Edgar Rice Burroughs
Tarzan of the Apes

Samuel Butler
Erewhon
The Way of All Flesh

George Washington Cable
The Grandissimes

Abraham Cahan
The Rise of David Levinsky

Cao Xueqin
The Story of the Stone, Volume 1: The
  Golden Days (Chapters 1–26)
The Story of the Stone, Volume 2: The
  Crab-Flower Club (Chapters 27–53)
The Story of the Stone, Volume 3: The
  Warning Voice (Chapters 54–80)
The Story of the Stone, Volume 4: The
  Debt of Tears (Chapters 81–98)
The Story of the Stone, Volume 5: The
  Dreamer Awakes (Chapters 99–120)

Lewis Carroll
Alice's Adventures in Wonderland and
  Through the Looking-Glass

Rosario Castellanos
The Book of Lamentations

Baldesar Castiglione
The Book of the Courtier

Willa Cather
Coming, Aphrodite!
My Ántonia
O Pioneers!
The Song of the Lark

Margaret Cavendish
The Blazing World and Other Writings

Benvenuto Cellini
Autobiography

Miguel de Cervantes Saavedra
Don Quixote
Exemplary Stories

Geoffrey Chaucer
The Canterbury Tales
The Canterbury Tales: The First Fragment
Love Visions
Troilus and Criseyde

Anton Chekhov
The Duel and Other Stories
The Fiancée and Other Stories
The Kiss and Other Stories
Lady with Lapdog and Other Stories
The Party and Other Stories

Charles W. Chesnutt
Conjure Tales and Stories of the
   Color Line
The House Behind the Cedars
The Marrow of Tradition

G. K. Chesterton
The Club of Queer Trades
The Man Who Was Thursday:
   A Nightmare

Erskine Childers
The Riddle of the Sands

Kate Chopin
The Awakening and Selected Stories
Bayou Folk and A Night in Acadie
A Vocation and a Voice: Stories

Chrétien de Troyes
Arthurian Romances

John Cleland
Fanny Hill: Or, Memoirs of a Woman of
   Pleasure

Albert Cohen
Belle du Seigneur

Colette
Chéri and The Last of Chéri
The Claudine Novels
Gigi and The Cat
The Ripening Seed
The Vagabond

Wilkie Collins
Armadale
The Law and the Lady
The Moonstone
No Name
The Woman in White

Joseph Conrad
Almayer's Folly
Chance
Heart of Darkness
Lord Jim
The Nigger of the "Narcissus"
Nostromo
A Personal Record and
   A Mirror of the Sea
The Rescue
The Secret Agent
The Shadow-Line
Tales of Unrest
Typhoon and Other Stories
Under Western Eyes
Victory
Youth/Heart of Darkness/
   The End of the Tether

Benjamin Constant
Adolphe

Captain James Cook
The Journals of Captain Cook

James Fenimore Cooper
The Deerslayer
The Last of the Mohicans
The Pathfinder
The Pioneers
The Prairie
The Spy

Stephen Crane
Maggie, A Girl of the Streets
The Red Badge of Courage and
   Other Stories

Sor Juana Inés de la Cruz
Poems, Protests, and a Dream

Auobna Ottobah Cugoano
Thoughts and Sentiments on the Evil of
    Slavery

E. E. Cummings
The Enormous Room

Richard Henry Dana, Jr.
Two Years Before the Mast: A Personal
    Narrative of Life at Sea

Dante
The Divine Comedy, Volume 1:
    Inferno (Hell)
The Divine Comedy, Volume 2: Purgatory
The Divine Comedy, Volume 3: Paradise

Robertson Davies
Fifth Business

Daniel Defoe
A Journal of the Plague Year
Moll Flanders
Robinson Crusoe
Roxana

John W. De Forest
Miss Ravenel's Conversion from
    Secession to Loyalty

Thomas De Quincey
Confessions of an English Opium Eater

Charles Dickens
Barnaby Rudge
Bleak House
The Christmas Books, Volume 1: A
    Christmas Carol/The Chimes
The Christmas Books, Volume 2: The
    Cricket on the Hearth/The Battle of
    Life/The Haunted Man
David Copperfield
Dombey and Son
Geat Expectations
Hard Times
Little Dorrit
Martin Chuzzlewit
The Mystery of Edwin Drood
Nicholas Nickleby
The Old Curiosity Shop
Oliver Twist

Our Mutual Friend
The Pickwick Papers
Selected Journalism, 1850–1870
Selected Short Fiction
Sketches by Boz
A Tale of Two Cities

Denis Diderot
Jacques the Fatalist and His Master
The Nun
Rameau's Nephew and
    D'Alembert's Dream

John Dos Passos
Three Soldiers

Fyodor Dostoyevsky
The Brothers Karamazov
Crime and Punishment
The Devils
The Gambler/Bobok/A Nasty Story
The House of the Dead
The Idiot
Netochka Nezvanova
Notes from the Underground/The Double
Poor Folk and Other Stories
Uncle's Dream and Other Stories
The Village of Stepanchikovo

Theodore Dreiser
Jennie Gerhardt
Sister Carrie

Alexander Dumas
The Count of Monte Cristo
The Three Musketeers

Maria Edgeworth
The Absentee
Castle Rackrent and Ennui
Ormond

George Eliot
Adam Bede
Daniel Deronda
Felix Holt: The Radical
Middlemarch
The Mill on the Floss
Romola
Scenes of Clerical Life
Selected Essays, Poems, and
    Other Writings
Silas Marner

Erasmus
Praise of Folly

Wolfram von Eschenbach
Parzival

Richard Fariña
Been Down So Long It Looks Like
    Up to Me

Fanny Fern
Ruth Hall: A Domestic Tale of the
    Present Time

Henry Fielding
Joseph Andrews/Shamela
Tom Jones

F. Scott Fitzgerald
The Beautiful and Damned
Jazz Age Stories
This Side of Paradise

Gustave Flaubert
Bouvard and Pécuchet
Madame Bovary
Salammbô
Selected Letters
Sentimental Education
Three Tales

Theodor Fontane
Effi Briest

Ford Madox Ford
The Fifth Queen
The Good Soldier

E. M. Forster
Howard's End
A Room with a View
Selected Stories

Anatole France
The Gods Will Have Blood

Sir James Frazer
The Golden Bough, Abridged Edition

Harold Frederic
The Damnation of Theron Ware

Mary E. Wilkins Freeman
A New England Nun

William Gaddis
Carpenter's Gothic
JR
The Recognitions

Elizabeth Gaskell
Cranford/Cousin Phillis
Gothic Tales
Mary Barton
North and South
Ruth
Wives and Daughters

William H. Gass
Omensetter's Luck

Stella Gibbons
Cold Comfort Farm

Charlotte Perkins Gilman
Herland, The Yellow Wallpaper, and
    Selected Writings

George Gissing
New Grub Street
The Odd Women

William Godwin
Caleb Williams

Johann Wolfgang von Goethe
Elective Affinities
Maxims and Reflections
The Sorrows of Young Werther

Nikolai Gogol
Dead Souls
Diary of a Madman and Other Stories

Oliver Goldsmith
The Vicar of Wakefield

Ivan Goncharov
Oblomov

Sir Edmund Gosse
Father and Son

Gottfried von Strassburg
Tristan

Henry Green
Loving/Living/Party Going

Graham Greene
Brighton Rock
A Burnt-Out Case
The Captain and the Enemy
Collected Essays
Collected Short Stories
The Comedians
The End of the Affair
England Made Me
A Gun for Sale
The Heart of the Matter
The Last Word and Other Stories
Loser Takes All
The Man Within
The Ministry of Fear
Our Man in Havana
The Power and the Glory
The Quiet American
Stamboul Train
The Third Man and The Fallen Idol
Travels with My Aunt
Twenty-one Stories

Lady Isabella Gregory
Selected Writings

Zane Grey
Riders of the Purple Sage

Jacob and Wilhelm Grimm
Selected Tales

Knut Hamsun
Hunger
Mysteries
Pan

Thomas Hardy
Desperate Remedies
The Distracted Preacher and Other Tales
Far from the Madding Crowd
The Hand of Ethelberta
Jude the Obscure
A Laodicean
The Mayor of Casterbridge
A Pair of Blue Eyes
The Pursuit of the Well-Beloved
    and The Well-Beloved
The Return of the Native
Tess of the D'Urbervilles
The Trumpet-Major
Two on a Tower
Under the Greenwood Tree

The Withered Arm and Other Stories
The Woodlanders

Joel Chandler Harris
Uncle Remus: His Songs and His Sayings

L. P. Hartley
The Go-Between

Jaroslav Hašek
The Good Soldier Švejk

John Hawkes
The Lime Twig/Second Skin/Travesty

Nathaniel Hawthorne
The Blithedale Romance
The House of the Seven Gables
The Marble Faun
The Scarlet Letter
Selected Tales and Sketches

O. Henry
Selected Stories

Herman Hesse
Siddhartha

Ernst Theodor Hoffmann
The Life and Opinions of the
    Tomcat Murr
The Tales of Hoffmann

Homer
The Iliad
The Iliad: A New Prose Translation
The Odyssey

Anthony Hope
The Prisoner of Zenda and
    Rupert of Hentzau

Gerard Manley Hopkins
Poems and Prose

William Dean Howells
A Modern Instance
The Rise of Silas Lapham

Victor Hugo
Les Misérables
Nôtre-Dame of Paris

Elspeth Huxley
Red Strangers

J. K. Huysmans
Against Nature

Saint Ignatius of Loyola
Personal Writings

Gilbert Imlay
The Emigrants

Elizabeth Inchbald
A Simple Story

Washington Irving
The Legend of Sleepy Hollow
    and Other Stories

Henry James
The Ambassadors
The American
The Aspern Papers and
    The Turn of the Screw
The Awkward Age
The Bostonians
Daisy Miller
The Europeans
The Figure in the Carpet and Other Stories
The Golden Bowl
The Jolly Corner and Other Tales
The Portrait of a Lady
The Princess Casamassima
Roderick Hudson
The Spoils of Poynton
The Tragic Muse
Washington Square
What Maisie Knew
The Wings of the Dove

Jerome K. Jerome
Three Men in a Boat and Three Men on
    the Bummell

Sarah Orne Jewett
The Country of the Pointed Firs and
    Other Stories

James Weldon Johnson
The Autobiography of an Ex-Colored Man

Samuel Johnson
The History of Rasselas, Prince of
    Abissinia
Selected Writings

James Joyce
Dubliners
Finnegans Wake
A Portrait of the Artist as a Young Man

Juvenal
Sixteen Satires

Franz Kafka
The Transformation ("Metamorphosis")
    and Other Stories

Jack Kerouac
On the Road

Rudyard Kipling
The Jungle Books
Just So Stories
Kim
Plain Tales from the Hills

Heinrich von Kleist
The Marquise of O— and Other Stories

Choderlos de Laclos
Les Liaisons Dangereuses

Madame de Lafayette
The Princesse de Clèves

William Langland
Piers the Ploughman

Ring Lardner
Selected Stories

Nella Larsen
Passing

Mary Lavin
In a Café

D. H. Lawrence
Aaron's Rod
Apocalypse
The Boy in the Bush
The Fox/The Captain's Doll/The Ladybird
Lady Chatterley's Lover
Mr. Noon
The Prussian Officer and Other Stories
The Rainbow
Sons and Lovers
Twilight in Italy and Other Essays
The Woman Who Rode Away
    and Other Stories
Women in Love

Mikhail Lermontov
A Hero of Our Time

Primo Levi
If Not Now, When?
The Monkey's Wrench

Matthew Lewis
The Monk

Sinclair Lewis
Babbit
Main Street

Jack London
The Assassination Bureau, Ltd.
The Call of the Wild, White Fang, and
    Other Stories
Martin Eden
Northland Stories
The Sea-Wolf and Other Stories
Tales of the Pacific

Longus
Daphnis and Chloe

Anita Loos
Gentlemen Prefer Blondes and But
    Gentlemen Marry Brunettes

H. P. Lovecraft
The Call of Cthulhu and Other Weird
    Stories

George MacDonald
The Complete Fairytales

Joachim Maria Machado de Assis
Dom Casmurro

Bernard Malamud
The Fixer
God's Grace
A New Life

Sir Thomas Malory
Le Morte D'Arthur

Heinrich Mann
Man of Straw

Klaus Mann
Mephisto

Thomas Mann
Death in Venice and Other Tales

Katherine Mansfield
The Garden Party and Other Stories

Alessandro Manzoni
The Betrothed (I promessi sposi)

Marguerite de Navarre
The Heptameron

Marie de France
The Lais of Marie de France

Charles W. Marurin
Melmoth the Wanderer

W. Somerset Maugham
Cakes and Ale
Collected Short Stories,
    Volumes 1, 2, 3, and 4
Liza of Lambeth
The Magician
The Moon and Sixpence
Mrs. Craddock
The Narrow Corner
Of Human Bondage
The Painted Veil
The Razor's Edge
The Summing Up

Guy de Maupassant
Bel-Ami
Pierre and Jean
Selected Short Stories
A Woman's Life

François Mauriac
Thérèse

Herman Melville
Billy Budd and Other Stories
The Confidence-Man
Moby-Dick: Or, The Whale
Pierre: Or, The Ambiguities
Redburn
Typee

George Meredith
The Ordeal of Richard Feverel

Iris Murdoch
A Fairly Honourable Defeat
The Sea, the Sea

Charles de Montesquieu
Persian Letters

William Morris
News from Nowhere and Other Writings

Multatuli
Max Havelaar: Or, The Coffee Auctions of
    the Dutch Trading Company

R. K. Narayan
The Guide
Malgudi Days
The Man-Eater of Malgudi
The Rāmayāna
A Tiger for Malgudi
The Vendor of Sweets

Thomas Nashe
The Unfortunate Traveller and
    Other Works

Gérard de Nerval
Selected Writings

Frank Norris
McTeague: A Story of San Francisco
The Octopus: A Story of California
The Pit: A Story of Chicago

Margaret Oliphant
Miss Marjoribanks

Dorothy Parker
Complete Stories

Thomas Love Peacock
Nightmare Abbey/Crotchet Castle

Petronius and Seneca
The Satyricon/The Apocolocyntosis

Plutarch
Essays

Edgar Allan Poe
The Fall of the House of Usher and Other
    Writings
The Narrative of Arthur Gordon Pym of
    Nantucket
The Science Fiction of Edgar Allan Poe

Jan Potocki
The Manuscript Found in Saragossa

Abbé Prévost
Manon Lescaut

Mary Prince
The History of Mary Prince

Marcel Proust
Swann's Way

Alexander Pushkin
The Queen of Spades and Other Stories
Tales of Belkin and Other Prose Writings

Thomas Pynchon
Gravity's Rainbow
Vineland

Eça de Queirós
The Maias

Francisco de Quevedo
Two Spanish Picaresque Novels

François Rabelais
Gargantua and Pantagruel

Ann Radcliffe
The Italian

Samuel Richardson
Clarissa
Pamela

Susanna Rowson
Charlotte Temple and Lucy Temple

Leopold von Sacher-Masoch
Venus in Furs

Ignatius Sancho
Letters of the Late Ignatius Sancho, an
    African

Friedrich Schiller
Mary Stuart

Olive Schreiner
The Story of an African Farm

Bruno Schulz
The Street of Crocodiles

Sir Walter Scott
The Antiquary
The Heart of Midlothian
Ivanhoe
Kenilworth
Old Mortality
Rob Roy
Waverley

Catharine Maria Sedgwick
Hope Leslie

Lucius Annaeus Seneca
Dialogues and Letters

Varlam Shalamov
Kolyma Tales

Mary Shelley
Frankenstein

Shen Fu
Six Records of a Floating Life

Sir Philip Sidney
The Countess of Pembroke's Arcadia

Upton Sinclair
The Jungle

Isaac Bashevis Singer
The Certificate
The King of the Fields

I. J. Singer
The Brothers Ashkenazi

Charles A. Siringo
A Texas Cowboy

Tobias Smollett
The Expedition of Humphry Clinker

Somadeva
Tales from the Kathāsaritsāgara

**Sir Richard Steele and
Joseph Addison**
Selections from The Tatler and The
    Spectator

Wallace Stegner
Angle of Repose
Wolf Willow

Gertrude Stein
Three Lives

John Steinbeck
Burning Bright
Cannery Row
Cup of Gold
East of Eden
The Grapes of Wrath
In Dubious Battle
The Long Valley
The Moon Is Down
Of Mice and Men
Once There Was a War
The Pastures of Heaven
The Pearl
The Red Pony
A Russian Journal
The Short Reign of Pippin IV
Sweet Thursday
To a God Unknown
Tortilla Flat
The Wayward Bus
The Winter of Our Discontent

Stendhal
The Charterhouse of Parma
Love
Scarlet and Black

Laurence Sterne
The Life and Opinions of Tristram Shandy
A Sentimental Journey

Robert Louis Stevenson
Dr. Jekyll and Mr. Hyde and
    Other Stories
In the South Seas
Kidnapped
The Master of Ballantrae
Treasure Island
Weir of Hermiston

Adalbert Stifter
Brigitta and Other Tales

Elizabeth Stoddard
The Morgesons

Bram Stoker
Dracula

Harriet Beecher Stowe
Dred
The Minister's Wooing
Uncle Tom's Cabin: Or, Life Among the
  Lowly

August Strindberg
Inferno/From an Occult Diary

Francis Stuart
Black List, Section H

Bamba Suso and Banna Kanute
Sunjata

Jonathan Swift
Gulliver's Travels

Sir Rabindranath Tagore
The Home and the World
Selected Short Stories

William Makepeace Thackeray
The History of Henry Esmond
The History of Pendennis
The Newcomes
Vanity Fair

Flora Thompson
Lark Rise to Candleford: A Trilogy

Henry David Thoreau
A Year in Thoreau's Journal: 1851

Leo Tolstoy
Anna Karenin
Childhood/Boyhood/Youth
The Death of Ivan Ilyich and Other
  Stories
How Much Land Does a Man Need?
  and Other Stories
The Kreutzer Sonata and Other Stories
Master and Man and Other Stories
Resurrection
The Sebastopol Sketches
War and Peace

Thomas Traherne
Selected Poems and Prose

Anthony Trollope
Barchester Towers
Can You Forgive Her?
Dr. Wortle's School
The Eustace Diamonds

Framley Parsonage
He Knew He Was Right
The Prime Minister
The Small House at Allington
The Warden
The Way We Live Now

Fanny Trollope
Domestic Manners of the Americans

Ivan Turgenev
Fathers and Sons
First Love
Home of the Gentry
On the Eve
Rudin
Sketches from a Hunter's Album
Spring Torrents

Mark Twain
The Adventures of Huckleberry Finn
The Adventures of Tom Sawyer
A Connecticut Yankee in King Arthur's
  Court
Life on the Mississippi
The Prince and the Pauper
Pudd'nhead Wilson
Roughing It
Tales, Speeches, Essays, and Sketches
A Tramp Abroad

Sigrid Undset
Gunnar's Daughter
Kristin Lavransdatter I: The Wreath
Kristin Lavransdatter II: The Wife
Kristin Lavransdatter III: The Cross

Giovanni Verga
Cavalleria Rusticana and Other Stories

Giambattista Vico
New Science

Gore Vidal
Duluth
Kalki
The Messiah
Myra Breckinridge/Myron

Virgil
The Aeneid
The Aeneid: A New Prose Translation

Voltaire
Candide
Zadig/L'Ingénu

Jacobus de Voragine
The Golden Legend

Rebecca West
The Return of the Soldier

Edith Wharton
The Age of Innocence
The Custom of the Country
Ethan Frome
The House of Mirth
The Reef
Summer

Phillis Wheatley
Complete Writings

Patrick White
The Cockatoos
A Fringe of Leaves
The Living and the Dead
Riders in the Chariot
The Vivisector

Oscar Wilde
Complete Short Fiction
De Profundis and Other Writings
The Picture of Dorian Gray

John Wilmot, Earl of Rochester
The Complete Works

Owen Wister
The Virginian

**Mary Wollstonecraft and
Mary Shelley**
Mary/Maria/Matilda

Virginia Woolf
Jacob's Room
Night and Day
The Voyage Out

William Wordsworth
Selected Prose Writings

W. B. Yeats
Short Fiction

Anzia Yezierska
Hungry Hearts

Yevgeny Zamyatin
We

Émile Zola
L'Assommoir (The Dram Shop)
L'Assommoir
La Bête Humaine
The Debacle
The Earth
Germinal
Nana
Thérèse Raquin

Against Slavery
American Local Color Writing, 1880–1920
Beowulf
Beowulf: A Prose Translation
A Celtic Miscellany
The Classic of Mountains and Seas
The Death of King Arthur
Early American Writing
Four Stories by American Women
The Greek Alexander Romance
King Arthur's Death: Morte Arthure/
    Le Morte Arthur
The Quest of the Holy Grail
Romantic Fairy Tales
The Song of Roland
Tales from the Thousand and One Nights
Three Gothic Novels

NATURE CLASSICS

John James Audubon
Selected Journals and Other Writings

Mary Austin
The Land of Little Rain

William Bartram
Travels

Rachel L. Carson
Under the Sea Wind

George Catlin
North American Indians

Gerald Durrell
My Family and Other Animals

**Meriwether Lewis and
William Clark**
The Journals of Lewis and Clark

Peter Matthiessen
Blue Meridian
The Cloud Forest
The Snow Leopard
The Tree Where Man Was Born
Under the Mountain Wall
Wildlife in America

Gavin Maxwell
Ring of Bright Water

John Muir
The Mountains of California
My First Summer in the Sierra
Travels in Alaska

Sigurd Olson
Songs of the North

John Wesley Powell
The Exploration of the Colorado River
    and Its Canyons

John Tanner
The Falcon

Henry David Thoreau
Cape Cod
The Maine Woods

Gilbert White
The Natural History of Selborne

PHILOSOPHY

Thomas Aquinas
Selected Writings

Hannah Arendt
Between Past and Future

Aristotle
The Art of Rhetoric
The Athenian Constitution
De Anima (On the Soul)
Ethics
The Metaphysics
Poetics
The Politics

Francis Bacon
The Essays

George Berkeley
Principles of Human Knowledge and Three
    Dialogues Between Hylas and Philonius

Ancius Boethius
The Consolation of Philosophy

Jean-Anthelme Brillat-Savarin
The Physiology of Taste

Sir Thomas Browne
The Major Works

Edmund Burke
A Philosophical Enquiry into the
    Origin of Our Ideas of the
    Sublime and Beautiful

Thomas Carlyle
Selected Writings

Marcus Tullius Cicero
The Nature of the Gods
On the Good Life

Confucius
The Analects

René Descartes
Discourse on Method and Related
    Writings
Discourse on Method and The
    Meditations
Meditations and Other Metaphysical
    Writings

Ralph Waldo Emerson
Selected Essays

David Hume
Dialogues Concerning Natural Religion
A Treatise of Human Nature

William James
Pragmatism and Other Writings

Søren Kierkegaard
Either/Or: A Fragment of Life
Fear and Trembling
Papers and Journals: A Selection
Sickness unto Death

François de La Rochefoucauld
Maxims

John Locke
An Essay Concerning Human
　　Understanding

Lucretius
On the Nature of the Universe

Sir Charles Lyell
Principles of Geology

Marcus Aurelius
Meditations

Mencius
Mencius

**John Stuart Mill and Jeremy
Bentham**
Utilitarianism and Other Essays

Michel de Montaigne
The Complete Essays
The Essays: A Selection

Friedrich Nietzsche
Beyond Good and Evil
The Birth of Tragedy
A Nietzsche Reader
Thus Spake Zarathustra
Twilight of the Idols and The Anti-Christ

Blaise Pascal
Pensées

Georges Perec
Species of Spaces and Other Pieces

Plato
Early Socratic Dialogues
Gorgias
The Last Days of Socrates:
　　Euthyphro/The Apology/Crito/Phaedo
The Laws
Phaedrus and Letters VII and VIII
Philebus
Protagoras and Meno
The Republic
The Symposium
Theaetetus
Timaeus and Critias

Plotinus
The Enneads

Jean-Jacques Rousseau
A Discourse on Inequality
Reveries of the Solitary Walker
The Social Contract

Arthur Schopenhauer
Essays and Aphorisms

Lucius Annaeus Seneca
Letters from a Stoic

Henry David Thoreau
Walden and Civil Disobedience
A Year in Thoreau's Journal: 1851

Voltaire
Philosophical Dictionary

Mary Wollstonecraft
A Vindication of the Rights of Woman

Xenophon
Conversations of Socrates

Early Greek Philosophy
German Idealist Philosophy
The Laws of Manu

POETRY

Anna Akhmatova
Selected Poems

Ludovico Ariosto
Orlando Furioso, Part I and Part II

Farid ud-Din Attar
The Conference of the Birds

Matsuo Bashō
The Narrow Road to the Deep North and
　　Other Travel Sketches
On Love and Barley: Haiku of Bashō

Charles Baudelaire
Baudelaire in English
Selected Poems

William Blake
The Complete Poems

Elizabeth Barrett Browning
Aurora Leigh and Other Poems

Robert Browning
Selected Poems

Robert Burns
Selected Poems

George Gordon, Lord Byron
Don Juan
Selected Poems

Lewis Carroll
The Hunting of the Snark

Catullus
The Poems of Catullus

Samuel Coleridge
The Complete Poems
Selected Poems

Sor Juana Inés de la Cruz
Poems, Protest, and a Dream

Dante
La Vita Nuova

John Donne
The Complete English Poems

T. S. Eliot
The Waste Land and Other Poems

Robert Frost
Early Poems: The Boy's Will, North of
    Boston, Mountain Interval, and Other
    Poems

Johann Wolfgang von Goethe
Selected Verse

Lady Isabella Gregory
Selected Writings

Thomas Hardy
Selected Poems

George Herbert
The Complete English Poems

Hesiod and Theognis
Hesiod and Theognis

Friedrich Hölderlin
Selected Poems and Fragments

Homer
The Iliad
The Odyssey

Gerard Manley Hopkins
Poems and Prose

Horace
The Complete Odes and Epodes
Horace in English

Horace and Persius
The Satires of Horace and Persius

James Weldon Johnson
Complete Poems
God's Trombones: Seven Negro Sermons
    in Verse
Lift Every Voice and Sing

Ben Jonson
The Complete Poems

Juvenal
The Sixteen Satires

John Keats
The Complete Poems: Second Edition
Selected Poems

Jean de La Fontaine
Selected Fables

Jules La Forgue
Selected Poems

Le Comte de Lautréamont
Maldoror and Poems

D. H. Lawrence
Complete Poems

Li Po and Tu Fu
Poems

Henry Wadsworth Longfellow
Selected Poems

Osip Mandelstam
Selected Poems

Andrew Marvell
The Complete Poems

Edna St. Vincent Millay
Early Poems

John Milton
The Complete Poems
Paradise Lost

Marianne Moore
Complete Poems

Pablo Neruda
Twenty Love Poems and a Song of
   Despair

Gérard de Nerval
Selected Writings

Omar Khayyám
The Ruba'iyat of Omar Khayyám

Ovid
The Erotic Poems
Fasti
Heroides
Metamorphoses
Ovid in English
The Poems of Exile

Dorothy Parker
Complete Poems

Pindar
The Odes

Alexander Pushkin
Eugene Onegin

Arthur Rimbaud
Collected Poems

Edwin Arlington Robinson
Selected Poems

Lucius Annaeus Seneca
Seneca in English

William Shakespeare
The Sonnets and A Lover's Complaint

Edmund Spenser
The Faerie Queene
The Shorter Poems

Robert Louis Stevenson
Selected Poems

Jonathan Swift
Complete Poems

Algernon Charles Swinburne
Poems and Ballads and Atalanta in
   Calydon

Sir Rabindranath Tagore
Selected Poems

Alfred, Lord Tennyson
Idylls of the King
Selected Poems

Theocritus
The Idylls

Thomas Traherne
Selected Poems and Prose

Marina Tsvetayeva
Selected Poems

Virgil
Aeneid
The Eclogues
The Georgics

Phillis Wheatley
Complete Writings

Walt Whitman
The Complete Poems
Leaves of Grass

William Wordsworth
The Poems, Volumes 1 and 2
Selected Poems

**William Wordsworth and Dorothy
Wordsworth**
Home at Grasmere

Sir Thomas Wyatt
The Complete Poems

Beowulf: A Verse Translation
A Celtic Miscellany
The Earliest English Poems,
   Third Revised Edition
The Epic of Gilgamesh
English Romantic Verse
Medieval English Verse
The Metaphysical Poets
The Nibelungenlied

Nineteenth-Century American Poetry
The Penguin Book of First World War
  Poetry
The Penguin Book of French Poetry,
  1820–1950
The Penguin Book of Modern African
  Poetry
The Penguin Book of Renaissance Verse
  1509–1659
The Penguin Book of Restoration Verse
The Penguin Book of Victorian Verse
The Poem of the Cid
Poems of Heaven and Hell from
  Ancient Mesopotamia
Poems of the Late T'ang
The Psalms in English
Sir Gawain and the Green Knight

RELIGION

Adomnán of Iona
Life of St. Columba

Anselm of Aosta
The Prayers and Meditations of St. Anselm

Farid ud-Din Attar
The Conference of the Birds

Saint Augustine
City of God
Confessions

Bede
The Ecclesiastical History of the English
  People

**Bede, Brendan, and Eddius
Stephanus**
The Age of Bede

John Bunyan
Grace Abounding to the Chief of Sinners

Meister Eckhart
Selected Writings

Wolfram von Eschenbach
Parzival

Eusebius
The History of the Church

Saint Ignatius of Loyola
Personal Writings

William James
The Varieties of Religious Experience:
  A Study in Human Nature

Julian of Norwich
Revelations of Divine Love

Lao Tzu
Tao Te Ching

Michel de Montaigne
An Apology for Raymond Sebond

R. K. Narayan
The Rāmayāna

John Henry Newman
Apologia pro Vita Sua

Blaise Pascal
Pensées

Teresa of Ávila
The Life of St. Teresa of Ávila by Herself

Thomas à Kempis
The Imitation of Christ

Leo Tolstoy
A Confession and
  Other Religious Writings

William Tyndale
The Obedience of a Christian Man

Jacobus de Voragine
The Golden Legend

The Bhagavad Gita
Buddhist Scriptures
The Cistercian World: Monastic Writings
  of the Twelfth Century
The Cloud of Unknowing and Other
  Works
The Dhammapada
Early Christian Lives
Early Christian Writings: The Apostolic
  Fathers
Hindu Myths
The Koran
The Koran, Revised Edition

Poems of Heaven and Hell from Ancient
  Mesopotamia
The Psalms in English
The Rig Veda
Speaking of Siva
The Upanishads

SAGAS

Snorri Sturluson
King Harald's Saga

Beowulf
Early Irish Myths and Sagas
Egil's Saga
Eyrbyggja Saga
Hrafnkel's Saga
Laxdaela Saga
The Mabinogion
Njal's Saga
The Saga of King Hrolf Kraki
The Saga of Volsungs
Orkneyinga Saga: The History of the
  Earls of Orkney
Seven Viking Romances
The Vinland Sagas and The Norse
  Discovery of America

SCIENCE

Charles Darwin
The Origin of Species
The Voyage of the Beagle: Charles
  Darwin's Journal of Researches

Sir Charles Lyell
Principles of Geology

TRAVEL

Christopher Columbus
The Four Voyages

Charles Dickens
American Notes for General Circulation
Pictures from Italy, 1850–1870

Henry Fielding
The Journal of a Voyage to Lisbon

Gustave Flaubert
Flaubert in Egypt

Gerald of Wales
The Journey Through Wales/The
  Description of Wales

Johann Wolfgang von Goethe
Italian Journey

Graham Greene
In Search of a Character
Journey Without Maps
The Lawless Roads

Alexander von Humboldt
Personal Narrative of a Journey to the
  Equinoctial Regions of the New World

Henry James
The American Scene
Italian Hours

**Samuel Johnson and
James Boswell**
A Journey to the Western Islands of
  Scotland and The Journal of a Tour to
  the Hebrides

D. H. Lawrence
D. H. Lawrence and Italy: Twilight in
  Italy/Sea and Sardinia/Etruscan Places
Sea and Sardinia
Sketches of Etruscan Places
Twilight in Italy and Other Essays

Sir John Mandeville
The Travels of Sir John Mandeville

Shiva Naipaul
North of South: An African Journey

Marco Polo
The Travels

John Steinbeck
The Log from the *Sea of Cortez*
A Russian Journal
Travels with Charley in Search of
  America

Robert Louis Stevenson
In the South Seas

J. M. Synge
The Aran Islands

Henry David Thoreau
A Week on the Concord and Merrimack
    Rivers

Rebecca West
Black Lamb and Grey Falcon: A Journey
    through Yugoslavia

**Mary Wollstonecraft and
William Godwin**
A Short Residence in Sweden, Norway,
    and Denmark and Memoirs of the
    Author of A Vindication of the Rights
    of Woman

Colonial American Travel Narratives

The Adventures
of Augie March
by Saul Bellow
0-14-771507-5

The Age of Innocence
by Edith Wharton
0-14-771164-9

Alice's Adventures in
Wonderland and Through
the Looking Glass
by Lewis Carroll
0-14-771401-X

Anna Karenin
by Leo Tolstoy
0-14-771187-8

The Awakening
by Kate Chopin
0-14-771200-9

Candide by Voltaire
0-14-771189-4

Cousin Bette
by Honore de Balzac
0-14-771273-4

Crime and Punishment
by Fyodor Dostoyevsky
0-14-771372-2

David Copperfield
by Charles Dickens
0-14-771544-X

Fifth Business
by Robertson Davies
0-14-771592-X

The Fifth Queen
by Ford Madox Ford
0-14-771429-X

Great Expectations
by Charles Dickens
0-14-771272-6

Herzog
by Saul Bellow
0-14-771508-3

The House of Mirth
by Edith Wharton
0-14-771309-9

Howards End
by E. M. Forster
0-14-771468-0

The Inheritance
by Louisa May Alcott
0-14-771275-0

Jude the Obscure
by Thomas Hardy
0-14-771188-6

Kristin Lavransdatter
trilogy
by Sigrid Undset
0-14-771466-4

Les Misérables
by Victor Hugo
0-14-771308-0

Moby-Dick
by Herman Melville
(Includes The Loss of the
Ship *Essex* and In The
Heart of the Sea)
0-14-771495-8

My Ántonia
by Willa Cather
0-14-771198-3

On the Road
by Jack Kerouac
0-14-771444-3

Pride and Prejudice and
Sense and Sensibility
by Jane Austen
0-14-771154-1

A Room with a View
by E. M. Forster
0-14-771467-2

The Portrait of a Lady
by Henry James
0-14-771165-7

The Sea, The Sea
by Iris Murdoch
0-14-771593-8

The Secret Garden
by Frances
Hodgson Burnett
0-14-771399-4

The Song of the Lark
by Willa Cather
0-14-771398-6

The Woman in White and
The Moonstone
by Wilkie Collins
0-14-771546-6

Wuthering Heights
by Emily Brontë
0-14-771199-1

Available in packs of 10
at no charge.

YEAR	WINNER	LIFE DATES	NATIONALITY
1907	Rudyard Kipling	1865–1936	British
1913	Sir Rabindranath Tagore	1861–1941	Indian
1920	Knut Hamsun	1859–1952	Norwegian
1921	Anatole France	1844–1924	French
1923	William Butler Yeats	1865–1939	Irish
1925	George Bernard Shaw	1856–1950	British
1928	Sigrid Undset	1882–1949	Norwegian
1929	Thomas Mann	1875–1955	German
1930	Sinclair Lewis	1885–1951	American
1933	Ivan A. Bunin	1870–1953	Russian
1934	Luigi Pirandello	1867–1936	Italian
1946	Hermann Hesse	1877–1962	Swedish
1948	T. S. Eliot	1888–1965	British
1952	François Mauriac	1885–1970	French
1962	John Steinbeck	1902–1968	American
1971	Pablo Neruda	1904–1973	Chilean
1972	Heinrich T. Böll	1917–1985	German
1973	Patrick White	1912–1990	Australian
1976	Saul Bellow	1915–	American
1978	Isaac Bashevis Singer	1904–1991	American

Frances Burney
Journals and Letters

**William Bligh and
Edward Christian**
The Bounty Mutiny

Giacomo Casanova
The Story of My Life

Miguel de Cervantes
*Don Quixote

Charles Dickens
*American Notes for General Circulation
*The Old Curiosity Shop

Arthur Conan Doyle
The Hound of the Baskervilles
The Sign of Four
A Study in Scarlet

James T. Farrell
Studs Lonigan

Theodor Fontane
*Effi Briest

Andre Gide
The Immoralist

H. Rider Haggard
She

Bret Harte
The Luck of Roaring Camp and
Other Sketches

William Dean Howells
A Hazard of New Fortunes

Henry James
Henry James: A Life in Letters
Selected Tales

Sheridan Le Fanu
Uncle Silas

H.P. Lovecraft
The Thing on the Doorstep

A. E. W. Mason
The Four Feathers

Robert Musil
The Confusions of Young Torless

Eugene O'Neill
Early Plays

Raymond Queneau
Zazie in the Metro

Ann Radcliffe
The Mysteries of Udolpho

Christina Rossetti
The Complete Poems

Walter Scott
The Bride of Lammermoor
Redgauntlet

George Bernard Shaw
*Major Barbara
*Pygmalion
*Saint Joan

**Mark Twain and
Charles Dudley Warner**
The Gilded Age

Hildegard of Bingen
Selected Writings

Max Weber
The Protestant Ethic and the
Spirit of Capitalism

**Isabella Whitney, Mary Sidney,
and Aemilia Lanyer**
Renaissance Women Poets

Oscar Wilde
*The Picture of Dorian Gray
The Soul of Man Under Socialism
& Selected Critical Prose

*Classical Literary Criticism

ALSO AVAILABLE

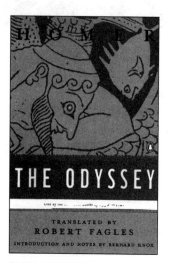

"A remarkably seductive achievement. In Fagles' hands this 'perennial poem of adventure' is again a work of entertainment, of majesty and epic beauty great enough to stun the senses."
— *Philadelphia Inquirer*

THE ODYSSEY
Homer
Translated by Robert Fagles
Introduction and
Notes by Bernard Knox
Literature / Poetry   5⅝ x 8⁷/₁₆
560 pp   French flaps
0-14-026886-3 $14.95

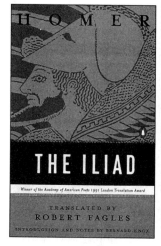

"Tremendous eloquence ... an *Iliad* primed for grandeur ... the result is a glory that can encompass that shuddering last month of the war ... a nobility and a sweep hitherto unknown in English *Iliads*."
—Douglass Parker, *The New Republic*

THE ILIAD
Homer
Translated by Robert Fagles
Introduction and Notes
by Bernard Knox
Literature / Poetry   5⅝ x 8⁷/₁₆
702 pp.   French flaps
0-14-027536-3 $15.95

PENGUIN BOOKS
www.penguinputnam.com

FROM PENGUIN

Jorge Luis Borges

COLLECTED FICTIONS
Translated by Andrew Hurley

"An unparalleled treasury of marvels."
— *Chicago Tribune*
Literature   5 1/2 x 8 7/16   French Flaps
0-14-028680-2   576 pp. $16.95

Jesse Fernandez

SELECTED POEMS
Edited by Alexander Coleman

"A surfeit of riches." — *San Francisco Chronicle*
Literature / Poetry   5 1/2 x 8 7/16   French Flaps
0-14-058721-7   496 pp. $17.95

SELECTED NON-FICTIONS
Edited by Eliot Weinberger

"Superb . . . indispensable to both the long-time Borges reader and the newcomer."
— *The Wall Street Journal*
Winner of the National
Book Critics Circle Award in Criticism

Literature / Essays   5 1/2 x 8 7/16   French Flaps
0-14-029011-7   576 pp. $17.00

"The glory of the Sagas is indisputable."
—Milan Kundera

"A testimony to the human spirit's ability not only to endure what fate may send it but to be renewed by the experience."
—Seamus Heaney

"One of the great marvels of the world of literature. . . . This is a dream come true." —Ted Hughes

THE SAGAS OF ICELANDERS
Preface by Jane Smiley
Literature   5 5/8 x 8 7/16   848 pp.
French Flaps   0-14-100003-1
$20.00

NEW FROM

ANNA KARENINA
Leo Tolstoy

Translated with notes by Richard
Pevear and Larissa Volokhonsky,
Introduction by Richard Pevear
Literature   6 x 9
864 pp.   0-670-89478-8

A dynamic new translation of one of the world's
greatest novels from an award-winning team

Praise for Pevear and Volokhonsky's
translation of *The Brothers Karamazov:*

*"Pevear and Volokhonsky have set a new
standard in the translation of
canonical works."*
—PEN/BOOK-OF-THE-MONTH CLUB
TRANSLATION PRIZE CITATION

*"Readers with no Russian can rest assured
that they are in the best of hands."*
—Michael Henry Heim, THE LOS ANGELES TIMES

FOR YOUR EYE ALONE
Robertson Davies

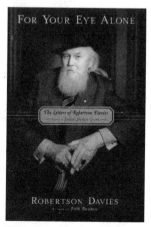

A fascinating collection that is
sure to delight his many readers as well
as connoisseurs of literary correspondence, *For Your Eye Alone* consists of letters written by Davies during the height
of his fame.

"Ingenious, erudite, entertaining…
Davies displays all the qualities of a
latter-day Trollope."— Anthony Burgess

Belles Lettres
6 ⅛ x 9 ¼   400pp.
0-670-89291-2

VIKING

FRAGMENTS
The Collected
Wisdom of Heraclitus

"In Brooks Haxton's fresh and lucid translation, the remains of Heraclitus's ancient wisdom are as arresting as mysterious notes slipped under your bedroom door by an anonymous genius who knows your every secret need."—Reynolds Price

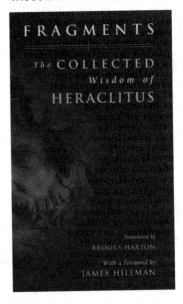

• Selected by the Book-of-the-Month Club

Translated by Brooks Haxton
Foreword by James Hillman
Philosophy/Poetry
4 ½ x 8   128 pp.   0-670-89195-9

DANCES FOR FLUTE AND THUNDER
Praises, Prayers, and Insults: Poems from the Ancient Greek
Translated by Brooks Haxton

Poetry
7 x 5   112 pp.
0-670-88728-5

"Intimacy, simplicity, intensity: like some of Whitman's late inscriptions, these breathtaking lyrics of Haxton's are really that: to be sung, to be intoned, as he says, or as Praxilla says, from the fifth-century BCE, 'to pierce and burn the heart.'" —Richard Howard

VIKING
www.penguinputnam.com

www.PENGUINCLASSICS.com

FEATURED
THIS WEEK

The Canterbury Tales: The First Fragment
Geoffrey Chaucer

The First Fragment of The Canterbury Tales contains some of Chaucer's most popular and widely enjoyed work. Chaucer introduces his pilgrims in The General Prologue, a set of speaking portraits that makes no attempt to conceal imperfections in human society, and the tales of the Knight, Miller, variety of human preoccupations, particularly romantic tale is alive with Chaucer's skills as a poet, as of comedy.

Internet zone

Click on a Classic

The world's greatest range of literature at the click of a button

... ce dedicated to the world's classic literature, of which Penguin have been the leading publisher in the English-reading world for over fifty years. The series now includes over 1600 titles, from the earliest creation myths to the masterpieces of the twentieth century.

ADVANCED SEA...

KEYWORD SEAR...

Welcome to Penguin Classics, the largest on-line resource dedicated to the world's classic literature, of which Penguin have been the leading publisher in the English-reading world for over fifty years. The series now includes over 1600 titles, from the earliest creation myths to the masterpieces of the twentieth century.

KEYWORD SEAR...

▶ NEW RELEASES
Browse the most recently p...
Penguin Classics.

▶ CLASSICS SCREEN...
Download our beautiful fre...
screen saver.

▶ HISTORY OF PENGUI...
CLASSICS

▶ NEW RELEASES
Browse the most recently
Penguin Classics.

▶ CLASSICS SCREEN S...
Download our beautiful fre
screen saver.

▶ HISTORY OF PENGUI...
CLASSICS

FEATURED
THIS WEEK

The Canterbury Tales: The First Fragment
Geoffrey Chaucer

The Canterbury Tales: The First Fragment
Geoffrey Chaucer

The First Fragment of The Canterbury Tales contains some of Chaucer's most popular and widely enjoyed work. Chaucer introduces his pilgrims in The General Prologue, a set of speaking portraits drawn with a loving that makes no attempt to conceal imperfections. The pilgrims represent human society, and the tales of the Knight, Miller, Reeve and Cook show variety of human preoccupations, particularly romantic and sexual love.

TITLE INDEX

H

I

J

K

L

M

N

O

P

S

T

U

V